"For nearly thirty years Arthur C. Danto has made his philosophical presence felt both within academic circles and in a more amorphous entity, the intellectual public. Forceful, intelligent, and learned, that presence pervades his writings, whether advancing new positions (particularly in philosophy of history and aesthetics), interpreting other philosophers (e.g. Nietzsche, Sartre), grappling with current issues in epistemology and philosophy of language, or criticizing art for *The Nation*. Always mindful of his analytical *Ps* and *Qs*, Danto nonetheless possesses a literary style and sensibilities, rarely equaled by academic philosophers, that take philosophical analysis to its limits and often refashion its insights. In his care even old ideas acquire freshness and a place in contemporary concerns. Indeed, few philosophers stand better equipped to survey the 'wide horizons' of philosophy, a task risking at once excessive commonplaces for the specialist and excessive allusions for the uninitiate.

"In *Connections to the World*, Danto undertakes the risk and essays a broad look at what philosophical inquiry consists of and how it proceeds. Through forty brief chapters, divided roughly into four decades, he considers the 'whole of philosophy' as a 'single text that counts itself content as well as container,' and broaches the major topics that have captivated Western philosophers since Antiquity. (He also occasionally introduces an argument from the Orient for a comparative, clarifying perspective.) These topics sift into three components of the 'basic cognitive episode' (subjects, representations, and the world) and three relationships between them (understanding, truth, and causality). Some might question the value of this broad view, and recommend instead reading the 'greats' in their own words or plunging directly into the minutiae of a philosophical debate. Yet Danto's richly textured description serves to convince readers, particularly those having experienced only a close brush with philosophy—perhaps drawn by the flame but fearing immolation, or simply interested but intellectually engaged elsewhere—why they ought to read Plato, Wittgenstein *et al.*, and why narrow arguments sometimes yield momentous consequences...."

—Michael E. Hobart,
*Metaphilosophy*

# CONNECTIONS TO THE WORLD

## OTHER TITLES BY ARTHUR C. DANTO

*Analytical Philosophy of History*

*Nietzsche as Philosopher*

*Analytical Philosophy of Knowledge*

*What Philosophy Is*

*Analytical Philosophy of Action*

*Mysticism and Morality*

*Jean-Paul Sartre*

*The Transfiguration of the Commonplace*

*Narration and Knowledge*

*The Philosophical Disenfranchisement of Art*

*The State of the Art*

# CONNECTIONS TO THE WORLD

## The Basic Concepts of Philosophy

Arthur C. Danto

PERENNIAL LIBRARY

Harper & Row, Publishers, New York
Grand Rapids, Philadelphia, St. Louis, San Francisco
London, Singapore, Sydney, Tokyo, Toronto

*The Library of Congress has catalogued the hardcover edition as follows:*

Danto, Arthur Coleman, 1924-
   Connections to the world.

   Includes index.
   1. Philosophy—Introductions.   2. Philosophy,
Modern—20th century.  I. Title.
BD21.D36   1989    100     88-45571

ISBN 0-06-015960-X

ISBN 0-06-091641-9 (**pbk.**)
90  91  92  93  94  FG  10  9  8  7  6  5  4  3  2  1

*For my brother Bruce*

# Contents

# PART III  Knowledge

# PART IV  The World

# Preface

A COMMONPLACE AND CHARACTERISTIC EPISODE in the lives of cognitive beings—of ourselves, animals, perhaps some machines, and possibly gods and angels if there are any—consists of the world causing us to represent it in a way that is true. Such episodes are as routine and incessant as respiration or digestion; and evolution, which gave us our cognitive as it did our metabolic structures, must underwrite—through our survival as individuals and as a species—the truthfulness of our representational systems. For the life of a cognitive being does not consist solely of a series of basic cognitive episodes—we are not passive instruments on which the world plays representational melodies—and representation is standardly and smoothly translated into actions, upon whose success our continuation depends. The possibility of illusion is a by-product of our cognitive architecture, to be sure, and falsehood is as much the dark companion of truth as death is of life. Still, if we are satisfied with statistical frequency, the preponderance of true over false representations must be stupefyingly great. In part this must be due to the fact that very few of their cognitive translations impinge on the consciousness of the beings they define. Like most of what takes place in body and in brain, the life of representation takes place without our being aware that it *is* taking place. Our basic cognitive competence is a piece of biological inheritance over most of which we exercise no control whatever.

It is no doubt a blessing of nature that so little of the impression that the world makes on us should be registered as an object of conscious awareness. In part this is due to the extreme inefficiency this would impose on the conduct of our cognitive affairs—think how little time we would have left over if we had to tend to what happens to what we have eaten once we have put it in our mouths. And even this degree of residual efficiency would be reduced were we obliged to determine, on the basis of representations that had become conscious, whether these were caused by what would make them true if they are true, and hence if it is safe to act on the information we believe these representations disclose. The philosopher Descartes acknowledged as much when he turned his back on what he termed a "rash impulse of nature"—the belief that his representations correspond to their causes—and undertook the dangerous meditations on certainty with which modern philosophy properly began. The question for Descartes was whether one could deduce from one's representations alone that there is anything outside ourselves that causes us to have them and of which they are true. Had nature allowed us to begin our existence in the way in which Descartes began his *Meditations,* we would have been among its most ephemeral experiments. It is a felicity of adaptation that the mechanisms of representation should be segregated from conscious meditation, or perhaps that those representations that do cross the threshold into consciousness should be but marginally relevant to our animal existence. But this is tantamount to saying that it was a fortune of evolution that our species did not begin with philosophers. It is biologically safe to philosophize only when we have become stable as a species. Descartes's decision to meditate on the cognitive reliability of his representations only when he could do nothing more practical—he was snowbound and immobilized—is a metaphor for this truth.

The basic cognitive episode, as I have called it, is composed of three components and three relationships, and inasmuch as these are the fundamental concepts of philosophy, it might be worth dwelling on them before our image becomes clouded with detail. The components are the subject, the representations, and the world:

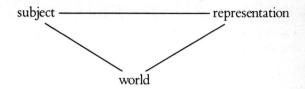

The relations are between the world and the subject, between the subject and its representations, and between the representations and the world. The first relation is that of causality, and the third that of truth. Together these constitute, philosophically speaking, our connections to the world. The second relation concerns our connection to ourselves and I shall, shortly, sketch some of the ways in which philosophers have supposed this connection must be analyzed. For the moment, all that matters is that it is as a representing being that we are connected to the world in terms of causality and truth—*inside* the world, one might say, under causality and outside the world under the truth-relationship. In daring to ask whether he was justified in believing that his representations answered to causes outside himself, Descartes was calling into question his (our) connections to the world. In answering his question with a qualified affirmation, Descartes supposed that he had discharged the philosophical task of reconnecting us to the world. But, in the first moment of his meditation, all he felt he really knew was that he was a being with representations that, for all he could tell, would be just as they were whether or not there were a world to cause them or make them true. And were he to fail in his reconnective enterprise, he would have to end where he began, as a being with representations or, as he put it, an *ens cogitans*—a thinking being, certain of nothing else.

Descartes looms large in this book and, indeed, my picture of the basic cognitive episode owes a great deal to him: It was he who defined our structure in the terms my first paragraph takes for granted. Nevertheless, it is worth stressing right at the beginning that pretty much every basic philosophical position may be defined against the triadic structure of subject, representation, and world. Bishop Berkeley, for example, thought the basic cognitive episode, as I have sketched it, far too rich. He sought to define the world in terms of our representations, so that his picture of things is made up of two components—subject and representation—and just a single relationship between them. Even this narrowed picture was too wide by half to his successor, David Hume, who reduced the subject to its representations, yielding a world that was composed of representations alone: a single component and no relationships other than the relationships among representations themselves. Other philosophers, earlier and later than Hume, found the subject—or self—to be the only reality, its representations being but illusions. So again, just one component and no further relationships beyond those spurious ones that trap the self in its own dreams and from which mere recognition of this fact is required to liberate it. This was a view that held sway in India and, in an exotic form, in nineteenth-century Germany.

A different array of erasures and reductions becomes available to philosophers who, for various reasons, find excessive the view that between the world and ourselves stands a screen of representations— that we relate indirectly to the world through the mediation of representations. There are, according to these philosophers, only subjects and objects in the world, and the basic cognitive episode consists of the former addressing the latter in its own terms, directly and without the mediation of representations. Eliminating the offending component obviously eliminates two relationships, but even this has been regarded as excessive: There are views, most notably defended in modern times by Jean-Paul Sartre, according to which there is no subject between which and the world some relationship holds; there is only the world, with the subject itself as one of its components, a thing among things. And in a comparable reductive spirit, if not advanced in quite the same words, is the materialistic view of the world as consisting merely of matter, the rest being a system of distinctions that have no objective residency in things as they are. This extreme materialism is a mirror image of the Indian philosophy that there is only the subject or self, everything else being phantasm.

The extreme views—that there is only the subject, or only the world, or that what there is is but a system of representations—are obviously the most exciting and the most challenging, since it requires elaborate and ingenious argumentation to achieve reductions so at odds with our ordinary expectations of the way we and the world must be if we are indeed cognitive beings. But it is important to stress that whether one believes there are three basic components and three fundamental relationships, or two basic components and only one relationship—or that there is only one thing out of which whatever there is is framed—the world as we experience it remains exactly the same. The ascetic Hindu who believes there is only the self has a body that must be fed and it is located in a world of sun and rain, amid animals and plants and beneath the stars, which are experienced by him the same as by the materialist or by the idealist, whose view is that everything is mental through and through. The fierce controversies between contending philosophies disturb not a single leaf and cast not a troubling shadow over the world as we live in it as cognitive beings. As we shall see over and over again in the text that follows, philosophical differences seem at once momentous and negligible.

It remains to be said that our lives do not consist of dense sequences of basic cognitive episodes, and a number of philosophical positions consist of rejecting rather than reducing the terms in which such episodes are defined. At the very least the subject is modified by the episodes it lives through, and so, marginally, is the world, so that cognition itself makes a difference to the scenes and actors. Experience is not a moment-by-moment chronicle of representation succeeding representation, but a textured tapestry woven in such a way that world and subject cannot be separated from the fabric that unites them. And truth is less a relationship between representation and reality than a force that keeps the tapestry from unraveling. Little matter whether we endorse this alternative to the standard array or not: The substance of philosophy remains as before— subject, representation, and the world, and especially the connections between the first and the last. It is for these reasons that I have named the book as I have.

*Connections to the World* grew out of and replaces *What Philosophy Is,* which appeared in 1968. Like its predecessor, it seeks to put the whole of philosophy into a single text that counts itself content as well as container—a nutshell that enfolds itself. The basic concepts of philosophy are, as this preface has suggested, few and fundamental. Still, just because every philosophical position defined in those narrow terms leaves the world as it finds it—since each makes not a single internal difference to the world we are obliged to live in—philosophy, for all its simplicity, is necessarily abstract and remote. But it is precisely this that makes it possible to house it in its entirety in a single short book. Each of the four main divisions, and each of the forty subdivisions, ruthlessly condenses jungles of difference and detail. Because the professional lives of philosophers are passed in the knotted overgrowth of argument, example, distinction, and imagination, the perspective afforded by the elevated position this book makes available may seem almost desperately bland. The jungles are there for those who relish short vistas and lurking logical dangers. But there is something thrilling in wide horizons as well, and we all owe it to ourselves now and again to make the total survey. I hope this book serves as a guide to the heights and distances.

We are what we owe: a book, like a life, is the product of its debts. Not every debt, in this sense, is an obligation, and I am anxious to acknowledge certain acts which do not so much penetrate the substance of this book, but contributed to its existence.

I am above all grateful to Hugh Van Dusen for his friendship and support, and for his great humanity. His enthusiasm, confidence, and editorial sensitivity are unmatched.

It was Hugh who suggested I find a piece of modern art for the cover of this book, and inevitably my mind turned to Robert Motherwell, one of the deep painters of the century. His etching *At The Edge* is a powerful image, and one nicely relevant to the content of a book called *Connections to the World,* for the image relates to its own edges in two main places, just as we connect to the world in two main ways. And if the image be read as an abstract representation of the self, one could hardly wish for a more suitable representation than the kind of fluid knot made by a form composed of its own connections. I am grateful to Robert for his friendship, and for his great generosity in allowing me to use this beautiful work to embellish and epitomize my book.

I dedicate this book to my brother Bruce Danto, who with his wife Joan assumed certain family responsibilities at a moment when, had I been required to deal with them myself, this book could certainly not have been written.

A. C. D.
New York City, 1988

# PART I

# The Singularity of Philosophical Thought

# 1

# Philosophy and Its History

PHILOSOPHY HAS OFTEN BEEN THOUGHT of as a kind of art or as a kind of science, but its history, by comparison with the histories of either art or science, exhibits a curious discontinuity. Each moment of philosophical advance seems to regard itself as a completely new beginning, which appears to require a correspondingly complete repudiation of everything that came before, including all the previous new beginnings, each of which was to place philosophy at last on suitable and enduring foundations. It is characteristic of the great philosophical thinker to discover that everything that went before rested on some hopeless and fundamental mistake. So the past of philosophy is kept alive by the need of those who mean to advance the subject to disengage themselves from their predecessors by some monumental refutation. The exposed error then points the way to a new path to be followed, a new landscape of the mind to explore. As a general rule, the philosopher will attempt, all alone, to solve all the problems, or to show how all of them can be solved. Of course the philosopher will have followers, who for a while will take their problems from the founder's program, and devote themselves to its establishment and consolidation. But almost never is there any subsequent interest in the work of those underlaborers in the service of an original philosophical vision, and everyone waits for the next visionary to come along, who will show us how to liberate ourselves from the past and begin afresh, build anew, design a bold new structure to house us in a universe the whole previous suite of philosophers had radically misconceived. So there is no body of accepted data handed down from generation to generation, no accumulation of knowledge, no progress, but instead an almost comic replacement of those who replaced their forerunners by those who will in turn be replaced in a precarious position at the proclaimed apex of total understanding of which philosophy is supposed to consist. The great works of philosophy are often works of astonishing brevity, considering the vast perspectives they open up, and in which whatever is philosophically visible is philosophically seen.

No view of philosophical thought could be adequate, I should think, which did not account for the curious rhythms of the history of philosophy—the perpetual return to beginnings, the internal urgency of having to dismiss as mistaken the entirety of the tradition save those who may have anticipated one's own breakthroughs, the magisterial laying down of the few simple hidden truths that up to now have defied discovery. For example, the mistakes of the past must have been easy to make and almost impossible to discover, by contrast with theories in the history of science that may have been wrong but often and even typically show considerable ingenuity on the part of those who framed them, and are to be rejected only when theories of greater explanatory power, or more consistency with observations, are advanced. But the usual case in philosophy is suggested to have been by way of an illusion on the part of previous theorists, a deep mistaking of appearance for reality, of men having raised a dust, as Bishop George Berkeley once phrased it, and then complaining they could not see. Whatever may have been the trouble with a theory of the sort held by Priestley—to the effect that combustion is due to the release of a volatile component, known as phlogiston, in all combustible substances—it clearly was not a mistake of the sort whose paradigm might consist in confusing shadows of things for the things themselves. Nor could the overthrow of the phlogiston theory, through a famous crucial experiment by Lavoisier, be at all of the sort that consisted of showing his scientific opponents to have been taken in by appearance. But, as we shall see, in philosophy one has to show that the nature of one's own discovery explains how one's predecessors should have failed to see it—and this means that philosophical discoveries will be restricted primarily to things where a possible confusion of appearance with reality is thinkable.

And philosophical errors will, accordingly, be defined in just these terms. They are not mistakes of judgment, they are not hypotheses that are false or theories that are wrong, but theories instead based on a certain *kind* of wrongness, a kind that, once revealed, casts into almost total irrelevance any thought based upon them. But this means, in effect, that by contrast with the history of science, where what came before was a stage in the discovery of what we now know, as the present itself is a stage in what will come to be known, the whole history of philosophy will be treated by the new philosopher as so much illusion and, hence, not part of a cognitive development. The present is like awakening from a dream, and the dream is not part of waking experience but an aberration from it, belonging to an irrelevant realm of experience, a symptom of cognitive disorder rather than a piece of cognition in its own right. And this explains why the original philosopher feels that history begins with him. Begins and *ends* with him, it might be better to say, for, having shown the way, he has in effect shown all there is to show: The way leads to an end so conspicuous that it is almost pedantic actually to enter on the path. So, internally speaking, philosophy does not have a real history. It is given all at once and, if right, it need never be undergone again. Or, more dramatically yet, the history of philosophy is a long nightmare from which philosophy longs to waken, and from which it seems at any given point to the working philosopher that he *has* awakened—even if, from the cruel vantage point of his successors, it will instead seem as if he had been but part of the nightmare.

# 2

# *The Character of*
# *Philosophical Problems*

2-1  THE SUBJECT OF PHILOSOPHY, if this account of its history is true, must be such that mistakes of this order are possible in connection with it, and I will even at this early stage venture the thesis that a problem is not genuinely a philosophical problem unless it is possible to imagine that its solution will consist of showing how appearance has been taken for reality. I want to illustrate this with some examples that I shall later discuss in some detail.

2-2  *1.* There is a famous passage in the *Meditations* of Descartes, to which philosophers return again and again, in which Descartes finds that the experience he is having is indistinguishable from the experience he might have had if he were *to be dreaming* instead of awake. Since nothing internal to his experience will discriminate satisfactorily between the state of dreaming and being awake, everything he believes on the basis of that experience is immediately put in question. It is conceivable that his experience could be just as it is but had by a being without a body, or without there being a world for the experiences to be about. The difference between dream and waking is not like the difference between anger and sorrow, which we can learn to tell, or the difference between blue and yellow, which we scarcely need to learn to tell, or the difference between seeing a camel and seeing a giraffe, where each has distinguishing features. Indeed, there can be no differences internal to the experience, or the problem would not have the force it has. Any solution, accordingly—if there is to be one—must refer to factors external to experience, not part of experience, whatever these factors are to be.

2-3  2. Kant, who sought a criterion of moral conduct, insists that no such criterion can be found in the behavior of the agent alone. For the person may simply be acting in conformity to principles without knowing what these principles are—like a blind man, to use an image of Plato's, who has taken the right road by accident. Conduct is genuinely moral, then, only when it refers us to moral principles the agent actually uses—but nothing about the conduct itself will assure us that it is moral. So we can imagine two pieces of behavior, exactly alike, one of them moral and the other one not, and the mistake of supposing the one to be the other is easy to make and almost impossible to avoid.

2-4  3. David Hume, concerned with the analysis of causality, offers grounds for the possibility of imagining two universes exactly alike—one of them deterministic in that everything happens as a matter of necessity, and one of them a world of pure chance. In the one, matches light when struck because of the way the world is made. In the other, matches burst into flame on being struck just because they happen to do that, but anything else is equally thinkable, whether it ever happens or not. The two universes are absolutely indiscriminable, but the difference, though not internal (like the difference between two universes, one of which contained giraffes and the other did not), seems somehow momentous. So any difference is to be sought at right angles, so to speak, to the universes themselves.

2-5  4. The philosophical mathematician Alan Turing once imagined a case in which the output of a machine is indiscriminable from that of an intelligent human being. If, Turing argued, there could be no way, internal to the two outputs, of telling which was produced by the human, then either we would have to ascribe intelligence to the machine or withhold ascribing it to the human. If you believe that—comparability of output notwithstanding—there really is a difference between what machines and humans do, you will have to explain where the difference is located, since it is not to be located in the outputs.

2-6  5. Bishop Berkeley distinguished two sorts of fundamental realities—what he called "spirits," which are minds—and what he called "ideas," which are the objects of minds. It is impossible, Berkeley argued, for there to be images of spirits, for they are nonspatial. He also argued that God is a spirit, who must accordingly be unpicturable, unimaginable, indeed invisible. But that means that a universe in which God exists could not be told apart from a universe from which God is totally absent. The presence or absence of God seems to make no difference to how minds experience the world, and if the difference seems momentous even so, then somehow we must think of God as outside the universe. Spinoza thought God was identical with the universe, which again would mean that there is nothing internal to the universe, no inner differentiating feature, and hence no conceivable observation on the basis of which we can tell that God exists. The world of the atheist and the world of the believer would look exactly alike.

2-7  6. The artist Marcel Duchamp created works of art that looked in every outward particular exactly like ordinary objects that were not works of art at all: dog combs, urinals, bottle racks, bicycle wheels, and the like. Indeed, these readymades, as he termed them, had been mere real things before they became works of art by Duchamp, who after all did not make the combs or snow shovels— what would be the point of that?—though he made the works of art. It had seemed down the ages that works of art must be importantly different from mere real things, from which they could easily be told apart. Duchamp showed that the difference, because after all philosophical, was not one that meets the eye.

2-8  The differences between dream and waking, between moral conduct and conduct that merely resembles moral conduct but is morally neutral, between determinism and chance, between thinking beings and mere machines or works of art and mere real objects—or between universes in which God is respectively present and absent— are differences of a different sort than those that divide pairs of things that happen to resemble one another a great deal, such as identical twins, or two products off the same assembly line, or two insects of the same species. The philosopher Leibniz believed it to be a truth of reason that two numerically distinct things, however much they resemble one another, must differ at some point or they would not be *two* things. So, we may be assured, if Leibniz is right, the two insects have at least one unshared feature. Such a feature may be extremely difficult to identify, however, and for practical purposes we may wish simply to create a difference—dress the twins in different-colored skirts, color code the product for quality control, and irradiate the insect we are anxious to track. Still, in each of these cases, the pairs of things belong to the same *kinds,* whereas the philosophically distinct pairs seem to belong to quite different kinds: Yet, in a way, they seem to have everything in common, in the sense that the history of a universe of necessity might be indiscernible from the history of a universe of chance, just as a waking person's sequence of experiences resembles in every particular that of a dreamer. And, though Leibniz's principle assures us that Duchamp's snow shovel differs through *some* feature from the snow shovel that is not a work of art, that feature surely could not make the difference between a work of art and a mere real thing. I mean, suppose the actual difference consisted of a difference in weight of, say, a millionth of a milligram?

2-9 Consider a case in which two things of quite different kinds resemble one another so far as the eye can tell. Usually differences between kinds are very obvious, such as the difference between males and females of our species, based on the usual primary and secondary sexual characteristics—voice, body form, and the like. A man undergoes a transsexual operation and declares him-herself to be a woman, as for all legal purposes she is. But this individual is an athlete who decides to compete against women in athletic events, in which it is argued that she has natural and unfair advantages because of certain muscularities carried over into her new sexual identity. At this point it may be necessary to invoke criteria of being female not ordinarily employed, in order to exclude this person from the events in which it is said she has no right to participate, though otherwise female. A sex-change operation leaves chromosomes unaltered, and females have two X chromosomes. At the level to which we have descended, the person is male, even if in most of the practices of life we accept the female classification. But until science made the discovery about chromosomes, there would have been no way of solving the problem. If males and females compose what we may call natural kinds, then there is some basis in reality for differentiating them, and it will require science to say what this basis is.

2-10   The philosopher Hilary Putnam has imagined the possibility of a Twin-Earth, exactly like Earth itself in every respect, including counterparts of you and me, counterparts of the room in which this book—or its counterpart—is being written or read: Whatever takes place on Earth has its counterpart occurrence on Twin-Earth. Any of us would feel exactly at home were we to be transferred there, so long as our counterpart were simultaneously transferred here, so that there would be none of those Shakespearean confusions to which two individuals of the same face and figure give rise. And yet Earth and Twin-Earth differ, but in ways rather like those in which females and transsexualized males differ in the previous example.

2-11   Water, on Earth, is $H_2O$, but water on Twin-Earth is XYZ. At the level of experience, water and Twin-Earth water are exactly of a piece: transparent, thirst quenching, hospitable to fish and frogs, subject to pollution by acid rain. And yet, at the molecular or some submolecular level, they differ. Putnam meant his example to show that *water* must ultimately have different meanings on Earth and Twin-Earth, and this will depend on what science finally has to say about the composition of water—but the important feature for us is that the difference between the two Earths is finally for science to determine. But, once more, you would not expect a chemist to emerge from his laboratory triumphantly waving a computer print-out on which he has circled the place where his researches have shown that Duchamp's snow shovel differs from an ordinary snow shovel. In whatever way their differences are hidden, it will not be for science to penetrate. They are different sorts of differences, hidden in different sorts of ways.

2-12 What I am suggesting, then, is that philosophical problems arise in connection with indiscriminable pairs, the difference between which is not a scientific one. I am supposing that the distinct kinds to which either member of such a philosophical pair belongs are not natural kinds, and that the philosophical way of dividing up the universe is very different—different in kind—from the way in which scientific analysis divides up the universe. If this is so, we might imagine having a complete scientific map of the universe in which all the natural kinds were identified and the differences between them made specific, without this helping to solve a single philosophical question. In a way, the difference between science and philosophy is a philosophical and not a scientific difference—in its way different from any of the differences that may divide the sciences from one another. The sciences, for example, may differ in point of subject matter, addressing different orders of fact. Philosophy may in that sense have no order of fact peculiar and proprietary to itself. Nothing less than the whole universe is its order of fact, for philosophical differences in a sense have to do with the question of what kind of universe it is, and differences between kinds of universes are not differences within the universes themselves (for there may, as in the examples we have discussed, *be* no such internal differences).

2-13 In any case, it is clear that mistaking one member of a philosophical pair for the other is a very easy thing to do, all the more so if no difference between them need ever be imagined as revealing itself in experience at all. Indeed, the differences are such that it might never have occurred to anyone to draw them. They are such that if it requires a special discipline to draw them, then philosophy might never have arisen as a discipline at all. Life could go forward perfectly well without these distinctions ever needing to be thought about. It is as if all the distinctions of concern to philosophy were at right angles to the set of differences it is the task of science to draw. And, hence, as if philosophical differences do not make the kind or kinds of difference that those accessible to science make in practice or understanding of the world. It is as if—just because there

would, in ordinary practice and understanding, be no way of noticing a philosophical difference—such differences have to be *revealed.*

2-14 "The whole function of philosophy," William James wrote in
*Pragmatism,* "ought to be to find out what definite difference it will
make to you and me, at definite instants of our life, if this world-
formula or that world-formula be the true one." But that implies,
and indeed the entirety of James's philosophy concedes as much, that
there is no way of telling whether this or that world formula should
be the correct one. It is only then, when there are two world
formulas incompatible with one another and each compatible with
everything known and knowable, that the question of "what definite difference it will make" arises. By this expression James meant
to designate such things as what it makes me feel happiest to believe,
or what it matters most to me to believe, or even what is good for
me to believe. This is what *pragmatic truth* more or less means, at
least in James. Pragmatism's only test, in his words, is "what works
best in the way of leading us, what fits every part of life best." And
if the belief in God, or in free will, should do this, then, James says,
pragmatism "could see no meaning in treating as 'not true' a notion
that was pragmatically so successful."

2-15 Wittgenstein said once that philosophy begins when language
goes on holiday, and James appears to believe that philosophy begins
when knowledge goes on holiday, having reached the limit of its
possible competence. It is striking that, in James's view, the most
important differences appear to make no cognitive difference at all
and answer, correspondingly, to no piece of knowledge that could
be acquired—for if we could acquire it, it would belong not to
philosophy but to some branch or other of positive science. It is, of
course, of the utmost importance to understand how this limit is to
be known, and whether it is a limit that belongs to us by virtue of
the mere circumstances of our being—that we cannot, for example,
as ordinary earthlings of flesh and blood, lift weights of a thousand
tons—or whether it is a limit for everyone everywhere, a limit on
knowledge as such. And it is a singular question of whether the
problem of drawing this limit belongs to philosophy or to some
branch of positive science. However this question is to be resolved,

whether the limit is absolute and logically impenetrable or contingent in such a way that we can coherently think someone (if not perhaps ourselves) might penetrate it, the fact remains that the issues of philosophy must be settled on some basis other than that of appeal to possible cognitions, even if not possible for us. The question immediately arises, then, whether philosophy is knowledge after all, if there is such a thing as philosophical truth—or whether, instead, philosophy is like a mood, a coloration of the whole of reality, rosy if we are optimistic and blue if we are pessimistic, but in any case not a separable part of the world. James appears to have believed philosophical differences to be of this order. And this means that the world of the optimist and the world of the pessimist—much, as we have seen, the world of the determinist and the indeterminist, the world of the dreamer like the world of the person who is awake, the world of the believer like the world of the atheist—are exactly alike, their differences being differences over the whole of their worlds, and not discernible within their tables of contents. It is as though philosophically different worlds turned more on faith than on knowledge, like the world of the religiously inspired.

2-16 And certainly it is here, at the boundaries between radically different but otherwise indistinguishable worlds, that philosophy itself must begin. This means that there cannot be something in one philosophical world that is lacking in another. It cannot be a philosophical possibility that a genuine division between philosophers can consist of the presence in one world and absence from another of some concrete thing. There can be no such thought as this—if giraffes are to be found, philosophy X is true and philosophy Y false—for the presence or absence of giraffes cannot be a philosophical difference. Each philosophy must be total, and each capable of explaining everything in one another's worlds, whatever it means to explain something in a philosophical way. A philosophical explanation must be one that explains the whole world as a whole.

# 3

## *Two Sorts of Illusions*

**3-1** PHILOSOPHY HAS REALLY ARISEN ONLY TWICE in the history of civilization, once in Greece and once in India. Both times it arose because some distinction between appearance and reality seemed urgent. In India, for example, it seemed of the utmost importance to insist that the world was not really as it appears to be at all, that all the distinctions we make ordinarily, all the things we believe exist, everything we care about or of which we are afraid, is but illusions, since reality has quite another character than that of anything we know. The Hindu thinker went on to argue that our salvation depends utterly on our penetrating the veil of illusion and grasping the true identity of the reality it obscures, as well as our own relationship to it. This inevitably generated a tradition of intense philosophical speculation, but it is reasonably plain that something like revelation, coupled with argument, rather than anything resembling observation or experience had to be relied on, simply because observation and experience belonged to the discredited world of illusion.

**3-2** The motivation for drawing such a distinction in Greece was somewhat different, but it very early occurred to Greek thinkers that the world as it appears to the senses must be radically different from the world we know through reason, and that the former, because of this discrepancy, must be illusory and in consequence not real. Nothing seems more obvious than the fact that apples fall, that animals run, that the sun rises and sets, that the world is in constant motion. But these commonplace things run athwart compelling arguments to the effect that motion is impossible. So the commonplace things must be illusory, and reality must be such that motion is deeply excluded: Reality is logically changeless. *example of this*

3-3 In both traditions, the thinkers were obliged to give a characterization of reality, of what it meant for something to be real. And, indeed, in both cultures this question set the agenda, which the philosophers were to follow on distinct but parallel tracks. Those tracks are followed today by philosophers: They define what philosophy is, in the sense that if it is not on a track that leads back to Greece or India, it is hard to see how it can be philosophy.

3-4 My concern at this stage is not to follow these tracks for any distance, but merely to stress that the distinction between appearance and reality, however it is characterized, is not the same as distinctions that resemble it as we draw them in the routine courses of the world. We teach our children, for example, to distinguish the things it will be important for them to distinguish if they are to have a safe and happy passage through life: between plants and animals, between the different sorts of trees and fishes, between what is useful and what is dangerous. The numbers, kinds, and ways of distinguishing among things will vary from culture to culture, but at no point will it be necessary to make the radical and wholesale sort of distinction that locates the whole world as we experience it on one side, and on the other, something more real than it. Our distinctions are within experience, not between the whole of experience and something else. Of course, within experience, a kind of distinction between appearance and reality will naturally arise. (Bedouins will have to learn about mirages, for example.) And, since there cannot be a human life lived in the absence of water, and because bodies of water are to be found everywhere, everyone will have some experience of reflecting surfaces, and hence with duplicates of things provided by the natural mirror of water. That those reflections are not real, while what is reflected *is* real, is a lesson everyone must learn: Narcissus fell in love with his own reflection, but only because he believed it was someone else in the water, looking up at him. Again, human life requires some modicum of light, so shadows are part of what we naturally experience. In the normal course of sleep, dreams occur, sometimes of great vividness, and it requires special explanations to distinguish dreams from memories that not all cultures possess: In some cultures, dreams are believed to be just memories of experiences had when outside one's body in sleep. And there can be few cultures in which there are no pictures, and the distinction between pictures of animals and animals themselves will tax a culture's conceptual resources. It is important that dreams, pictures, shadows, reflections, and illusions be distinguished from real things, without any of this giving rise to philosophy.

3-5 It may be true that these distinctions, *within* experience, provide the *models* philosophers would need for their speculations that there exists a comparable distinction *between* experience, taken as a whole, and something more real than it. If there were no experience we could point to for drawing a distinction between illusion and reality within experience, the Hindu would be unable to make intelligible his claim that experience as a whole is illusion. Were there no available distinction between shadow and substance, Socrates would have been unable to mount a metaphor for maintaining that the whole experienced world of sense is but a shadow cast by the real world grasped through the intellect.

# 4

## *Philosophical Kinds*

4~1

*T*HE ABRUPT AND TOTAL GENERALIZATIONS drawn by the ancient speculative philosophers may be misguided; they may simply be inspired artifacts of routine distinctions allowed to spill wildly outside the circumstances in which it was useful to have drawn them; but at this early stage in my exposition, my concern is only to say that it is just such distinctions as these, whatever their proper scope, which marked off the special area of philosophical thought. In the case of Plato, for example, it might reasonably be argued that had it not been for the advent of illusory art—art in connection with which it would be possible to make the mistake of believing one were experiencing a real happening or a real thing rather than the imitation of one in dramatic presentation, sculpture, or painting—the problem of drawing distinctions as he did would never have arisen, of defining knowledge in contrast with mere belief, of characterizing reality in contrast with mere appearance, and the rest. But, having this task forced upon him, Plato had no choice but to work the entire thing out, with appearances on one side and reality on the other, with answers to the question of what the relationships between the two must be, of how we are to mark the differences in cognitive access to either, and of what difference it may make in our lives if we get it wrong. The entire Platonic system, bold as it is, consists of just a few relationships between just a few fundamentally different kinds of things. Vast in its scope and imaginative in its execution as his system was, it is easy to see how a single person, having first sensed the need for such a system, should have been able, all alone, to work it out in its entirety, at least in principle—easy to see how the whole system could be set out in just a few pages.

4-2 Well, to understand what philosophy is requires that we understand the kinds of things between which these relationships hold and what these relationships are. It has been claimed that the whole of Western philosophy is but a set of footnotes to Plato. In a way this is true: Plato was among the first, if not the first, to have grasped the structures that exercise philosophical thought, and having done so to discharge the entire task, all at once, as though there were nothing save details to work out and objections to be met. But in a way it is false: Anyone who undertakes philosophy is going to have to deal with all the same kinds of things and all the same kinds of relationships, hence is going to have to discover what Plato discovered, without this being a comment on Plato. In a way, and this is the last of my initial observations, philosophy—if its subject is to be just these things and just these relationships—is going to be essentially the same whoever discovers or rediscovers it. And that, if true, would account at last for the strange cadences of the history of philosophy, which seems to consist of the same drama reenacted over and over again, as though in compliance with the same choreography—as though philosophers were constrained to tread the same magic circle, to realize one or another of the very few positions logically available. Plato's system is rather a full array, but it is possible to imagine a more meager structure than his—everything is appearance, or appearance is reality, or the distinction between appearance and reality is spurious or nonsense—which will nonetheless be argued for, insisted upon, over and over again.

4-3 The Hindus held a belief in reincarnation, according to which the soul is born again in different bodies and is obliged to live different lives. The differences from lifetime to lifetime may be considerable: The differences between men and women, rich and poor, weak and strong, talented and graceless, healthy and sick, kings and commoners—or between gods and humans—seem vast from the perspective afforded by the position into which one has been born. But these differences even out over the (very) long run of which karmic rebirth consists, until finally one life seems so little different from another that the Hindu is overwhelmed by the almost nauseating monotony. After a time the thing is not to aspire to a better form of life but to no form of life at all, with the most supreme good imaginable that of breaking out of the cycle of rebirth radically and definitively, never to be born again. Philosophy in its way is like this, granting that the number of philosophical systems seems fewer than the number of kinds of possible lives lived in the immense time spans the Hindu metaphysician enjoyed projecting. There are grave and substantial differences from system to system, at least as viewed from the perspective of any single system that sees its rivals as fatally wrong. And yet, in an important sense, there is a cloying sameness from system to system, the same array of distinctions coming up again and again, so that a thinker like Santayana, without quite recognizing the horror of the claim, was able to say that under whatever sky he would have been born, he would have come up with the same philosophy! Imagine a great scientist saying this about his or her science. Or a great artist. The art historian Heinrich Wölfflin said, taking history seriously, that not everything is possible at every time. Philosophy seems immune from this historicity. Santayana is right: The same philosophy is always possible. In a way no other philosophy is possible at all, save in terms of minor variation. This is why philosophy is always beginnings, and why all beginnings seem essentially alike.

# 5

## *Philosophy as Pathology*

**5-1** A DISCIPLINE WHOSE CHARACTER is given by this extreme repetition, in which in the nature of the case the same structures appear and reappear like the figures on a carousel, may come naturally to be regarded less as genuine thought than as the pathology of thought, a kind of disease, just as the Hindu thought of life itself as a kind of cosmic illness. And just as the Hindu sought a radical cure for the disease exemplified by even the healthy, happy, and fulfilled life, there have been radical thinkers who have sought to get rid of philosophy, to stifle once and for all the propensity to think that way at all. There is an interesting question whether this is to take a position outside the cycle of positions, or whether this is one of the positions, part of the cycle, part of what one longs to escape from rather than escape itself. As though it may be true that philosophy only arises here and there, but it is never true that it dies, at least not by internal decay. Of course it could be extirpated by external causes—that is, people could just lose interest, or terrible sanctions could be ruthlessly applied.

**5-2** Whether inside or outside the cycle of philosophy, antiphilosophical philosophies have marked the present century. Twentieth-century philosophy has characteristically conceived philosophy itself, in its most general terms, as something to be dealt with and dissolved so totally, discredited so completely, that there will never be philosophy again. Thus the whole of Western philosophy is conceived of as a great aberration, a rupture of an intimate connection between man and being, according to Martin Heidegger, and we must return to this healing unity if we are to be saved. Philosophy must devote itself, according to John Dewey, to the practical problems of human life and abandon any pretense of having problems of its own. Philosophy must address itself to the clarification of scientific concepts, according to the logical positivists, for whom science alone offers the possibility of knowledge and understanding and exemplifies practices any deviation from which is nonsense. Philosophy must return to the distinctions of daily experience and study rather than impugn the structures through which ordinary men and women relate to the world—such was the recipe of phenomenology. Philosophy, as it has been practiced for millennia, begins only when language goes on holiday, was the thought of Ludwig Wittgenstein, as we said. His follower, J. L. Austin, encouraged philosophers to return from their obscurities and examine ordinary language, which houses all the distinctions the species has found it important to frame, and which holds the answers to all sensible questions if we consult it with care. If we add to this array of positions the exaltation of simple persons in Marxism and Maoism, ours has been a century in which, by deliberate opposition to philosophers, the common man has been celebrated.

5-3   The death of philosophy has been, then, the constant message of contemporary philosophical writing, but with this dark forecast have come, and always as consolation, the programs that—if followed instead of their traditional wayward paths—mean philosophers will find themselves doing something useful for mankind. Although there is little agreement on the program, little agreement, for that matter, on what precisely was the cause of death, there has been small dissent in regard to the morbid fact. Nevertheless, there is a serious question of whether the coroners of philosophy have succeeded in performing their autopsies without resurrecting the dead. For it is almost as if the distinctions offered as the cause of philosophy's demise reappear in the explanation of it—almost as though one cannot pronounce philosophy dead save through the mouth of philosophy itself. This would have a profound consequence, it seems to me, if true: It would mean that one cannot talk intelligently about philosophy save from *within* philosophy, so there can be no rational escape from philosophy at all. After all, Heidegger did not turn his back, he summoned us to reencounter being. The positivists did not close the books and take up test tubes. The phenomenologists did not become psychologists and sociologists. Austin did not study and contribute to linguistics or lexicography. Dewey did do a number of practical things—he set up systems of education and headed commissions—but we study his pragmatism—his philosophy—unless, as historians, we study his practice. You cannot cure the mind of philosophy without using philosophy.

5-4 If there is anything to this paradox, it suggests two possible courses of action. One is simply to stop philosophizing, to stop in particular philosophizing about philosophy and do something else. A stronger version of this path is not to allow anything to be said about philosophy, and to hope for a kind of universal stupefaction. This would be the intellectual equivalent of the way in which the Chinese militants sought to deal with the crime of intellect during the Cultural Revolution: Send the intellectual to live the hard, grinding existence of the peasant in the hope that the propensity to intellectualize will expire through fatigue and brutalization.

5-5 The other way is to accept the fact that the internal dissolution of philosophy inherits all the features we have been ascribing to philosophy itself. For one thing, there remains the distinction between appearance and reality, for it has certainly seemed to philosophers that they were doing something serious and important, though it now turns out that it only appears that they have. They supposed that they were advancing real truths, but in fact they only appeared to be doing that, since their propositions were not real propositions but apparent ones, and their problems were not real problems but pseudoproblems, as the positivists used to say. And the solution to the problems of philosophy seems at once as simple and as elusive as philosophers who make new beginnings have always supposed their solutions to be. Sometimes, as with the positivists, all it takes to solve the problem is to distinguish meaningful from meaningless utterance, a problem and a solution that seemed to have evaded thinkers for two millennia! Of course, meaningless utterances have to resemble meaningful ones very closely indeed if the fact that they are meaningless has not been noticed. It is not as though the utternaces of Plato looked like something as meaningless as "blah blah blah blah blah"—or as ill formed as "cats when catch from tertiary" or "winged under over single wooden simple." They were almost as indiscernible from meaningful utterance as dreams are supposed to be from waking experience. And how long can it take to solve the problems of philosophy if all it takes is the laying down of the criteria of meaningfulness? Ten pages would seem to be a lot. Ten lines ought to do it, details and objections aside.

# 6

# ✳ Wittgenstein and Plato

6-1

NO WORK OF TWENTIETH-CENTURY PHILOSOPHY better exemplifies the features I have been discussing than the curious *Tractatus Logico-Philosophicus* (1922) of the Viennese thinker Ludwig Wittgenstein. The *Tractatus* consists of seven propositions, together with a number of observations, of gradedly different degrees of importance, on all but the final proposition—"Whereof one cannot speak, thereof must one be silent"—which stands alone. The book as a whole is about ninety small pages in all, and the author writes at the beginning that the truth of the thoughts it communicates is "unassailable and definitive." (Wittgenstein not many years later changed his mind completely.) There is a further consideration, namely that his work shows "how little has been done when these problems have been solved." The reason is that the problems are philosophical problems, and what Wittgenstein means to do is to show that they are no problems at all but puzzles believed to be problems—muddles believed to be mysteries—because the philosophers who addressed them did not see that they were due to a certain kind of illusion. So Wittgenstein's intentions are diagnostic and in a way therapeutic. Construing philosophy as a set of symptoms of the wayward intellect, his aim is to relieve us of the agonies they cause by showing their illusoriness.

Perhaps no better way can be found of grasping his meaning than recalling some parallel claims made at times by great religious thinkers. The teaching of the Vedantic school of Hinduism, for example, often proposed that the problems that beset men and women are not real problems at all but illusions to be seen through. Imagine, to use a classical Indian example, a length of rope someone sees as a snake. Believe it to be a serpent, frightening if not dangerous, and all manner of feelings arise together with plans for dealing with it—but when it is seen for what it is—a mere length of rope—the potential dangers dissolve and the feelings subside, since they were grounded in illusion. By comparison with dealing with a real snake, very little has been accomplished in showing that it was not real. All that is involved is a certain minimal displacement of perception and intelligence. And yet the change is momentous when things are seen for what they are. The *whole world,* the Hindu thinker goes on to insist, is illusory in this sense, and the problem is not to deal with the problems to which it appears to give rise but to see through them to a different order of reality. If we compare the achievement of these thinkers to the practical activities of snake hunters, their achievement is minimal. But in terms of the radical restructuring of vision, their achievement is immense. They have solved no problems as such, simply showed there were no problems to solve. For Wittgenstein the problems of philosophy are like the problem of the snake: There *was* no snake, and so no problem. "The deepest problems," he wrote, "are really *no* problems."

Wittgenstein supposed that what appeared to be the problems of philosophy were due, one and all, to the fact that philosophers did not understand "the logic of our language." Language, or the failure to understand its logic, interposes between thinkers and proper thoughts a set of disguises, and with the disguises the problem is to penetrate them and recover the thought they conceal. For this, of course, one must first recognize that they *are* disguises, just as the problem, the solution to which is a *cure,* is for the neurotic to recognize that he is sick. There really is, then, no ambition any longer to be a philosopher, understood as one who takes problems as real ones, but to do something altogether different, namely to rectify the language of philosophy: to show how one's predecessors had been systematically bewitched by language. One must develop a strategy for identifying these bewitchments and displaying their utter illusoriness. The result of this will not be more philosophy, for there is no point in more philosophy, no point in laying out and defending a set of philosophical theses. "Philosophy," Wittgenstein claimed, referring to his new rather than to the old sense of the term, "is not a theory but an activity." The activity consists of elucidations of what is being said behind what one thinks is being said. "The result of philosophy is not a number of philosophical propositions but to make propositions clear." *Analytical* philosophy, as it came to be called, was just such a program of logical clarifications.

I have stressed a comparison between Wittgenstein and religion, as well as emphasized the prominent role in his thinking of the idiom of appearance and reality, in order to show the deep continuities between his thought and the thought of the tradition it was his aim radically and totally to subvert. For Plato, too, the preoccupations of men and women with the world are not as serious as they take them to be, because the world itself is but a set of appearances to be seen through. We are bewitched by the senses, as Wittgenstein supposes we are bewitched by language. And though ordinary persons so bewitched would not think of themselves as philosophers, they are victims of a philosophical mistake, consisting of taking appearance for reality. What is frightening in the world has as little substance as the snakes of Indian philosophy, and its pleasures are correspondingly shallow. The Hindu thinker places alongside the snake-rope example the one of the piece of mother-of-pearl someone believes to be a piece of silver. The jubilation of finding it cannot survive the recognition of its worthlessness. In just this sense, Plato argued, the triumphs and exultations elicited by the good things of this world—riches, power, sexual joy—are but the result of shadows in which we ought finally not to believe. The true philosopher sees through them, cannot be tempted by them or distracted—which is why Plato proposes, with an air of paradox, that the philosopher should be king. Nothing could corrupt him in the world over which he rules because the things of that world are, to him, utterly without substance.

Plato conveys an image of the human condition as one of being imprisoned in a cave, an image that in a sense has to seem false to those who hear it, for they are able to distinguish, within experience, the differences between being in a cave and being outside it, as between being in prison and being free. Clearly, in the terms they have learned to use, they are not in caves or prisons at all. But Plato wants to say that their imprisonment consists exactly of their incapacity to recognize their condition for what it is: Their *resistance* is the problem. There are, of course, illusions by which we continue to be taken in when we know they are illusions, unlike the rope taken for a snake. We will always see the moon as larger on the horizon than when directly above our heads, even though we know it subtends the same angle. We will always see the stick immersed in water as bent, even though we know it is straight. As long as we have senses, we will continue to see and feel things as we do, whatever knowledge prescribes. In a way we can only escape the prison in moments of understanding, not in life. Even so, the ordinary people of whom Plato speaks have not attained that understanding, and so do not understand the sense in which the senses are a prison. For the conditions of understanding this are incompatible with the beliefs they have—that reality is as it appears. So the philosopher who tells them otherwise has to sound insane. It was in part because of the gibberishness of his message to the understanding of those most in need of grasping it that the philosopher becoming *king* must strike those people as crazy—as Plato was aware that it would.

The sum of what the prisoners know consists, if they but knew it, of shadows projected onto the walls of their cave. Those shadows are the touchstones of intelligibility for beings in their circumstances, and they explain the meaning of their words with reference to those shadows. But for just this reason they have no resources for saying that what they know are shadows. This is a statement about their experience made from *outside* that experience. All they know is what is inside their experience, though they cannot so much as say this, since the concept of *outside,* which *inside* presupposes, is inaccessible to them. When philosophers speak as commen men and say that nothing is intelligible that cannot be defined in terms of sense experience, they are making this statement about experience from the outside, as it were, which means that they are not speaking as common men at all. When, as we shall see, philosophers dismiss Platonic philosophy as nonsense because it refers to things indefinable in terms of sense experience, they really remain philosophers through taking a stand from outside experience. If they are right, they are wrong, for how is *their* language intelligible? It does not refer to what we see and hear but refers to *referring* to what we see and hear.

# 7

## *Inside and Outside the World*

IT IS THE VERY ESSENCE OF PHILOSOPHY to undertake to characterize a certain domain from outside it—experience, as in Plato, from outside experience; language, as in Wittgenstein, from outside language—and hence to say things that cannot be explained in terms that derive their meaning from inside those domains. At best, distinctions within the domain furnish metaphors for what the philosopher cannot say directly. *Inside* and *outside* are themselves perhaps metaphors in this sense. It is not a disfigurement of philosophy that it should resort to metaphors, since what it means to say is after all true and could be seen as true if we could occupy a position, as the philosopher pretends to do, outside the domain he seeks to characterize. It is only when the domain is as wide and total as experience or language that this is rendered difficult to conceive. If we lived in a perfectly fluid world, it would be difficult to describe the world for what it is, since we would know only what is fluid. But if fluids have differing degrees of viscosity, a metaphor might enable us to say something about the world from outside the resources it allows. Even if we cannot say it directly, however, it remains true that the world we want to characterize is a fluid world.

Wittgenstein, in this respect, was as much a philosophical visionary as Plato was, with an audacious and external theory of the world he also thought he could not directly express. Roughly, his vision was this: The world is composed of the total set of facts. He drew an important distinction between facts and things. The world does not, in his view, consist of such things as roses and robins, but *facts* about roses and robins—the *fact* that roses are red, the *fact* that robins eat worms, and so on. It is the facts that make the world a world. So it is clear, or clear enough, what he is trying to say: He wants an explanation of how it is that the world is intelligible. To say it consists of facts is a way of giving that explanation. For facts correspond to sentences, and when we understand a sentence, we understand what fact would make it true. So the world being said to be composed of facts explains how we are able to describe the world. The understanding of the world and the understanding of language are of a piece.

7-3  Wittgenstein supposed it to be the task of science to represent the various facts that make up the world, and speaks of "the total natural science" as the set of all sentences that corresponds to what facts there are. It is as though to each fact there is a sentence and to each true sentence a fact, and the total natural science is a kind of mapping of the one onto the other. There is a question of what kind of fact *this* statement describes, and hence whether this statement is part of the total natural science; and it is not difficult to appreciate that in a way, in describing the relationship between science and the world, one is doing so from a position outside science. I shall return to this. I shall return, too, to the thought that, whatever its status, the picture of science that Wittgenstein gives is a very restricted one. Science, it may be said, does not just record the facts, it explains them. (And it is worth a moment's reflection to contrast scientific explanation, which makes this or that fact intelligible, with the essentially philosophical explanation Wittgenstein is concerned with, which asks how to explain the intelligibility of the world). In any case, it is Wittgenstein's thought that an essential contrast exists between philosophy and science because there are, in the world, no facts for philosophy to record—philosophy lies outside the total natural science. Since there are no philosophical facts, there is nothing for philosophical propositions to be true of or false of, and Wittgenstein is insistent that the utterances of philosophy are neither true nor false. If being true or false in a straightforward way is the criterion for a proposition's being meaningful, as many of Wittgenstein's followers proposed, then it follows immediately that the sentences or propositions of philosophy are not meaningful. And this is just what Wittgenstein declared: "Most propositions and questions, that have been written about philosophical matters, are not false but senseless. We cannot therefore answer questions of this kind, but only state their senselessness." And for Wittgenstein, as for many who followed the path he was breaking, just here is the final disposition of philosophy, which adds and can add nothing to our knowledge. How could it, if there are no facts of philosophy? Science and science alone can contribute to knowledge. The best philosophy can hope to do is to explain how science does this. The only task for philosophy is the clarification of science.

7-4 Now, Plato certainly would have insisted that there are philosophical facts, or at least things of a kind philosophy is uniquely equipped to deal with. And these things, or facts, would have been brought in by him in specific response to the very question Wittgenstein himself supposed it necessary to postulate the existence of facts in order to be able to answer: What accounts for the world being intelligible? Wittgenstein's answer to this was that the world is made up of facts, and facts themselves have certain forms. The forms that facts have are the very forms that propositions have; so much so, indeed, that Wittgenstein was prepared to say that a proposition is a *picture* of a fact, drawing on that feature pictures have that enables them to represent things, namely that they share the same form. This is known as Wittgenstein's Picture Theory of Meaning, and this is not the place to discuss it further. I bring it in mainly to extend the parallels with Plato. Plato supposed that the world we inhabit, cavelike and imprisoning as it must be, is nevertheless marginally intelligible. The cave dwellers, for example, living among shadows, are able to find structures among and between the shadows, so they are in the end capable of integrating their experiences in some more or less coherent way. On the basis of certain experiences, they are able to anticipate others and so build up structural hypotheses by which they can live. It never occurs to them to ask how the world they know allows them to do this, but Plato has an answer. It is that outside the shadow world is a real world, composed of forms, or, as he called them, ideas. These forms exist in a world of their own, and they, by comparison with the shadows, are fully real. They never change, though the shadows change without cease. And the shadows have the structures they have because they are penetrated by the forms. Science, as Plato understood it, grasps the forms in appearances. Philosophy assures that science is possible by explaining what science does, which is to grasp the forms that underlie all of experience. In an odd way, appearances are intelligible in the same way that—for Wittgenstein—facts are, by sharing structure with something whose intelligibility may be assumed: forms in the case of Plato, propositions in the case of Wittgenstein. Or, better, forms in the case of Wittgenstein too, for we understand, according to him, language and world together by grasping the forms they share.

1-5  Wittgenstein himself would have been exceedingly severe with Plato. He would have seen in Plato's postulation of forms exactly the sort of bewitchment of which, according to his harsh diagnosis, philosophy always consists. "Philosophy is not one of the natural sciences," he wrote. "The word 'philosophy' must mean something that stands above, or below, but not beside the natural sciences." But, of course, philosophers have always said something like this. The positivists, having no information of their own to offer, saw philosophy as below the natural sciences, carrying out essentially domestic chores of clarifying the language with which information is primarily given. "Handmaidens to science" is the way they conceived of themselves, by sharp contrast with "Queen of the Sciences," which is the role philosophy had traditionally and arrogantly assigned itself, answering the most fundamental questions that there are—namely how science itself is possible, which means in effect what conditions must be satisfied if the world is to be intelligible to science. Plato saw philosophy as the deepest science thinkable or, if not a science, then deeper than science. But so must Wittgenstein have felt this, that philosophy is something above the sciences, explaining how in the end they are possible. And he, too, offers an account of how the world must be if they, the sciences, can be.

7-6 Instead of this Wittgenstein makes a sharp and unanticipated turn. He says that philosophy is nonsense, which means that the *Tractatus* itself must be nonsense, if it is philosophy. And Wittgenstein had the courage of his convictions and went on to say that the very book in which philosophy is stigmatized as nonsense is nonsense in its own right—which ought to mean that even the claim that philosophy is nonsense is nonsense, if it is a philosophical claim. At the end of the book he proposes that we throw the book away. Like a ladder that we have climbed to get where we are and has no further use, it should be discarded. Of course ladders are for going up *and* for going down, but Wittgenstein evidently never thought of descending, and in this he was unlike Plato, who believed the philosopher must at some time descend into the cave to disclose the things he knows to his colleagues lost in the shadows. Now there is no way in which he can translate what he has come to know into a language they understand, for all they know are shadows. They do not know and cannot say, save in terms of metaphor, that these are shadows. They cannot grasp, except again in metaphor, what the philosopher is trying to tell them. Strictly speaking, what he has to tell them is nonsense relative to their language. And in a way this is exactly the case with Wittgenstein. The statements the *Tractatus* makes about science cannot be put into the language of science. Relative to that language, which is directly about the world, what philosophy says is nonsense. The scientist in Wittgenstein is like the cave dweller in Plato: For both of them philosophy cannot be understood. The difference is that Plato thinks of his cave dwellers as intellectually inferior for being unable to grasp philosophy: They then have to be led by a person whose reasons they cannot comprehend (and of course the entire apparatus of forms may but be a metaphor for the general principles that govern the world and that the philosopher in the nature of his calling can grasp, the rest of us living in the swarm of detail that obscures the truth). Wittgenstein, in a mysterious inversion of his own achievement, declares the *philosopher* to be inferior since what he says is not science. If science is the measure of what is sayable, philosophy is unsayable, even when it says that science is the measure of what can be said. But why should we accept this criterion? There is something very odd about a book that insists on its own incoherence when we evidently understand it well enough to know what it claims. And if it lays out a theory of understanding that entails, if it is true, that it cannot be understood, then it is incoherent in an internal, contradictory way. Why then should we accept it? But if we reject it, where does it leave philosophy and the relationship between philosophy and science?

# 8

## The Intelligibility of the World

8-1

*L*ET US SEEK THROUGH AN EXTENDED EXAMPLE to force a distinction between science and philosophy by attending to how
different their respective answers must be to the question of how
the world is, if it is to be understood. Modern cosmology has
concerned itself with a question close enough to this one for us to
use its speculations to this end. It has asked what the case must be
if the universe is to be cognizable, which in effect is to ask: How
must the universe be if cosmology itself—the science that puts that
question—is itself to be something that takes place in that universe?
8-2 It is striking that cosmology situates itself within the universe it
seeks to understand and sees its own existence as among the problems
it undertakes to solve. It rarely happens that a science asks such
questions about itself, or treats science itself as a problem for science,
to be answered in the same way in which it answers the other
questions that fall within its domain. The usual procedure, by
contrast, is for science to forget that it exists or to treat itself as
scientifically invisible. In many cases this will not greatly matter.
There is not likely to be a special law for falling physicists: Physicists
who leap from the rim of the Tower of Pisa will fall at the same
rate as any other lump of matter. But psychology, one would think,
would want an explanation of how the minds of psychologists
particularly work. The theory of evolution ought to be able to

explain how it itself evolved. If a science puts forward a theory that makes it impossible that the putting forward of that theory could be understood, then there is something internally wrong about that theory, just as there is a fault in a philosophy that argues that philosophy, itself included, is unintelligible. Psychology has been flagrant in this regard, holding views of its subject that make radically unclear what it means to hold views. But cosmology is exemplary, in regarding itself as part of its problem and in seeing, between itself and its subject, an internal relationship. It almost resembles philosophy in this self-consciousness. It does so, in fact, in a way that prohibits us from advancing as a criterion of philosophy the fact that it *is* an internal problem for itself.

8-3   Cosmologists have discussed what they term the Anthropic Principle, which rests, as I understand it, on the thought that the world we inhabit is one of a number of physically possible worlds, though the only world in which cosmology itself should exist. Cosmologists speculate, for example, that if a few of the basic constants that figure in the laws of nature were only slightly different—if nuclear force were marginally stronger or weaker than it actually is—the universe in consequence would be sufficiently different so that there would be no beings in it capable of knowledge. The Anthropic Principle makes it sound, after all, just as if the universe were designed with us in mind, like the Garden of Eden. The universe evolves, for example, just because gravity is precisely as weak as it is. Its vast scale is physically presupposed if anything like an evolutionary process is to take place within it on even one planet circling around only one of the $10^{24}$ stars that make up its stellar population. Some writers have even hastily inferred that a being just as great as we conceive God to be must exist in order that in a world as huge and unwieldy as ours is, there should be such creatures in it as us. We are, to be sure, not directly fashioned, like Adam, from a handful of dust. But we may very well be composed of the ashes of exploding stars. Of course, this biblical analogy is just fantasy, and in fact an analogical argument to the existence of the kind of God that is required would rest on a kind of idolatry, as we shall see when we come to consider arguments for the existence of God. Still, it is instructive to think that the universe could not be different than it is, if it were to become revealed, cognitively, some ten to twenty billion years after its explosive beginning, to a portion of itself—us.

8-4 The cosmological procedure, then, is to deduce all sorts of possible universes, to be set alongside the actual universe in thought, and to deduce the physical consequences that would bear on the existence of cognitive beings such as ourselves. And it may be that nothing in the universe could be different if there were to be cosmologists in it. The philosopher F. H. Bradley once said, in parody of a thought of Leibniz, "This is the best of all possible worlds, and everything in it is a necessary evil." The Anthropic Principle is something like that. Other worlds are possible, but *we* depend upon our world being exactly the way it is.

9-5 Now in truth all the possible worlds are intelligible to us, existing in the present world. They would be intelligible to cosmologists existing in them, except there could be none. All the infinite possible worlds are intelligible because we could describe them. And what philosophers would be concerned with is how a world must be if it is to be described. And it is here that philosophers, concerned with that question, begin to bring in factors all the worlds, the actual one and all its possible alternates, must share, if they are to be intelligible. Whatever the measure of gravitational force, if a world is to be intelligible it must, in Wittgenstein's view, be composed of facts and in Plato's view be penetrated by forms. The cosmologists may tell us what the facts are or, if we think of laws of nature as forms, what the forms must be. But that there are facts and forms seems not to be a cosmological fact, and indeed does not seem in any way to depend on the sorts of physical conditions with which the cosmologist deals. There cannot be cosmological evidence for their existence. Or rather, one might say, the possibility of cosmology is evidence for their existence, just because cosmology is intelligible. And it seems genuinely curious that we can say such things without knowing any science at all—that we should, not knowing a thing about our world or any other, cavalierly insist what things any world must have if it is to be understood. On what should we base such inferences?

8-6   I can see no basis for them other than what seems to follow, at best, from a theory of what makes understanding possible, whatever it is we seek to understand. And it is very much as though the philosophers had erected, alongside the structures of science, a structure invariant to all such structures because it is the structure of science itself. Entities such as facts or forms could not be scientifically demonstrated just because the very practice of science must presuppose them. They are invariant to all possible scientific theories. But that makes them not in the least scientific, and if science is the measure of intelligibility, these are really unintelligible entities. It would have been a kind of impatience with postulating entities such as these that turned philosophers against themselves—rightly, in my view—for insisting on the existence of things for which there could not in principle be a shred of differentiating scientific evidence. It is as though, in analyzing what it is for something to be intelligible, philosophers deduced how the world must be from that alone.

8-7   Usually, I believe, philosophical practice has proceeded from certain assumptions of how our understanding of the world must relate to the world if that understanding is to be true. Oddly, in my view, philosophers have supposed the world must have the structure of understanding itself if it is to be understood. Or that, if the structure of the understanding should be linguistic, then the structure of the world should itself be linguistic, if the world is to be understood. That the world and language must share a form, as a picture and its subject must share a form, is a natural theory if that assumption should be granted. But why should we grant it? Is it not conceivable that the world could be any way whatever, consistent with our arriving at an understanding of it? Just as all possible universes are consistent with the possibility of cosmological representation, even if only one of them could have cosmologists *in* it?

# 9

# The Structures of Philosophical Thought

9-1

FOR PLATO, TO UNDERSTAND THE WORLD is to grasp the forms that the things in the world exemplify or embody—of which these things are, in Plato's term, "appearances." This account involves three components—subjects, the world, and forms—and three distinct relationships—between subjects and forms, subjects and appearances, and forms and appearances. Thus the subject grasps the forms, which in Plato is a kind of intellectual intuition. Things appear to the subject, chiefly through the senses. The forms "penetrate" or "participate" (again Plato's terms) in those appearances. However picturesquely Plato, a stylish thinker, embroidered on these components and relationships, they constitute the substance of his mature philosophy.

For Wittgenstein, at least in the *Tractatus,* to understand a proposition is to know how the world must be if the proposition is true. Again there are three components—subjects, propositions, and the world, conceived of, as we saw, as sets of "facts"—and three relationships—understanding, which holds between subjects and propositions; truth, which holds between propositions and facts; and knowledge, which holds between the subjects and the facts that make the propositions the subjects understand true. Subtracting for the eccentricities of the text (the brilliant obiter dicta that make the text worth reading even if we reject the philosophy), the essentials of Wittgenstein's philosophy are to be found here. He himself rejected the entire edifice of understanding and the world in his later philosophy, but he had different concepts of understanding, of language, and of the relationship between language and reality when he did so. I shall have occasion to discuss the differences in a later section.

The components and relationships we find exemplified in Plato as in Wittgenstein appear again and again in philosophy. Descartes, only for instance, regards understanding as a relationship between the self—the "I"—and the subject's mental representations. His problem is whether, from this understanding, I can achieve knowledge, namely whether my representations, which he termed "ideas," are true. When they are true, and when what makes them true explains the fact that I have the representations in the first place, then I can claim to possess knowledge. But there are the components—self, representation, and reality—and the relationships—understanding, truth, and explanation.

Many philosophers have advanced philosophies that seek to eliminate one or another component and, accordingly, one or another relationship. They try to collapse the distinction between self and reality or between representation and reality. For Jean-Paul Sartre the self is just a thing among the things that make up the world. For Bishop Berkeley no coherent distinction is to be drawn between ideas and things. Of course, when these reductions are attempted, complexities are required to appear somewhere in the system to indicate the fact of their elimination. Sartre has to introduce consciousness in place of the ego but then resists reducing consciousness to its objects. Berkeley, for whom reality is just our representations, has to explain how I can misrepresent if there *is* nothing for me to misrepresent or represent. So the same steady array of components and relationships defines the structure on which any philosopher must work.

I shall accordingly venture the conjecture that philosophy is just the effort to understand the relationships between subjects, representations, and reality. Of course this means that the picture philosophy presents of selves, representations, and reality will be exceedingly thin and abstract, for in truth the philosopher is to be concerned with these components only insofar as they impinge on one another in terms of the essential philosophical relationships. Thus, characteristically, the self is going to be addressed primarily in its capacities as understander of representations and as cognizer of the world. There is more to us than this, as there is more to life than these, but what does not touch upon these matters will not finally be of great interest to philosophy.

9-6 To be sure, knowing ourselves and the world we inhabit to be infinitely richer than any philosophy can possibly represent limits the interest philosophy may have for us. Nevertheless, the structures—being those of knowledge, understanding, and being—are very basic and, in compensation for the austerity of the picture they yield of the world and ourselves and our relationships, there is comfort of a kind in recognizing that if we arrive at some truths in these matters, they would be truths for any order of cognitive being in any world whatever, and not just parochial features of human beings on Earth. We may or may not be the only such creatures, that being for science to say. All philosophy can offer is that if there are beings of this order other than us, they are our philosophical kin, for the structure of understanding must be the same in any universe—and the limits of understanding will fall indifferently on Alpha Centaurians, if they exist, and us.

# PART II

# Understanding

# 10

# *Vehicles of Understanding*

10-1

"To UNDERSTAND A PROPOSITION," Wittgenstein wrote, "means to know what is the case, if the proposition is true." Understanding a proposition, according to this elegant formulation, is knowing what its meaning is, and its meaning must then be the conditions under which it is true. So understanding a proposition, for Wittgenstein, consists in grasping these truth-conditions.

10-2 It is perhaps best at this point to consider only quite simple propositions—those expressed, in effect, by simple declarative sentences with a subject and a predicate, like "The street is wet" or, slightly less simple, with two subjects related in a certain way, like "Othello loves Desdemona." To understand such propositions as these is in effect to know to what the subject refers, and to know what property or relationship the subject must have if the proposition is true. One need not know that the proposition *is* true, only what the case would have to be if it were. As a general rule, in order to know whether a proposition is in fact true requires something further than understanding alone can yield. I well understand "The street is wet," but whether this in addition expresses something I *know* will require some activity beyond the mere grasping of meaning—looking out the window, say, to see whether or not the street is wet. As a general rule, then, understanding does not entail knowledge in this sense. We understand most of the propositions in a book of history, and we also know them to be true if the author is to be trusted. But we also understand the propositions in a fictional story, and while the mechanisms of understanding are the same in the two cases, the one text gives knowledge while the other does not, being fiction—and the distinction between history and fiction takes us well beyond anything compassed by meaning and understanding alone. As we shall see, the distinction between knowledge and understanding is of the greatest philosophical importance. In this part of this book, I mean so far as possible to keep questions of knowledge segregated from those of understanding. Here as elsewhere, it is exceedingly difficult to talk about any part of philosophy without talking about every part of philosophy. And in fact even this minimal characterization of propositional understanding is going to shape the way in which we think about the question of knowledge.

10-3  Wittgenstein, for reasons somewhat peculiar to his theory of language at the time, thought that a proposition was a sort of picture—a picture of a "fact"—so that propositional and pictorial understanding were of a piece for him. And in a way it does seem easier to understand how we understand pictures than how we understand propositions. Recognizing what a picture is of, for example, seems to call on the same sorts of perceptual skills that enter into recognizing things as such—the same neural pathways may be activated in the recognition of a picture of a tree as in the recognition of a tree itself, whereas nothing like this seems plausible for understanding the word *tree*. To understand *tree* requires a special kind of learning and perhaps a special sort of association of *tree* with trees. But as a general rule we do not need to learn how to recognize pictures of trees as long as we can recognize trees. Even animals are able to recognize pictures of things, though animals show no signs of linguistic competence whatever.

10-4  In any case, Wittgenstein perhaps thought of pictures this way: A picture shows how the world must be if the picture portrays the world the way it is. Of course it does not show that the world in fact *is* that way. Imagine a picture which shows the Empire State Building side by side with the Eiffel Tower. The picture shows two structures side by side, but of course those two structures are not really side by side at all, and stand in different cities. Still, pictures enable us to identify persons and scenes easily enough, and when the person or scene matches the picture, we can say, without too greatly stretching the concept, that the picture and the thing or scene so relate to one another, that the picture is true. A "false" picture in this sense shows the world other than the way the world really is.

10-5 There are many reasons to reject the thought that propositions are pictures, and hence to doubt the pictorial theory of meaning on which this assimilation would depend. Even so, there is a parallel of an important sort between pictures and propositions, and one could offer a formulation of pictorial understanding much like Wittgenstein's—"To understand a picture means to know what is the case, if the picture is true." And once more, simply understanding a picture in this way will not yield knowledge that the picture is true—that the world is the way the picture shows it to be. The picture shows a possible state of affairs that is actual only if the picture happens to be true.

10-6 We might say at this point that to understand a picture is to know what it is a picture of. But the word *of* is fraught with philosophical treachery, and it will be a helpful inoculation at this point to show how it is so. Take perhaps the most familiar sorts of pictures we have—ordinary snapshots. We say, "This is a picture of my dogs, Charlotte and Emilio." And indeed the snapshot shows two glowering dogs. The "of" seems to connect the piece of film and the two dogs in a certain way. Snapshots are such that light reflected from an object sets up photochemical processes that cause an image that looks like the object to form on a surface. So a photograph consists of an image that is caused by what it resembles. And so to be *of* that object means to be caused by what the picture resembles. But then, obviously, if this is what *of* means, you cannot know what a photograph is of without knowing that there are things that cause it to have the shape it has, and without knowing what these things look like—pictorial understanding would ipso facto yield knowledge of the snapshot's truth. But there are certainly a good many pictures of things where nothing like this is true. There is a picture of the Holy Trinity by Masaccio in Florence—but was it really caused by the Holy Trinity, and does the Holy Trinity, if it exists, really look as Masaccio depicted it? The answer is clearly no, and the *of* in "picture of the Holy Trinity" must differ in force and meaning from the *of* in "snapshot of my dogs," since the latter *of* carries causal information about the way the world is. The first *of* simply refers to the picture's content or subject, without enabling us to know whether anything in the world answers to that content or pictorial subject. The second sense of *of* does tell us about the world. But then, clearly, it is false that a snapshot is "of" my dogs if I have no dogs and the photograph has been doctored in some way. But even if God did not exist, even if there is nothing that "The Holy Trinity" denotes, Masaccio's painting would still be "of" the Holy Trinity.

10-7 The one notion of *of* more or less classifies the picture: There are pictures of dogs, of clowns, of houses, of trees. The second use of *of* connects the picture and the world in terms of representational adequacy. So in general we can understand a picture—that is, clas-sify it together with other pictures or identify its content, without knowing anything further. The Unicorn Tapestries at the Cloisters in New York is a "unicorn picture"—it is *of* an animal we know does not exist. Understanding it pictorially is knowing how the world would look if there were unicorns in it and the picture were true. But there are no unicorns. The picture in this sense is false. Well, "Unicorns are savage" is a "unicorn sentence" as those tapes-tries are unicorn pictures. It is, as a sentence, about unicorns.

10-8 I now want to designate as "vehicles of understanding" whatever there is that admits both these senses of *of*—whatever has meaning or content and whatever may be true or false. To understand such a vehicle, then, is to grasp its meaning or content, and this we may follow Wittgenstein in supposing consists of knowing what would be the case if it were true. I speak of these as "vehicles" because they bear a cargo of meaning, but the expression is deliberately ugly in order to draw attention to what I want to talk about, and because there is no expression I know of in English that has as examples everything I would want to consider vehicles of understanding. We have no term, for example, which designates the two main kinds of vehicle we have so far discussed, pictures and propositions. But these are in no sense all the vehicles of understanding there are. There are, for example, names. Yahweh is one of the names of God, one of the ways we refer to the very being we also call God or the Almighty or even He who shall be nameless. So these names have a common content. And if God exists, they are in fact names of him. But of course it does not follow (as we shall later argue) from the fact that we understand the names that there exists a being whose names they are. Understanding what *God* means does not entail that God exists, nor hence that the name is, in the somewhat stretched sense we must allow, "true."

10-9 Philosophers have used different things as vehicles of understanding in different eras. Propositions, or sentences, have come in recent decades to be the favored example, and it is with the meaning of propositions and with their truth that philosophers have mainly occupied themselves. Slightly earlier in time, philosophers were more concerned with signs or with symbols; and signs, too, admit both senses of *of.* Something can be a sign of X without there having to be an X for it to signify in the second sense. Smoke is certainly a sign of fire, but on any given occasion there may be smoke without fire, as with a smoke-making machine. Sneezing is certainly a sign of head cold, but we cannot be certain that a given sneezer on a given occasion in fact is suffering a head cold, for he may be in the grip of hay fever or have taken snuff. Words, as signs, mean what they mean without it following that on any given occasion of their use there exists something that they are descriptions of in the second sense of *of.*

10-10 When we move further back in time, we find philosophers using other vehicles of understanding, such as images, impressions, and most especially "ideas." The term *idea* was introduced into English by John Locke—much as I have introduced the term *vehicles of understanding*—as a term of art. Though the word has long entered ordinary speech, *idea* (except as a translation of the word in Plato) did not exist in English before Locke—it does not appear either in Shakespeare or in the King James Version of the Bible. Locke took it over from Descartes, who again used it in a novel way, to refer to whatever I experience, or whatever might be the content of a mental state. When, for instance, I think of a unicorn, Descartes would say that there is an idea that is the object of my thought, and unicorn is what the idea is of. It has—all ideas have—a content of one sort or another. When I desire a warm drink, there is an object of my desire, once again termed an idea by Descartes, which has a warm drink as its content. *All* ideas are ideas of something in the first sense of *of* and so qualify as vehicles of understanding. And all ideas equally can be ideas of something in the second sense of *of* as well: There may in fact be things in the world that correspond to the ideas of them that I have. For Descartes, as we shall see, one of the great problems of philosophy—the problem with which he is most closely identified and that in fact gave shape to philosophical analysis ever since his fateful writings—was how we are to proceed from the first sense of *of* to the second. How are we to infer, on the basis of having an idea of a world filled with such things as houses and trees and rivers and mountains, that there *is* a world filled with houses, trees, rivers, and mountains *of* which these ideas are true? And as before, it will be important to stress that understanding, which is grasping the content of ideas, is distinct from knowledge, which is to know that an idea with a given content is in fact true. How to move from understanding to knowledge is for Descartes the aching problem of his philosophical masterpiece, the *Meditations*. Still, something like Wittgenstein's formulation may easily enough be adjusted to fit the case of ideas. To understand an idea is to know what the case must be if the idea is true. But this also is not to *know* that the conditions of truth for a given idea are met. And so our ideas could be understood just as we understand them, and none of them in fact be true.

10-11 Propositions, pictures, names, signs, ideas, appearances—for to be an appearance is to be an appearance of something, leaving it always open if the thing itself really appears or not—not to mention impressions, concepts, and images, are all vehicles of understanding as I mean for that expression to be used. Perhaps this does not exhaust the list of cases. Forms, in Plato's sense, certainly are vehicles of understanding, for to be a form is to be a form of something. And yet the form may have no exemplars of which, in the second sense of this crucial proposition, it is the form. Plato fails to mention the form of unicorn, but if, alongside the other forms that compose the furniture of Plato's heaven, there is such a form, it lacks exemplars in the world, and so is an empty or unrealized form. But the form of chair, to use his famous example, has exemplars wherever men and women sit down on something other than the ground.

10-12 I will now stop using the ugly expression and replace it with another. Whatever I have called a vehicle of understanding I shall now designate a representation. All representations are of something, and it is always open to question whether there exists something outside the representation that the latter represents and of which it is true. Some representations are psychological, but of course not all of them are. Pictures exist in the imagination, but also in museums and in picture books. Propositions are units of language, forms (in the Platonic sense) are in a world of their own, ideas may be in the head, impressions are in the senses, appearances are always to someone. I want the concept of representation to cut across all these differences. Wherever they are to be housed, representations are the central components of philosophical thought. For me the problems of philosophy, one and all, are problems of representation. If Wittgenstein's formulation is accepted, then to understand a proposition is to represent something in such a way that one knows what is the case if it is true. In fact, it is to represent it through a proposition—or a picture if we accept Wittgenstein's curious theory that propositions have a pictorial form.

10-13 Everything in philosophy, I believe, falls out of the distinctions drawn in this small section. Thus the philosophical picture of us as men and women is a picture of beings that represent—beings that understand representations and that aspire to truth. If the representations are propositions, we are linguistic; if they are signs, we are sign users; if they are ideas, then it is as beings who have ideas that we will be conceived by philosophers. And the philosophical picture of the world itself has often been specified by the specific vehicle of understanding a given philosopher should take as central to his program. For Wittgenstein, for example, the world is "the set of facts, not things," and a "fact" was something a pictorial proposition showed. Facts and propositions were made for one another, and Wittgenstein simply supposed the world had the same shape as the language with which we represent it. It was, for him, as for legions of other thinkers, as if language could not represent the world unless the world itself were somehow linguistic in its structure, and hence as though language and world mirrored one another. Nietzsche once contended, "We shall not get rid of God until we have gotten rid of grammar," and he meant by this formulation that what we believe the world to be is a function of our grammar, so much so that the division of the world into objects and properties is an artifact of the circumstance that propositions are compounded of (grammatical) subjects and (grammatical) attributes. So if we changed the grammar, we would change our picture of reality and indeed of ourselves and our relationship to reality. Nietzsche went on to argue that the world itself has no structure, that it is infinitely plastic and takes whatever form we give to it. It was as if, from the undeniable fact that the world is not made of words, Nietzsche went on to insist that it had no structure whatever—as if unless it had a grammatical structure it had *no* structure (whereas it has the structures, not themselves artifacts of language, that science finds it to have).

10-14 All of this takes us far beyond the topic of understanding. These exotic views are mentioned in order to make plausible the claim that the concept of representation, and the concept of understanding that goes with it, is so central a component in philosophy that it is easy to appreciate someone who insisted that if there are no representations, philosophy itself has come to an end. Someone unhappy with philosophy as a human enterprise might then attack the concept of representation as the keystone around which the entire edifice would collapse if it were removed. On the other hand it is extremely difficult to suppose there are no representations—for what have we been doing but representing things at every step in this section? Surely the propositions that compose the past several pages represent the thoughts and arguments of a wide class of philosophers. And how have we understood them?

# 11

## *Verification*

WITTGENSTEIN'S DEFINITION of propositional understanding connects together, in a single striking formula, several philosophically central concepts: meaning and truth, understanding and knowledge. But "to know what is the case, if it is true" brings us, the proposition, and whatever makes the proposition true together in a single, striking episode of cognition. It suggests that to understand is to be able to tell whether there is truth or not. Or, inversely, that failure to be able to tell is one with failure to understand. The proposition "the street is wet" represents the street as wet, and understanding is knowing how to check the proposition out against the condition of the street and to see if it *is* wet.

We shall soon see that this representationalist picture of language can be contested, on the ground that language has many uses other than to describe things. Still, description must be pretty central, and the simple declarative sentence must be crucial for a number of the other uses. Consider, just for contrast, questions and commands. "Is the street wet?" certainly has "the street is wet" at its core, and unless one understood that, one could not understand the question, whatever else there is to a question beyond its descriptive core. And similarly with commands such as "Wet the street!" Unless we understood what state of the world constituted compliance with the command, we could hardly understand what was being asked of us. The meaning of a question is a function of its indicative answers, and the meaning of a command is given by the indicative that represents compliance. So for the moment we will confine linguistic understanding, and propositional understandability, to being able to tell whether a proposition is true.

A number of philosophers, known as logical positivists (or logical empiricists), much under the influence of Wittgenstein, drew from his formulation the idea that a proposition was meaningful only if it was verifiable. That is, to understand a proposition meant, for the positivists, knowing how the proposition was to be verified or knowing what observations would verify the proposition to some degree. Their model for meaningful discourse was the language of science, and their general belief was that scientific meaning was inseparable from scientific observations. So they would somewhat modify Wittgenstein's formula to read: To understand a proposition is to know how the proposition is to be verified. And this in effect was, for them, to know what experiences would be required for one to say that the proposition was true or confirmed to some significant degree. With the simple declarative sentences of ordinary language, such as, "The street is wet," little more is required for verification than a glance or, if one is being especially circumspect, a touch. For the street might look wet but in fact be dry, having recently been paved with glass. But verification need not have meant *conclusive* verification, which the positivists were ready to agree seldom was achieved outside, at least, the range of propositions that referred to certain inner states, such as being in pain, where there is little beyond just feeling the pain that would be required to know the proposition that one is in pain to be true. It seemed to them quite consistent with science that we should rarely be altogether certain that a proposition was true beyond question. Perhaps that is why they substituted verification for truth in Wittgenstein's formula.

The verification need only be in principle, as far as they were concerned, for there were propositions they would concede as meaningful though practical impediments made their verification out of the question. At that time, it would scarcely have been believed that we might circle the moon and see whether there were mountains on its other side—for "the other side of the moon" was something one never hoped to see: The moon always showed the same face to the observers on Earth. Still, one knew what would be required to be able to tell whether the proposition was meaningful: One just circled the moon and looked for mountains. Similarly, we may not hope ever to visit the past, but we would, if we could, observe Caesar crossing the Rubicon or Columbus discovering America. So propositions about times and places we never expected to occupy remained meaningful since we knew in general what it would be like to verify them.

Some verificationists took a rather more radical view than this. For them, a proposition was not just meaningful if verifiable: Its meaning *was* its verification. That is, what a proposition means consists of the set of observations through which it would be verified. "The street is wet" requires analysis along the following lines. First, "the street" would have to be defined in terms of some set of observations, whatever observations would be required for one to say something was a street. And "is wet" similarly would be analyzed into certain looks and feels that composed the standard sorts of observations verifying wetness. It was almost as though a sort of dictionary were presupposed, in which there were terms or expressions that were meaningful just in case their meaning would be given in terms that refer to experiences of one sort or another.

The motive for this somewhat radical move lay in the fact that a good bit of the vocabulary of science consisted of terms whose references could not be directly observed but that were defined through certain operations or observations. What, precisely, is blood pressure? It is the pressure of blood against the walls of arteries and veins and capillaries, but reference to blood pressure refers us to the sorts of observations involved in telling what a person's blood pressure is, and hence in using a sphygmomanometer. This seemed to suggest that the meaning of the term finally must consist in those operations and observations we learn about when we learn to *take* blood pressure. Consider a proposition like "The enzyme renin affects blood pressure and electrolyte homeostasis by catalyzing the formation of angiotensin I from circulating angiotensinogen." A rather large body of theory must be mastered in order to verify, hence to understand, this proposition—I certainly don't know what it means, but I have faith that the authors of the scientific article from which I took it do, and that enough others understand it to be able to see if it is true and duplicate this result.

The identification of meaning with verification sometimes leads to very odd results. Some theorists saw little difference between things like blood pressure, which we could not observe directly, and historical episodes, which we could not observe directly either. Still, just as *blood pressure* refers us to readings on the sphygmomanometer, *Caesar* refers us to certain documents—to inscriptions, coins, statuary, papyruses, and the like. The next step was simply to define Caesar in terms of these, and then to say that "Caesar crossed the Rubicon" refers us to observations we would make in archives and libraries and museums—so that the sentence, which seemed to be about a man who performed an action in the past, is *really* about what the historian will find in the future if he undertakes certain operations. And there is something fairly absurd in the claim that propositions about the past are really about the future. Still, a great many scientists were prepared to endorse comparable views, the most familiar perhaps being behaviorism, according to which propositions about mental states, especially the mental states of others, which we cannot ourselves observe, must finally, if they are to be meaningful, refer us to what we can observe. And these would be behaviors not only of animals but other humans. Thus, in effect, to say that someone is angry means, in the implied lexicon of behaviorism, that he is flushed, clenches his jaw, makes loud, rude noises, stamps his feet, and so on. What else, the behaviorist might say, could we mean by the term *anger* than just such things as these?

We shall have opportunity to discuss these radical analyses. Let us for the moment, however, forbear asking what meaning is, or how it is to be understood, and confine ourselves merely to questions of meaningfulness, which were what mainly concerned the positivists anyway. All they wished to insist on was that unless a proposition is verifiable, in principle and to some degree, and hence connects us to experience that will verify or falsify it, it is not a meaningful proposition at all. Indeed, they said abusively, it was not a real proposition in such a case but a "pseudoproposition"—something that looked like a proposition but, being meaningless, was simply nonsense.

For the positivists, the propositions of philosophy, unless they were disguised science and hence implicitly verifiable, were 'pseudo-propositions' one and all—portentous nonsense masquerading as deep wisdom. Their aim was to rid the world of philosophy or, more properly, of metaphysics, once and for all. This was to be achieved by demonstrating its nonsense—and this was to be achieved by making it palpable that no observation could be imagined that would contribute to the verification or falsification of the metaphysical utterance. The verifiability criterion, then, was a sharp blade, designed to cut the philosophical excrescences from the surfaces of discourse, leaving only positive knowledge behind. And this would be provided by science, whose essence was making observations. It was, to be sure, a minimalistic picture of science, but for the positivists this minimum was all that was required to draw the line between science and philosophical nonsense as they felt it must be drawn. For them, the verifiability criterion was almost laughably simple and at the same time exceedingly generous. Anything that could not meet its not especially demanding conditions hardly could be taken as cognitively serious at all. Any philosopher of a certain age can recall the great alarm that was felt in universities when the verifiability criterion was brandished by the brash outriders of the positivist movement. It was as though the deepest beliefs of philosophy were under threat. And the verificationists themselves greatly relished being deflationist, dismissing as so much noise utterances about being, essence, the absolute, pure spirit, and the like.

Very few philosophers today, openly or consciously at least, subscribe to verificationism, though it continues to determine a great deal of philosophical thought and to underlie many of the characteristic moves in contemporary philosophy. The reason it was abandoned was not that philosophers stopped believing in it (for I am uncertain that they did), but because no way was ever finally found to formulate it that did not carve away, along with the metaphysics the positivists so detested, a great deal of science. In part this was because of certain leakages in logic that enabled as much by way of metaphysical terminology to flow in as anyone could wish—where the leaks could not be plugged without sacrificing features of logic the positivists knew could not be dispensed with if logic was to be the language of science. Many of these leakages were quite trivial, but logic itself was not trivial, and so, bit by bit, the verifiability criterion was given up.

As verificationism collapsed, so to speak, under the weight of clever but finally unavailing modifications in the original robust criterion, a certain relief began to radiate outward in philosophy departments throughout the world. Not only did the demise of the criterion mean that one could practice metaphysical speculation with impunity, but that certain dangers to matters far more central to human life than metaphysics were diminished. One of the consequences felt to be most frightening by philosophers—and not by philosophers alone—was that the verifiability criterion appeared to rule out as nonsense a good bit of language that seems absolutely central to human welfare, namely the language through which our moral beliefs are expressed. As "moral propositions" could not be verified, they had to be dismissed as nonsense—and any philosophy that consigns to this category the values and commandments of moral existence has to sound threatening.

# 12

## Feeling and Meaning

THE ABSOLUTE FAVORITE EXAMPLE of metaphysical nonsense, according to the positivists, was a sentence in Martin Heidegger's *What is Metaphysics?*": *Das Nichts nichtet*— "Nothing nothings" or, in the paraphrase of a Cambridge wit, "Nothing noths." How, Carnap loved to ask, holding the sentence up by a corner and displaying it with hilarity, could one verify *this?* What conceivable experience could conduce to the belief that it either was true or false? Oddly enough, it was introduced by Heidegger with rather a powerful description of the experience in which nothingness was revealed as that which—we lack a good English phrase for the verb *nichten* ("nihilates" is too Latin)—"nothings." Heidegger was interested in the Nothing because he saw it as providing the boundary for being; and its philosophical importance lay in the fact that being *as a whole* is brought to consciousness by Nothing. Science investigates "what is—and beyond that nothing." This sounds as though nothing were a certain kind of something off the coast of what-is—and hence nothing is not nothing after all. But Heidegger felt that we could not get a grip on what-is without seeing its boundary somehow, and he wanted to know where we get the idea of nothing. It is, he contended, revealed by a feeling, namely dread. In the experience of dread—which he contrasted with fear, which is always *of* something perceived as dangerous—nothing is *revealed.* I shall not pursue further what he means to say by saying that nothing nothings, except that this, too, is experienced through dread.

Heidegger, then, might say that, after all, *Das Nichts nichtet* is meaningful by the criterion of verifiability provided only that one is prepared to grant a certain cognitive dimension to feelings or moods (*Stimmungen,* as he termed them). But Carnap was unprepared to do this. When the positivists spoke of verification, they had in mind sense experience rather than emotional states. Their model of verification was a moment of chill objectivity, in which the laboratory scientist observes a needle gauge move or something turn color or a bell sound. Their model was scientific observation, which they construed narrowly as having a sensation. For them, a proposition was meaningful only if it could be directly tested by sense experience, like "X is red," or logically entailed by sentences that could be tested this way—"observation sentences" as they were called—and so could be verified in some degree. The pragmatist C. I. Lewis supposed that a proposition that could not be directly tested against experience was meaningful if it could be "translated" into a set of propositions that could be. The translation would never be complete, for such propositions entail an infinite number of such directly testable propositions, and so themselves are capable at best of some degree of verification short of absolute certitude. But "nothing nothings" is not testable by observation, nor does it entail any observation sentences that are directly testable in terms of the laboratory model favored by the positivists. Feelings, emotions, carry no cognitive weight at all. If they did carry cognitive weight, one of the most incendiary of the positivist's theses would collapse.

This was their thought: That the language of ethics had only *emotive* meaning but no cognitive meaning at all; its sentences were not really propositions (though again they looked as though they might be so far as grammar, or surface grammar, was concerned). Though it looked as though "X is good" has the same grammatical form as "X is red," in truth the latter is meaningful and the former is not, for the latter is testable against observation and the former is not. There is no answer to the question of what would it be like for "X is good" to be true, and so, strictly, it should be a sentence we do not understand and that accordingly is meaningless. But of course it is intelligible in some way when people say of something

X that it is good (though few people outside the novels of Hemingway just flatly say such things as "X is good"). So in some secondary sense it is meaningful. The positivists proposed that it was meaningful in the way in which lyric poetry is—it expressed a feeling on the part of the speaker. This was the Emotive Theory of Ethical Discourse.

So far as Carnap was concerned, poetry was simply a refined way of saying—or emitting—sounds like oh, oh, or ha-ha. With these noises we express feelings of astonishment or amusement. Indeed, to say that something is astonishing or amusing, by positivist lights, was to say it was the sort thing that caused us to emit such sounds as oh, oh, or ha-ha. Lyric poetry did nothing more, cognitively, than this. To be sure, we can address poetic discourse as revealing something about the person who voices it. It expresses his or her feelings, much as hives express, as symptoms, his or her allergy to salicylates. The poet may feel he is conveying something about the world— something true of something other than himself. But in fact he is not. And neither is the metaphysician, if, in charity, we treat him as a poet of sorts, believing himself to be conveying truths of the highest or deepest order. Metaphysics was, as a general rule, just bad poetry, and in this way Carnap might be prepared to tolerate Heidegger. But of course Heidegger himself did not believe he was expressing dread. He was, instead, saying that dread reveals, with as much validity as the sensation of red reveals red, an objective emptiness. But that is the delusion of the metaphysician, the therapeutic positivist would say: He is taken in by the grammatical parities between discourse that is cognitively meaningful and discourse that is cognitively empty. Carnap in fact had some good things to say about Nietzsche, who really did write poetically rather than barbarically.

Crude, let us say deliberately provocative, as the deflationist idiom of positivism was, it yielded an initial example of a theme that became extremely prominent in analytical philosophy, namely that not all language is essentially descriptive. There are different kinds of meanings as functions of different kinds of uses, and while description was the use central to science, expression was the kind of use central to morality. Of course, a great many theorists were prepared to agree with the positivists in insisting that moral language is not descriptive, while reluctant to endorse, because they thought it false, the thesis that moral language merely expresses feelings. Noncognitivism in ethical theory has a long history. Spinoza famously denied that "good" and "evil" answer to anything objective in the universe. For him the world is neither objectively good nor objectively evil, and this might have given him grounds for saying that such sentences as "X is good" are neither true nor false. Sartre, obsessed as he was throughout his life with moral questions, was noncognitivistic in his attitude toward moral reality, insisting there is none. Nietzsche himself believed that moral beliefs but express the will to power of their users. Wittgenstein said explicitly, "In the world there are no values—and if there were, they would be of no value." For Wittgenstein, indeed, it was true that the whole point of morality would be lost if it were but a cognition of something objective and resident in the world. But whether Spinoza, Sartre, Nietzsche, or Wittgenstein would have gone on to acquiesce in the Emotive Theory of Discourse or Meaning is another matter altogether. Agreeing that moral language is not descriptive, they might have disagreed that all it does is express the speaker's feelings. We may use moral language to guide people or to goad them into doing what society requires of them. We may use it to persuade them, as if *saying* something that is good were a reason why they should endorse or pursue it. We can use it to lobby with. In truth, the question of what the use of moral language is, if it is not descriptive, is finally sociological or sociolinguistic. It is something we can find out about by conducting tests. It is a scientific rather than a philosophical question. But noncognitivism, as it is termed, really is a philosophical position, and it is worth tracking it for a while in order to show why. For there are cognitivists in moral theory too.

The positivists, in advancing noncognitivism, were certainly doing more than analyzing language. They were doing something philosophers, indeed metaphysicians, always have tried to do: They were saying what the world contains. They were saying what there is and what there is not. But unlike scientists, who say what there is or what there is not on the basis of experience or observation, they sought to do this by the analysis of language. Their view was that moral language is of the wrong sort to express truth or to correspond with facts. They did not search the world over for values, and indeed it would be odd if values were rare and difficult to locate, like neutrinos. They play too intimate a role in the daily lives of normal men and women everywhere in the world. If they were anywhere, they would be everywhere that human beings are. But in fact they are nowhere and we have, the positivists would say, been bewitched by the outward grammatical accidents of the language of morals into believing that they are there, like shapes and colors. The positivists were in effect doing philosophy through the analysis of language, coarse textured as their account may have been.

Even so, noncognitivism is disquieting in a certain way. It has certain consequences that are disruptive, in a sense, of moral life. It is not a theory we can fully integrate with moral life as we practice it, and to this degree it may be said that it has certain moral as well as certain metaphysical implications. For one thing, it gives a radical analysis of moral argument. When we are arguing about whether something is good, it may seem as though we are exchanging views when in fact all we are doing is engaging in monologue, if even that. If I say $X$ is good, I am expressing my feelings. And if you say $X$ is bad, you are expressing *your* feelings. So it is as though I were to make the noises ha-ha and you to be making the noises boo-hoo. It would be as though I were laughing and you weeping. That is not an argument or a discussion. We confront one another as two lunatics might, one of whom laughs and the other of whom howls. Of course, this may have benign consequences. It may put an end to moral argument. Moral argument itself is usually (morally) preferred as the rational alternative to combat. But in fact it is no more rational than combat if all it is is mutually confronting ejaculations. These are, one might say, sophisticated ways of striking out, much as poetry is sophisticated wincing and moaning or giggling. And indeed there is no room for rationality in moral discourse at all. There is none because the language of morals is, if the positivists are right, "of the wrong logical sort" to yield conclusions to valid arguments.

An argument is valid when there is no consistent way in which the conclusion can be false while the premises are true, and we invalidate an argument by showing that it really is possible for this to happen—that it is logically consistent for the conclusion to be false when the premises are true. Imagine that we had what looked like an argument with a moral conclusion. It is true that there is no consistent way in which the conclusion should be false while the premises are true. But that is because moral propositions just cannot be false—so if this argument were valid for such a reason, so would all moral arguments be valid, including the one that pretends to deduce from these very premises the very opposite of the moral proposition we supposed followed from them.

In a famous observation, Hume points out that most moral descriptions suddenly move from description to exhortation—from statements about what is the case to injunctions about what we ought to do. But there is no logically deriving an "ought" from an "is"—there is no deriving an "ought" from as many "is's" as you choose—not only because there is a question as to whether imperatives themselves are capable of truth-values, particularly when the "ought" in question is moral, but because, even if that problem were overcome, there should be nothing in the conclusion of a valid deductive argument that did not appear somewhere in the premises—and if there were an "ought" among the premises, then the question of its standing and basis would arise. The mathematician and philosopher of science Henri Poincaré, expanding on Hume's discovery of a logical gap between the language of description and of injunction, drew the important consequence that science, capable at best of describing the world, cannot really tell us what we ought to do—so there can be no scientific basis for morality. What we ought morally to do is "up to us" to decide. We may decide this on the basis of facts, but the logical explanation of what the very notion of "basis" means remains to be given, and at least we know that it cannot be the kind of basis premises give us in deductive argument.

These problems affect any form of the noncognitivist position in ethical theory. The emotivist has yet a further problem in that he insists that what may look like the conclusion of a deductive argument, if indeed a moral proposition, in fact has to express the speaker's feelings. And this would be as though, having advanced the premises, "All ghosts are scary and all scary things are to be avoided," the reasoner suddenly screamed in terror. It would be an interruption rather than a completion of a logical process.

It might, against these difficulties, seem quite to the point to see what cognitivism in ethical theory looks like, and see if it does not deal with ethical argument and moral reasoning in a way consistent with the possibility of rationality in moral discussion.

# 13

# Metaethical Controversy

COGNITIVISM, IN MORAL PHILOSOPHY, is the view that there are real moral propositions—propositions that are true or false, and even verifiable against experience—and that it is possible to have moral knowledge. But cognitivists are deeply divided between themselves over a matter that connects with a piece of philosophical structure that has an interest and importance beyond the sphere of moral philosophy itself. Where the issue of contention concerns the definability of moral terms, cognitivists are divided between what are termed "intuitionists" and "naturalists." The question is whether we can give definitions of moral terms that do not use some other moral term or terms in the defining expression. If we could, for example, define *good* in such a way that no moral term or expression played a role in the definition, then there would be no moral knowledge as such: Moral knowledge would instead be knowledge of whatever it was in terms of which the vocabulary of moral discourse had been defined. The philosophical importance of this can hardly be overestimated. Philosophers have always been deeply concerned to identify how many and what kinds of fundamentally different things or concepts there are. If the philosopher can show that a distinction heretofore thought fundamental can in fact be overcome, by definition or analysis, then a reduction in the basic inventory philosophers have supposed it their task to draw up would have been achieved. If moral language can be defined through or reduced to an idiom from which moral vocabulary has been eliminated, then moral distinctions are not among the fundamental distinctions it is necessary to draw in making a philosophical map of the world. So the naturalist in moral theory has two tasks to perform. He must show that there is such a thing as moral knowledge, but he also must show that moral knowledge is not ultimate or fundamental, since the terms of moral description can be defined away.

One leading naturalistic position, construed in these terms, is utilitarianism, which defines *good* and *bad* in terms of pleasure and pain, and *better* and *worse* as matters conducing to the greater or lesser preponderance of pleasure over pain in consequence of actions or policies. Whether something causes pain or pleasure seems as verifiable a matter as whether something causes comfort or discomfort. We all know how to give one another pleasure, we can all study how to increase the pleasure we give one another; and we all, alas, as the history of torture and torment shows, know how to cause one another pain and to increase the pain when we want to be particularly brutal and sadistic. These are empirical matters, as are issues of whether some policy will or will not conduce to the greater overall pleasure of sentient beings, for whom, in any case, moral questions seem uniquely applicable. If beings did not suffer, if they did not find things preferable to others in terms of suffering or felicity, it is very difficult to see what duties or obligations we would have to them. Morality has very little, one would think, to do with stones or clouds, save insofar as these have to do with beings capable of being made happy or unhappy as a consequence of what we do to stones or clouds. This, I think, is the underlying premise of utilitarianism.

Powerful and convincing as this premise is, many have doubted that utilitarianism altogether captures our moral views. It is, for example, not difficult to imagine a course of action that produces greater overall happiness than an alternative, but at the cost of doing something we would hesitate to call *morally* preferable to its alternative. A nephew makes a deathbed promise to his aunt to abandon something that gives him a great deal of pleasure, and she dies happier than she would have died had he refused to make the promise, which he now does nothing to keep. He is happier breaking the promise, the aunt is happier believing he made the promise—but is making a promise intending to break it really the morally right thing to do? It may be that there are reasons for preferring to do something other than the morally right thing—but that does not make what one does in *fact* the morally right thing, and it was the morally right thing that was supposed to have been analyzed—not something that it might even be reasonable to prefer doing rather than it. It is as though doing what increases pleasure is morally fine, as against decreasing it or increasing pain—but only if it really *is* morally fine. And utilitarianism, from this point of view, has made not a single step toward the analysis of moral language. But neither, it has been insisted by noncognitivists and intuitionists alike, can any other naturalistic theory. Their reasons, to be sure, will differ, even if both agree that moral language cannot be defined in naturalistic terms—the noncognitivist because moral language is not descriptive whereas naturalistic language is; the intuitionist, whose views are especially interesting, because the distinction between moral and nonmoral (or morally neutral) really is one of the basic distinctions philosophers are obliged to recognize. There really is, the intuitionist insists, moral knowledge. But it is knowledge different in kind from knowledge of other sorts and requires a special faculty on the part of those who understand it. This faculty is moral intuition. Let me now sketch out the argumentation likely to be used by these temporary bedfellows, whose disagreement with one another at this point is less important than the disagreement both have with the naturalist.

Here is an argument either of them might use. Consider the expression "good X" for any X in connection with which it makes sense to speak of it as good: a good dentist, say, or a good dog. In each instance there is no question that X is good only on condition that it possess a number of properties that we may call "good-making" properties for things of X's sort—"painless, knowledgeable and fast," and "not terribly expensive" if a dentist; "loyal," "alert," and "gets along with children" if a dog. Different things generate different lists—the properties that make for good dentists are not those that make for good cooks, nor are the properties that make for good cooks those that make for good painters, automobiles, mushrooms, shoemakers, or congressmen. So what can all these things have in common when they are called good *beyond* the fact that they are *called* good? And what can we mean by calling them that—what is the *use* of the word, why even do we have it in the language? Certainly it is clear that we are saying something beyond what we say about X when we itemize the properties in question, the ones that *good* singles out. Can it be that these all produce pleasure? Perhaps they all do, but once again, we seem to be saying something with the word *good* that "causes pleasure" does not say. If nothing else, the two expressions vary in force. And since this will be true for any property we might single out, translating "good X" into "an X that is F" leaves something behind and unaccounted for.

The noncognitivist and the intuitionist diverge at this point. For the former, the question is to examine what we do mean when we use the term—we are, after all, native speakers; it is, after all, our term. The issue is thoroughly empirical, and one suggestion is that we use *good* to recommend something. We do not add to the description; *good* is not a further descriptive phrase true of *X:* Its role is not descriptive at all. But language has uses that exceed descriptivity. And the fact is that in saying a dentist is good, we are recommending him to those who have need of a dentist. Perhaps one may disagree that this is exactly what we do, but then the issue is what else or other than recommending is being done, and the answer is to be found by investigation of linguistic practice.

The intuitionist has another argument. It was invented by G. E. Moore in a famous book, *Principia Ethica.* Suppose, Moore says, we attempt to define X in some such way as "causes pleasure." Can this really be what *good* means? No, Moore argues, since we can always ask if causing pleasure is good, whereas if *good* just meant "causes pleasure," the question would be, "Is causing pleasure causing pleasure?" to which the empty answer is yes. This is known as the Open Question Argument, and Moore used it to show that *good* is really indefinable. That is still consistent with the noncognitivists' claim, for which the question of whether it is definable is replaced by the question of what use it has. But Moore in fact went on to a different view—namely that goodness is a *quality* or property of things, by virtue of which they are good, but it is a simple property, like *yellow;* and just as we can only tell whether something is yellow by looking at it and seeing what color it is, so, Moore argued, we can only tell whether something is good by "intuition"—its goodness is revealed to a kind of moral perception. John Donne wrote: "If it were good it would be seen,/Good is as visible as green." And this was Moore's view—it is as though goodness were a palpable quality, like color (though he went on to elaborate that it was a "non-natural" quality, which rather obscured issues). It is as though the perception of moral qualities were a matter of having a special sense, much in the way in which aestheticians supposed there is a sense of beauty, sensitive specifically to the aesthetic qualities of things.

It might at this point be appropriate to ask to what degree either version of cognitivism is capable of dealing with the difficulties by which the noncognitivist is threatened. In a way the naturalist has no difficulty, inasmuch as, for him, there never is the leap over a logical gap from "is" to "ought," nor is there the problem that moral statements are not really propositions but expressions. They are already in the indicative, true or false in quite straightforward ways, and hence amenable to moral reasoning and moral argument. Moral debate is like scientific debate: It appeals to facts alone. The only remaining gap is between moral discourse and its proposed indicative "translation." Something is lost in the translation—as we saw, the specifically moral force of such words as *good.* And we may continue to ask whether and why such natural things as pleasure really are good, and as long as such questions make sense, naturalism fails. And the impasse means that both naturalism and noncognitivism fail in different ways: Each is inadequate in rendering some aspect of moral language or moral practice.

This, however, does not make the intuitionist the victor by elimination, for this position, too, faces insuperable problems, certainly in the version offered by G. E. Moore. It is true that Moore has an answer to the moral reasoning problem. We do not *argue,* as it were indirectly, that something is good or bad, we see that it is. You do not, similarly, reason to the conclusion that something is yellow—you look and see what color it is. Perhaps there are degrees of weakness in moral perception, as in color perception, which account for disagreements. After all, the same thing that tastes bitter to one tastes sweet to another. Moreover, because good itself is indefinable, a conclusion using *good* cannot occur in a moral argument in which it does not also occur in one of the premises—for conclusions are not supposed to have information in excess of that furnished by the premises. So rather than a defect, the difficulties noncognitivism encounters are what might have been expected in consequence of the simple nature of the quality of goodness. And intuitionism has an explanation of these consequences. For intuitionism it is genuinely a defect of naturalism that it maintains that it is really possible to employ moral reasoning or construct valid arguments with moral propositions as conclusions.

But then there are the difficulties peculiar to intuitionism itself, quite apart from its postulation of nonnatural qualities and "sixth senses." The difficulty turns on the idea of something being a *simple* quality, which connects us with a set of philosophical ideas I shall need to discuss in a moment. The distinction Moore was using was between simple and compound ideas, and an example of the latter would be the idea of a horse, which is compounded of a number of distinct components: A horse is a quadruped, has hooves, eats hay, and the like. In this sense, which is going to need a lot of defense later on, *yellow* answers to a simple idea, in that it has no components: It is not compounded of anything simpler than itself. Rather, it is one of the components out of which other ideas, like the idea of a banana, are compounded. Good is believed by Moore to be simple in this very sense. Something is yellow or it is not, and it cannot be partly yellow as something can be partly a horse (the way a centaur would be).

Now, the thought was that simple qualities, having no components, are really independent of one another. If shape, for example, were simple in this way—at least there are simple shapes—then we could imagine shape and color varying independently of one another: A red square can become a red circle with no alteration in color; a red square can become a yellow square with no alteration in shape. So far as simple qualities are concerned, then, two compounded things can be exactly alike, except for one single simple quality: A red sphere can be exactly like a yellow sphere except in point of color. Let us imagine, indeed, two spheres, exactly alike in a great many simple respects, but varying in just the one way that the first is yellow and the second is red. This seems logical enough, whatever difficulties we may have with the very notion of simple qualities.

But is it even conceivable that two things should be exactly alike with the sole difference that one is good and the other is not? Suppose we were to say that there are identical twins, absolutely indiscernible, with the sole difference that one is good and the other not—and then went on to see if we could just sense the goodness of the one, like a sort of fragrance? Or two students turn in examinations with the same answer, except that one is a good examination, and the other bad—or a third neither good nor bad, if goodness can be absent without badness being present? I think everyone would regard this as impossible, and that means that there is something really wrong with the idea of good being simple and hence indefinable. If two things differ in point of goodness, they *must* differ in some other way. And that other way in which they differ must be part at least of what it is to be good. This would open the door to naturalism, if naturalism did not have so many difficulties of its own.

This objection against Moore is terribly compelling and merits a few moments of contemplation. It connects with a principle that seems internal to moral belief and moral practice, namely that equals must be treated as equals: if two papers are just alike, or two horses, or two persons, one cannot consistently say that one is good and the other not. If the one is good, the other must be, if just like it or even if just relevantly like it. This logical feature of goodness entails, almost by itself, the notions of justice and equality that seem so central to human institutions—hence Moore's theory has consequences profoundly contrary to moral intuition. Nothing is as offensive to moral intuition as unjust, which is to say, unequal or unfair treatment. That explains why we are so offended by *arbitrary* treatment, where one person is punished for the same offense for which another is let off. Or where one person is rewarded where another is not, though each is equally deserving. Of course the world, of course existence itself, is unfair. Some persons do not have the lives others get, though there is little or nothing to distinguish them. Why some should prosper though others languish cannot be answered: It is no answer, or the only answer, to say, that is how it is with luck. But, then, *luck* itself is another word for the arbitrary or the irrational, and we do not want our moral institutions to be arbitrary. And that in turn explains why we subscribe to a rule of law, that no one should have power that he or she can use arbitrarily and unfairly. To be sure, it is not real power unless it *can* be used that way. In Calvinist theology, it is an abiding fear that the meritorious should be punished and the miscreants rewarded, contrary to the imperatives of our own moral practice. But anything else would constrain God. If God is *really* to be powerful and indeed all-powerful, God *must* be arbitrary. And that at last suggests that God cannot consistently be thought of as all-powerful and good. To be good he would be obliged to treat equals equally and to apportion rewards and punishments strictly. Sometimes the existence of evil is used as an argument against the existence of God. But a better argument may be based on the unfairnesses of existence and the sheer luck of the draw in life.

At one point it was believed that one could engage in the analysis of moral language without moralizing. Philosophers undertook metaethical investigations, of the sort I have sketched in this section and in the last, in the belief that in doing so they could remain neutral on any questions of a positive moral nature. I have tried to show that this is not possible, that each of the metaethical positions has moral consequences or violates one or another moral intuition—using the term now in a broader sense than did Moore. It is as though we cannot take a position "beyond good and evil," outside morality, and address moral language from without. Aristotle recognized as much, I believe, when he said we do not study ethics simply for the sake of knowledge, but in order to *become* good ourselves. There is an internal relationship, then, between the study and practice of morality that, while philosophically important to stress, may make ethical discourse a bad example to use to address the questions of understanding and meaning.

# 14

## Two Views of Language

*E*ACH CONTENDER IN THE METAETHICAL controversy appears to have seized possession of a feature of moral language—that *good* has a use or force different from the terms used to describe a thing in morally neutral language; that there are moral intuitions not altogether captured by naturalistic moral theories; that the moral qualities of a thing or act cannot be independent of its other qualities—and there is a strong inclination to see if there may not be some overall theory that captures these insights without falling into the errors and difficulties we have seen each contender do. No doubt a solution to the puzzles of metaethics would be a substantial philosophical contribution, but I shall not at this point press for this. Rather, I want to show that this controversy conforms to a structure that is quite widespread in philosophy, especially in analytical philosophy, ever since it seemed appropriate to distinguish the kind of meaning moral sentences appeared to have from that attributed to the "uniquely meaningful" language of science. And, if this is true, philosophical intelligence suggests that we postpone seeking a solution to one of the examples, even if it is a particularly vivid example of this structure, and see if there is not something quite general to say about the structure itself. For in truth it is a structure widely found in philosophical analysis, and counterparts to the three positions in metaethics are to be found in areas initially perceived as quite remote from ethics.

In the early 1950s, there was a school of analytical philosophy at Oxford, under the influence of a meticulous thinker, J. L. Austin, which came to be called the school of ordinary language philosophy. Its main inspiration came, I think, from Austin's proposal that there are a great many uses of language other than description—other than that linguistic role siezed upon as central to cognitive inquiry by the logical positivists—and the effort to assimilate the entirety of language to this role, and to regard sentences that do not conform as meaningless, is to commit a fallacy—namely what Austin termed the Descriptive Fallacy. And identification of uses other than descriptivity may in fact show the way out of problems that have baffled philosophers for centuries.

Consider the case of knowledge. Beginning with an influential dialogue of Plato's, the *Theaetetus,* philosophers have undertaken to analyze the concept of knowledge. In that dialogue, Socrates and his fellow discussants give a partial analysis—or definition—of what it is to know: It is to have a true belief plus some other conditions they in fact fail to find. I shall discuss this analysis in another section, but for now I want to say only that the missing condition in Socrates' analysis has not been identified to everyone's satisfaction and may never be identified. This may encourage other philosophers to wonder if knowledge really is analyzable at all, whether it is not perhaps simple and indefinable just as Moore thought good was. But Austin had a brilliant alternative proposal to make, namely that *know* may not be a descriptive term at all but had a use close examination of common speech would reveal. And his analysis came out this way: In saying "I know that P" I am not describing some special fact of an immensely important cognitive sort, an achievement at the very top of a scale of which "I believe that P" describes some lower segment. Rather, I am *performing an action* by means of these words: I am effectively *giving my word* that P is true. The performative account of meaning for this sentence resembles that for a sentence such as, "I promise that P." In saying, "I promise," I perform the act of promising, and do not describe some inner state for which philosophers bent on analysis might search. Words are what, among other things, I perform actions with, for example, in "I warn," I actually warn; in "I forbid," I in fact forbid. And Austin spent the remainder of his life, and devoted an important number of writings, to the careful identification of various "performatives," as he termed them.

With this move, it becomes plain that there is what one might call a noncognitive analysis of cognitive discourse. And hence the possibility of a metacognitive controversy in every respect like the controversy in metaethics. There are those who may disagree with Austin as to the precise use of "I know," while accepting that at least it is not descriptive. And then there are the descriptivists, as we may call them, who divide as to whether knowledge can be defined or analyzed, and hence is not among the basic or primitive concepts philosophers must deal with, or whether it is a basic concept and accordingly indefinable.

And the same array of possibilities opens up for any number of other terms and expressions. It may be asked whether *truth,* for example, is definable or not; and against this it may be urged that the thing to do is to see how in fact the word *true* is used in ordinary language—and the result of this is that when people say "P is true" they are in fact expressing agreement with someone who simply said "P." "P is true" has the force, more or less, of saying, "P: How true!" This analysis, ingenious indeed, was offered by P. F. Strawson, who dubbed it the Concessive Use. And there was a time during which use after use of philosophically crucial terms was identified, to the hopeful purgation of a wide class of philosophical questions. The question was, in each case, How would you teach the meaning of the term or expression to a stranger, or to a child? What you would do would be to instruct the child or stranger in the conditions under which the term or expression would be correctly used. So long as we stick with actual linguistic practice, we fall into no difficulties whatever. Philosophical problems arise only when we stray from the benign directives of the languages that define our forms of life. Such was the view of linguistic philosophy.

Behind all this begin to emerge the outlines of a whole theory of language different to a striking degree from that presupposed by the positivists. It is a theory developed in the later philosophy of Wittgenstein, and it is condensed in the characteristically memorable utterance, "Do not ask for the meaning; ask for the use." In his later investigations Wittgenstein gave a picture of language almost completely instrumental, in which sentences were like tools, to be used for this occasion and that purpose. A system of tools defines a kind of instrumental complex, and an instrumental complex for language is simply a form of life—what he termed a *Lebensform.* To understand a sentence now is not a question of knowing what must be the case if it is true; it is, rather, to know how to use it correctly. But with this new, instrumentalistic theory of language, the contrast between moral language and scientific language itself begins to give way. For what is to prevent our regarding scientific sentences as tools, as instruments to be employed in the form of life for scientists, tools there as much as test tubes are tools, or cloud chambers, or cyclotrons? And instead of the picture in the *Tractatus,* of language standing on the one side and the world on the other, with the former a representation of the latter and the latter what the former is true of, we find language as an instrument or set of instruments to be used on this occasion or that, and the concepts of truth and falsity give way to correct or incorrect employment. Wittgenstein's extreme followers went so far as to say the question of religious truth gives way to that of the use of religious expressions. It is not a matter of whether God exists but how *God* is used. It is used in certain ritually prescribed formulas in certain sacred places on the appropriate times by the right sorts of people. It may be doubted that religious persons feel that this is all there is to their belief in God—that it is a belief that *God* is used to address prayers to, as an accusative—but the use-theorists may retort that this is how the word was learned and so this is what the word must mean: specify the uses to which the word *is* put, and there is nothing further to do in order to say what the word means.

The metaethical controversy in a way simply dissolves, for the contrast it requires itself dissolves. The noncognitivist theory of ethical discourse gives way to a noncognitivist theory of discourse in general. If we are then prepared to be radical enough in seeking uses, that yields a basic dissolution of the metaethics controversy. Asked how we solve the question of moral reasoning, the answer would be simple: It is reasoning about uses of the word *good*. Discussion of whether to use it on one occasion rather than another would be like a discussion between carpenters as to when to use a certain tool or between cooks on when to use baking powder and when to use yeast. But then, it may seem, the distinction between use and description reappears, for surely one must have some way of describing correct and incorrect usage; and this seems to involve us with truth and falsity, just as before. It may not be altogether a deconstruction of the use theory to point this out, but it certainly seems a defect of some sort that the use theory can only be gotten to go through on the back of the theory it means to overthrow, namely the descriptive account of linguistic meaning, even if it should be confined to the truth or falsity of such propositions as these: "The sentence S is correctly used when C"—where C specifies the conditions of appropriate employment for S.

But why in fact should this be the only exception? Consider the Performative Theory of "I know." Does this really give the meaning of *know* in such a way that questions of definition no longer arise? Surely not. In a sentence like, "If I know that P, then Smith knows that P as well"—a simple conditional sentence—the expression "I know that P" clearly does not occur as a simple performative at all, but as a straight declarative sentence capable of admitting truth-values, much in the way in which "Smith knows that P" occurs. And much the same must be said with regard to "P is true" in a conditional such as, "If P is true then Q is false," where "P is true" states a condition for the falsity of Q: it does not express concurrence, as in a conversation, with what someone else may have said. Indeed, even "X is good" loses its expressive force when it occurs in conditional or in other larger sentential contexts. So the Use Theory of Meaning draws its initial plausibility from considering sentences taken one at a time, outside the larger discursive frameworks in which they might occur naturally; and in stressing the first-person forms, as in "I know that *P*," which may be performative in certain contexts, without it following that it is not descriptive, as "Smith knows that *P*" is descriptive.

Beyond this, it seems to me the Instrumentalist Theory of Language misrepresents our relationship to language completely, treating it virtually as a set of sentences whose use we learn to master, much as a stranger to a language learns to master the phrases in a phrase book. No doubt you would say to a stranger something like: "If you need to have a meal, tell the natives something like *J'ai faim* or *Je veux manger.*" It treats the sentences of the language very much as we would spontaneously treat the *words* of a language. Beyond question, we can imagine a complete dictionary for a language, one in which every word is included, together with its definition. And new definitions get added as new words get introduced and the dictionary requires updating. But can there even in principle be a reference work containing all the sentences of a language? It has been recognized, since the great work of Noam Chomsky, that the primary mark of linguistic competence is the capacity to create *new* sentences and to understand sentences one has never heard before. It is quite imaginable that the reader of this book has encountered not a single sentence the book contains before reading it. No doubt there will be sentences he or she does not understand—but you would not look them up in a phrase book as you would look up in a dictionary the words you do not understand. A theory of language that is incompatible with the central facts of linguistic competence cannot be an acceptable theory. We still may not understand how we understand sentences, but we at least know that the account of sentential understanding that assimilates language to use would be a bad account. For *it* would assimilate learning the sentences to a model rather like learning the vocabulary of a foreign speech. What it leaves out of account is a different procedure altogether, namely learning the *grammar* of that language, which in fact is like mastering a theory for the language in question.

Now there is, beyond question, a special place for a use theory of sentential meaning. A person may, let us imagine, learn a foreign language in school, and become fluent in expressing his thoughts in the language. Still, unless he actually visits the culture in which the language is spoken, there will be a great deal about the language he does not understand, namely the *extralinguistic* rules, almost a code of usage, which govern what we mean when we say certain things. There are words we do not use in certain contexts. And there are certain sentences we do use in order to perform certain verbal acts. There is a whole domain of ceremonial usage, for example: We know that quite different kinds of answers are expected to the question "How are you?" depending on whether asked by a doctor or simply by the superintendent, hosing down the sidewalk with no interest whatever in the minutiae of our digestion or our problems in getting enough sleep. We can, then, understand a language without understanding the culture in which the language is spoken—and the Use Theory of Meaning belongs to cultural understanding. It is in terms of the rules of culture that it makes sense, that it in fact is true that "to understand a language is to understand a form of life."

No doubt the philosophers who construe language purely as representation have forgotten that there is more to human life than simply saying what is true. They work with a severely reduced picture of what it is to use language. Still, it is far from plain that this reduced picture will not suffice for all our philosophical needs. Descartes, in his *Meditations,* imagines a situation in which he is absolutely isolated, in which no occasion could arise in which he need *use* language, in order to concentrate on the question, Which of the sentences he believes to be true *are* true? For purposes of that inquiry, the use theory of meaning has no application, though it might be interesting to point out that even in his self-imposed isolation, Descartes continues to use language as he had learned to use it in the commonplaces of life. Even so, for Descartes the philosophical picture is very much that of a single being, concerned to represent the world in such a way that there cannot be any contagion of error. It would be ridiculous to point out to Descartes that there is more to life than that—after all, a man does not seek isolation who believes he already is isolated. Descartes was a lover, a swordsman, an aristocrat, a scientist, a correspondent, a member of a religious community, a father—a person whose entire life and mode of being was penetrated by his social relationships. His speech almost certainly reflects the circumstances of his status as an aristocrat, as an educated man. He would not use the words with which he addresses Mersenne or Gassendi to address his servants or his mistress. Wittgenstein, in his later philosophy, gives us a picture of human beings who are in this sense penetrated by the form of life that goes with the language they have learned to use. And it is possible to set this picture against the Cartesian picture of the austere and isolated inquirer after truth. But the pictures are compatible and not exclusive of one another, roughly in the way that two models of understanding language—once through grammar and once through linguistic practices—are compatible with one another, simply because we do in fact use language in the ordinary transactions of life. But we could not learn language simply by mastering the rules under which we would say this or that sentence. When, in the course of social life, would I have occasion to use the sentence I last wrote?

So my sense is that the use theory of meaning is diversionary and that the large family of noncognitivisms has no philosophical significance. It has a sociolinguistic significance, beyond question. It is of the greatest sociolinguistic interest to have learned that I do something with "I know that P" beyond describing what someone else, speaking of me, would be saying when he says, "He knows that P." Or that in saying, "I promise," I am doing something in excess of what someone would be describing were he to say of me that "he promised." But I *am* also saying these things, and "I know that P" and "I promise that P" have a descriptive core, which is what knowledge or making a promise consists of. The data on which the noncognitivist draws are quite compatible with the data on which the cognitivists draw. They are saying something further, without it following that this further thing bears greatly on the questions it was hoped to solve.

This clears the field of one of the combatants in the metaethics controversy, leaving the intuitionist and the naturalist to fight the battle through. But at least room has been opened for the possibility of moral knowledge, however it is to be characterized. And it is plain that the meaningfulness of moral language is patently plain, even by the severest verificationist criteria. True, it may be very difficult to know how to verify a sentence like "X is good," but that may be because *good* occurs in it as a fragment, rather than a complete phrase. It has to be completed in some way, by saying more, namely what good thing it is that X is said to be. A good dentist? A good husband? A good hunter? Or what? Consider a sentence like "X believes." Unless context makes it plain, this is a fragment. To believe is to believe something, and until one makes explicit what X believes, one has said nothing, much in the way in which one has said nothing—until something more has been said—in saying that "X is." Is *what?* is what we have to know in order to respond intelligently. But once it is clear *what good thing* it is that X is said to be, there is no question that it can be verified or falsified, and hence that it is meaningful. Let it be a good husband. Then, of course, a lot is implied. X must be attentive, trustworthy, considerate, reliable, a provider. These are not at all the qualities of a good lover, and there is a great distance between being a good husband and a good lover, and a mistake is made in using the criteria for one as a measure of the other. A good husband is sexually responsive, but there are dangers in being a good lover that may be incompatible with the sexual obligations of the good husband. That may be a digression. The point to be made is different. It is that the force of Moore's Open Question Argument is blunted when we take whole expressions like "good husband" rather than the fragmentary "good." It sounds jarringly strange to say: "X is attentive, trustworthy, considerate, reliable, a provider, and sexually responsive to his wife—but is X a good husband?" For these are what it is to *be* a good husband: A man cannot be these and not be a good husband if he is a husband. To be sure, we may have left something out. But it is up to the questioner to say what it is. He may be saying there is more to being a husband than just this, but whenever he adds to these conditions the condition he implies is missing from our list, we can say what it is and verify that it is there. Of course there is room for contest: We can say that X is a good husband despite lacking some qualities or missing certain features. But if a woman were to say that X is a good husband though missing all the features I have listed, there would be a serious question of whether she was using the expression "good husband" correctly. Perhaps all she meant to say was that she loves X despite, or perhaps even because of, his failings. But that does not make him a good husband. What she really should be saying is that she loves him though he is a bad husband or even, such is the nature of human feeling, *because* he is a bad husband.

We have, then, blunted both the noncognitivist and the intuitionist arguments against the definability of good by refusing to treat *good* as an expression complete in itself: it is essentially adjectival. "Good F" is definable, or partially definable, but at least verifiable and meaningful. We do know, further, that if X is a good F, then Y must be a good F, unless there is some relevant property G that X has and Y lacks. So we have a lot of structure to work with as we go on to address the question of whether, finally, good is simple and unanalyzable like *yellow,* or is definable without remainder, like *horse,* into more elementary terms. But this requires us to broaden the domain of our investigation and to begin to think seriously about that difference.

In thinking about it we may keep in mind the following thought: Something may be a horse or may be yellow no matter what the world thinks about it. But is good of that sort? And if not, may it not be the case that just the sorts of considerations reemerge that we sought to bracket by saying they belonged not to representation but to use? That "X is a good F" makes no sense in abstraction from a social context, as "X is yellow" or "X is a horse" do?

# 15

## The Empiricist Theory of Understanding

IN CONTRASTING THE CONCEPT OF *horse* with the concept of *yellow*—and in insisting that the concept of *good* is like the latter rather than the former—Moore is tacitly endorsing a piece of philosophical structure that finds its most familiar embodiment in John Locke's *Essay Concerning Human Understanding*. It is indeed the structure of understanding itself, according to Locke, in that all our concepts are arrayed somewhere on a structure that in fact has two main constituents. There is an analytical component, which has something like the form of a dictionary, in that the concepts are related to one another through definitions. And then there is what we might term an input component, through which the analytical component is stocked. I suppose the analytical component would be the structure of understanding for any kind of being that can be said to understand at all, but the input component varies from being to being and in our case is constituted by our sensory modes—sight, hearing, taste, and the like. A being with none of our senses, but a set of senses we can scarcely imagine, might derive a type of input we also can scarcely understand—but its concepts would even so be arrayed on something like the same structure that defines what Locke is careful to call *human* understanding.

Let us consider the concept of *horse*—or better, because it is more tractable, the concept of *apple*. We have in fact acquired the concept *apple* through experiencing apples, which is to say through sight and taste and feel. Berkeley, who largely accepts Locke's structure, puts the matter vividly:

> A certain color, taste, smell, figure, and consistence having been observed to go together, are accounted one distinct thing signified by the name "apple:" other collections of ideas constitute a stone, a tree, a book, and the like sensible things.

For Berkeley, as for Locke, there is a lexical connection between the word *apple*— or between the idea of apple—and terms (ideas) referring to the specific color, taste, smell, figure, and consistency associated together in the overall experience of apples. So *apple* in effect resolves, lexically, into "round, red, tart, crisp, fragrant," and to understand what *apple* means is in effect to have had the sensory experiences the definition picks out. (Of course, there are green and mushy and sour apples, apples that are far from round, and so on, but let us remain with the paradigm case, the somewhat idealized fruits with which this discussion traditionally operates.) The *apple* to *red* connection, then, is lexical—but since red itself is regarded by both Locke and Berkeley as indefinable, the term *red* cannot be understood through a definition, and so understanding it must come some other way. That way, obviously, is through sense experience, and it would have been thought by both thinkers that there would be no other way. The idea of red is put into the understanding by the senses. And the idea of *apple* is composed of such sensory inputs. The latter Locke terms a compound, and the former a simple, idea. Since Moore was constrained by the Open Question Argument to the view that the idea of good was simple, and so indefinable, he was obliged to answer the question of how, if not by analysis, it is understood, and he was evidently enough of a disciple of Locke to suppose there must be some specific sense, or 'intuition,' through which we acquired it—a *moral* sense.

There would have been an alternative possibility, namely that the idea of good is *innate:* We simply enter the world with a moral understanding. Locke himself was vehemently opposed to the existence of innate ideas, and the first book of his *Essay* is polemically addressed to just that point. Locke argues that it would be inconsistent with the belief that God made us the way we are that he would have given us senses wherewith to acquire our basic ideas and then, redundantly, also stocked us with a set of innate ideas. If there were a noncontroversial moral sense, the same argument might have been mounted, so far as that argument is compelling, in the case of our ideas of colors. But in fact it is one of the most controversial aspects of Moore's thesis, and it would be far more acceptable were he to have viewed our moral sense as innate, as a disposition to do or avoid or value certain things. For all his aversion to innate ideas, Locke certainly regarded the senses themselves as original equipment, and hence the disposition to acquire simple ideas as something we bring into the world with us. The Chinese, who thought deeply on this subject, believed much the same thing about moral intuition. It was argued in classical Chinese philosophy that the most hardened criminal would spontaneously and so prereflectively reach out to rescue a child crawling toward the edge of a well. He would do this not for a reason—to get a reward or to sell or molest the child—but because he knows it to be the right thing to do, which he cannot help knowing, given his original nature. This natural disposition of human heartedness might even suggest that moral behavior is genetically coded. The problem, or one problem, with Moore is that his address to moral questions is too cognitive, too much a matter of saying which things are good through, in his view, recognizing them to be so. But knowing something to be good or right is ipso facto to have a disposition to do or avoid certain things—it immediately translates into action, as the great moral theorists of China appreciated. Plato, too, I think, believed that the idea of good was innate, but he held this because he held that most of our concepts were acquired in previous existences and merely remembered in this one.

In any case, that portion of the understanding that has the structure of a dictionary is composed, as it were, of two books. In the one would be all the compound ideas, like *horse* or *apple,* each with its definition. But the elements of the defining expression would refer to the first volume of the dictionary, and would consist of terms whose meaning is inseparable from sense-experience: *red, tart, round,* and the like. Let us call these basic terms, since none of the terms in the second volume would be intelligible without them. The two-volume dictionary might, I suppose, have a counterpart in the Chinese dictionary, which also has two parts, one consisting of a set of roots into which the other characters are analyzed. It is only that, in Locke and Berkeley and the empiricists generally, the roots of meaning are the senses.

Locke was well aware that there would be a disproportion in size between the two volumes. The volume of compound ideas was vastly larger than the volume of roots, as we would expect, and he was quite brilliant in recognizing that this discrepancy had to be accounted for somehow. Of the human understanding Locke asked (rather floridly), "Whence comes it by that vast store, which the busy and boundless fancy of man has painted on it with an almost endless variety?" His answer, in one word, was "experience," but that accounts only for how the volume of root ideas got stocked. His answer to the corresponding question for the second volume is given in the way he phrases the question: It comes from the "fancy" or the "imagination," which compounds higher-order ideas out of the materials furnished by the senses, producing all sorts of ideas whose constituents, unlike in the case of apples, are never experienced together—the idea of mermaids, or of centaurs, or satyrs, or the gods of Greece and Rome. Locke saw the problem almost as an engineer who, struck by the disproportion between output and input, must characterize the mechanism in such a way as to account for it, assuming that something does not come from nothing. It was an anticipation of Chomsky's thesis about language: Our linguistic output is infinite, but the input—the actual sentences we learn—is finite and even degenerate (we learn from slovenly speakers), and to account for the difference Chomsky postulated an innate grammar, a "language of thought" in which the language learner formulates a theory for his or her language. Locke instead postulates the imagination, and this, too, is innate. People with an impoverished imagination must get along with only the simple ideas: The logician Quine once wrote this piece of doggerel to characterize

> The unrefined and sluggish mind,
> Of *homo javanensis,*
> Could only treat of things concrete
> And present to the senses.

Imagination, in Locke, is primarily a synthesizing mechanism, compounding the materials with which sense furnished the mind into higher and higher fabrications. So the mind will contain things that exist nowhere outside it—ghosts and monsters and things never encountered in experience at all. Locke said, on the other hand, that one could not imagine a simple idea: One could not imagine red, for instance, or the taste of pineapple, which had to be experienced in order to be understood. And in a way we all must accept this. It would be difficult to imagine sexual experience or love unless one has experienced them—or pain, or what it is like to be tortured, or, to use an example made famous by a speculation of Thomas Nagel's, what it is like to be a bat. What would it be to experience the world sonically, as bats do, or as the blind do? Nagel supposes that for each sense, there is something that *it is like* to have that sense, and one simply does not and cannot know what it is like unless one is oneself so made as to have experiences of just that fundamental order.

Locke cites a blind man who volunteered the thought that scarlet must be like a blast on a trumpet, which suggests that through language certain cross-modal inferences are encouraged: He would scarcely have supposed pink were like the blast of a trumpet, and I am certain there would be considerable agreement were we to say what the musical counterpart to pink was. It cannot be an accident that certain harmonies and rhythms are called the blues, and that the blues connect with certain moods. Hume argued, in effect, that we can know what it is like to experience a certain color we in fact have not experienced if that color corresponds to a gap in a chromatic array and we have experienced the adjacent colors. Peter Geach once argued that a blind man understands what red means if he is able to answer certain grammatical questions regarding sentences in which *red* is correctly used; for example (I suppose), Can something be red and green all over at the same time? So there is considerable room for controversy regarding the simple ideas. What it is like to move an arm must be unimaginable or wrongly imagined by the paralyzed. What it is like to nurse a child is closed off to males, given their physiology, to understand directly.

But all these questions must refer us to another topic or set of topics—that of knowledge by direct acquaintance, and that of the philosophical nature of mind so far as such states as simple ideas are supposed to correspond to are in fact states of mind. For the moment my concern is not with these, but with the structural analysis of understanding, on the model of an analytical dictionary.

In logic and mathematics, there exist certain formal systems that have a sort of primitive vocabulary, a set of terms not defined within the system. Then there are other terms defined by these. Perhaps *point* and *line* are so related that a line is defined as a set of points, and parallel lines defined as disjoint sets of points, viz., sets having no common element. A rigorous deductive system, so far as its vocabulary is concerned, will contain no term not among the primitive terms or not explicitly defined by means of these. For such a system, the nonprimitive terms can always be eliminated from an expression in which they occur in favor of a perhaps more cumbersome expression using the primitive terms alone. There is a base, as it were, and a superstructure, and the superstructure may be eliminated, leaving only the base. To understand a term, then, is to be able to eliminate it, if it is in the lexical superstructure. But how are we to understand the basic vocabulary, the terms that are mutually noninterdefinable, or lexically independent of one another?

There are two answers, as we might expect. The first is that we simply do understand them, as though such understanding were innate. Something like this must have been believed by Euclid, whose own formal system of geometry is the model for this way of connecting up knowledge. The other is that we understand them only through some bridging definition that coordinates the basic terms with something outside the system: A point is the intersection of two lines, say. The basic, or primitive, terms in a formal system, indeed, can mean any number of things, depending on what coordinating definitions we find it useful to use; and each connected set of these definitions gives a sort of *model* for the formal system. Locke's theory of understanding is rather like the formal system so described, but he has a natural explanation of how we understand the basic terms, and this, of course, was his empiricism: We understand them through the experiences that cause us to have the relevant ideas in the first place. The understanding comes from outside the system. At least so far as the basic ideas are concerned, they are in the understanding only if they were first put there by the senses. Each new simple idea is an absolute augmentation of the base of human understanding. It is a limited base—limited as our senses are limited—but it is the ultimate furniture of the mind.

It was because they subscribed to more or less this account of understanding that the verificationists insisted that if we could not specify the experiences—the sense experiences—it would be required to have in order to verify a proposition, the proposition would be meaningless. It simply could not be understood. A proposition like "X is red" is easily understood if we know what *red* means. Very few sentences of science are as simple as that, but the logical positivists were convinced that however impoverished such basic "observation" sentences might seem, the whole of meaningful discourse rested on them. That meant that any sentence not itself an observation sentence must, if it was to be meaningful, be connected in some logical way—"translated into," was one way of representing this—with observation sentences. That meant that the terms of meaningful discourse related to one another lexically much as Locke insisted. If *apple* is a term with meaning, it translates into *red, round, tart,* and so on.

This may be as reductive a view of science as *Homo javanensis's* is a reduced view of understanding. But it clearly pivots, as so much of what we have been discussing pivots, on the central notion of definition. Definition is the analytical strategy through which we discover, almost as a prism enables us to discover the spectral colors, what the basic components of our understanding are—providing the understanding is really structured like an analytical dictionary. Perhaps it is not. Perhaps even the language of science is not structured as the logical empiricists have supposed it is. Even so, definition has played so crucial a role in the *philosophy* of understanding and meaning that we cannot really advance without taking some account of it. To that task I shall turn in the next section.

Before doing so, a somewhat general word might be pronounced on the concept of simplicity that played so crucial a role in the structures tacitly subscribed to by Moore, and that is explicit in the philosophy of Locke. The first is that the structure of understanding is represented as a kind of mosaic of irreducible units of meaning, these being the simple ideas or concepts or, linguistically, the simple, or basic, terms. The thought was that every idea or concept not itself simple—or any term not simple—was put together out of simples into which it can be dissolved—or into which it can be defined. There is, then, a kind of foundationalism for understanding, according to which understanding rests on these atoms of intelligibility. But there is a second notion of simplicity that connects with a foundationalism in the theory of knowledge, namely that there are simple or basic propositions—propositions known to be true but in such a way that there are no more elementary propositions *through* which they are known to be true. Just as every term not itself simple is *understood* through the simple terms, so every proposition not itself simple is *known* through some simple proposition or set of simple propositions. And usually, the crucial vocabulary for the basic proposition is the basic or simple terms of the foundations of understanding. Moore thought *good* a simple term and "X is good" a simple proposition. Philosophers, seeking the basic furniture of the mind, would, if he were right, have to take into their inventory the concept of good as philosophers concerned with the basic furniture of cognition would have to take into their inventory the basic ethical proposition that "X is good."

But there is a further sense of simplicity that Moore doubtless intended, namely that good was a simple *thing* or *quality*. And the thought was that like understanding and knowledge, the *world itself* is compounded out of simples. And to be sure, we do believe something like this to the degree that we believe in something like the atomic theory of matter—that there are fundamental particles out of which whatever there is is compounded by various physical forces. But philosophical pictures of the world are not quite like that, as we have already seen. In any case, Moore must have believed that through philosophical argument (and think how different such procedures are from those of science!) one had arrived at an item in the basic inventory of the world itself: that among the basic constituents of reality itself was Good. So the three dimensions of philosophy—as a theory of understanding, of knowledge, and of the world—seem to have the same architectonic structure.

This implies, I believe, that the structure in which simples play a foundationalistic role is one of the main and most compelling of the forms of thought in the philosophical way of thought. So much is this true that it would be difficult to articulate entire philosophical controversies, such as that over the nature of moral discourse, without taking this into account as one of the basic structures. It is a structure, for example, shared by the two forms of cognitivism. Both the intuitionist and the naturalist tacitly accept a structure in which, through definition, we can determine whether good is basic and therefore simple, or whether it can be defined away as not among the fundamental concepts or things, leaving moral knowledge essentially knowledge of pleasure or utility or whatever it is into which moral terms are to be resolved. But if this whole structure is itself an illusion, if this way of ordering concepts, propositions, and things has simply been allowed to spill beyond the boundaries inside which it has some natural application, such as the domain of formal or axiomatized systems, then whole philosophical continents dissolve away into nothingness. But this then makes the notion of definition that much more crucial, for it is definition, as we saw, that binds the basic terms into larger compounds. And if definition itself is vulnerable, so are the forces that are its counterparts in the theory of knowledge and the theory of the world.

# 16

# *Definition and Dialectic*

THE EYE IS AN EXTRUDED PART OF THE BRAIN, and the processes of vision are of such considerable complexity that Darwin, who knew only part of the story, was able to say how the mere thought of the eye caused him to turn cold all over. We know only part of the story today, but very little in visual experience as such discloses how complex a process is taking place when we see something. Vision takes place when quanta are reflected, or emitted, or refracted, or scattered by external objects and absorbed in the form of light waves by the retina, and neural images are caused. But none of this is part of the experience it explains. Consider the case of seeing yellow. This occurs when the cones of the retina receive light waves corresponding to about 580 nanometers. The eye in fact is sensitive to a range between 400 and 700 nanometers, and in ordinary vision there are three primary centers of color reception, sensitive, respectively, to 460 nm (blue), 530 nm (green), and 650 nm (red). Yellow is not, physiologically speaking, a primary color, but results from admixture. But no single mixture will give you yellow. Rather, there will be a whole range of distinct mixtures that produce the same color. On p. 96, for example, are three spectral distributions that will produce the color of lemon peel in daylight. Nothing internal to experienced yellow will discriminate between these distributions, any more than anything internal to that experience will disclose that one is experiencing light waves. The experience will be of something simple, quite as Moore contends, however

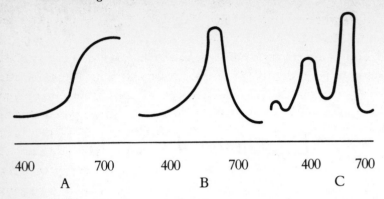

400        700        400        700        400        700

A                      B                      C

complex the physiology of what transpires. And the quality will be indefinable, not just despite, but because of, the fact that the experience of yellow is consistent with a whole range of distinct spectral distributions.

In a definition we will typically have two expressions, the one to be defined, which is referred to as the *definiendum*, and the expression through which it is defined, designated the *definiens*. The two expressions are supposed to be interchangeable, and hence are related to one another by the relationship of identity, graphically represented by "$=$." The usual view of "$=$" is that the expressions united by means of it into a definition are altogether interchangeable: In any context in which one of them occurs, it can be replaced by the other without changing the truth of that context. Now, identity has a number of interesting logical properties, among them what logicians call transitivity: If $X = Y$ and $Y = Z$, then $X = Z$. If transitivity fails, then identity collapses. But this makes it perfectly plain why we cannot define yellow with reference to spectral distributions. It is obvious that if yellow were defined in terms of $A$ or $B$ or $C$, then by virtue of transitivity, these would have to be identical with one another—which they clearly are not. So, though they severally cause the experience of spectral yellow, yellow cannot be identified with them. And so it is consistent with physiological complexity that yellow should be quite as simple as the empiricists supposed it was. And anyway, one might experience yellow without the eyes being involved at all—one might get hit on the head, or simply dream of daffodils.

So it is difficult to know in advance which terms or concepts are going to be indefinable. In a famous remark, Saint Augustine said about time that he knew what it was—until someone asked him what it was. With yellow it may be argued that we do not understand what it means—or what it *is*—unless we have experiences of a certain sort. Are there experiences of time? A dog seems not to notice the passage of time, much in the way in which very old humans seem not to—which is much the same as saying, perhaps, that they, like dogs, lack short-term memories. (That is why you have to make an immediate impression on a dog who has done something bad, for he will have forgotten that it even happened in a very short of time, and will be simply indignant at what he perceives as an injustice if you punish him without cause). But it would even so be quite contrary to our understanding of the concept to attempt to define time in terms of short-term memory—not least of all because we need the notion of time in order to define what it means to be short term, and the definition would go circular. Perhaps the most basic terms we have are those we need for any attempted definition of themselves, so that they are indefinable without circularity, whatever their relationship to experience. Kant, whose views on time are somewhat difficult to describe without a great deal of narrative, held that time is a *form* of perception, so that we experience things in time without there being an experience *of* time as such at all. Indeed, if time were experienced, it would be experienced *in* time—and there the circularity would appear. So Augustine's lament may have been due to the indefinability of time, time being a basic notion, fascinating though it would be to explain how we come by our knowledge of such basic things.

Sometimes in Plato one gets the sense that some among the terms he is attempting to define are basic because we seem to be appealing to them in the very act of seeking their definition. And in fact this whiff of circularity may be the best evidence we have that we are in the presence of one of the basic concepts—far more basic, in a certain sense, than the color concepts of which the empiricists made so much. Still, at this stage of our inquiry it is more important that we explore the anatomy of definition itself than its limits, and we have at least the two notions of identity and transitivity to guide us: The question is, What does it mean to say that $T = D$, where $T$ is the term to be defined (the "definiendum"), and $D$ its defining expression (the "definiens")? This is a difficult question for the obvious reason that nothing can be more basic to the concept of definition than the concept of identity itself, so that circularity of definition is hardly avoidable. So the best thing is to operationalize it slightly by asking how we would test for the truth of $T = D$, and perhaps one good test is asking native speakers whether they would agree that whatever is $D$ is *also* $T$. At least we would know that as a matter of linguistic practice, whatever is $D$ is also $T$.

Certainly this was the practice of Socrates, with whom the philosophical concern with definition began. He is seldom concerned with terms his companions did not use frequently and easily, certainly in their moral discourse; nothing could have been more central to their language than the terms under discussion in the Socratic dialogues—*justice, love, friendship, piety,* and the like. Plato clearly had a special motive in displaying his mentor and moral hero in these discussions—Socrates was executed for impiety, and it would be a bitter irony if there was sufficient disagreement on its meaning that those who condemned him of it did not display the kind of understanding consistent with putting a man to death. Of course, one might suppose that *piety* itself is indefinable, but in the great minor dialogue the *Euthyphro,* Socrates is able to demonstrate that the patterns of use of this crucial word are inconsistent—so even if indefinable, our intuition of the concept cannot be tremendously clear.

Consider the case in which, as it happens, a kind of definition really is arrived at at last: the case of *justice* in the *Republic*. In the first exchange between Socrates and Cephalus—a man who is clearly decent and responsible and concerned with doing the right things—definition $D$ of the term *justice* is offered: "Justice is telling the truth and paying one's debts"—just the kinds of things by which one assays probity in the world of business to which Cephalus belonged. But even Cephalus recognizes the inadequacy of the definition when it is pointed out to him that there are cases of which the description "paying a debt" is true that we would hesitate to describe as just. The famous example is returning a weapon to a man who has since gone mad. We *owe* him the return of his sword, beyond question, as it is his and he had lent it to us—but one does not in the name of justice put swords in the hands of madmen, any more than we give bombs to children whom we can only get to go to sleep by promising they can have anything they ask for and they ask for a bomb. As a native speaker, Cephalus applies the definiendum to what he will not apply the definiens—and that breaks the definition. This method is used often in philosophy—it is the method of *finding counterinstances*—and it is extremely powerful. So far as I know, it was a method invented by Socrates, though perhaps it was widely exercised in the sorts of legal debates that were so important a feature in the litigious form of life that belonged to Athens.

The dialogue proceeded to patch up this problem: Everyone recognized that a definition of justice that did not include paying one's debts and telling the truth would be defective, so that much of Cephalus's definition must be retained. The thing was to include this while excluding the difficult Socratic case, and the next attempt at definition, offered by Cephalus's son Polymarchus, does that—only it too falls to the methods of counterinstantiation. So the search continues: Each new definition retains what belonged to the previous one, excludes the difficulties it gave rise to, and of course corresponds to our intuitions as users of the word to begin with. It is our concept, after all, and we are finally the authorities on what the term can and cannot mean, even if we lack the analytical skills to find definitions on our own. Lexicography takes a certain sort of study, after all, even if Socrates is not exactly compiling a dictionary. As a matter of historical interest, the sequence of overthrown definitions in the first pages of the *Republic* illustrates what is known as dialectic. A thesis is stated, a contradiction is found, a synthesis is framed that overcomes the contradiction while preserving the thesis—and this goes on until we find ourselves with a contradiction-free thesis—a thesis to which there is no counterinstantial antithesis—and this will then condense and retain everything that came before. The belief that the world, or that history at least, exhibits a dialectical structure is based on a presumed analogy with what Plato would have supposed was the nature of thought. It is striking that thought, for Plato, is not something that takes place privately, in our heads, but publicly, in the marketplace of ideas in which his celebrated dialogues occur.

The implicit notion of definition, then, that emerges from the dialogues is this: $T = D$ if and only if there is nothing that is $D$ that is not also $T$. As we shall see, there are grave problems with this account, but the first problem at least is this: How do we know we have come to the end of counterinstances? Perhaps there are counterinstances we have not thought of or are simply not clever enough to point out to one another because the issue has become too complex. In certain philosophically interesting examples, as in the definition of knowledge, something like this may have taken place: We simply were not bright enough to make the next dialectical move. So what guarantee is there that the contradictions have all been ironed out and we are home free? Once this is seen as a problem, it is not difficult to proceed to the others.

The other problems stem from the assumption, first, that the meaning of a term or expression is what it stands for—an individual, in the case of a proper name like *Rome* or *George Washington,* a class of individuals in the case of a common noun such as *bird* or *bear*. Two terms, then, have the same meaning if they stand for, or name, the same individual or class of individuals. In the first instance, there are terms that have what logicians call empty extensions, terms that stand for nothing because there is nothing for them to stand for—*unicorn* and *centaur* and "human being twelve miles tall." We could, of course, following logical practice, say that these designate the null class, giving them something to mean—but then they would all have to mean the same thing, and this simply seems wrong, so far as meaning as anything to do with understanding is concerned. For we do not understand them as synonyms. We could perhaps enlist, as Nelson Goodman did, what he terms "secondary extensions." The primary extensions are the class of things a term stands for: The secondary extension of *unicorn* would be the unicorn pictures and unicorn descriptions, on the basis of which in any case we come to what understanding of unicorns as we possess. So the term *unicorn* differs from the term *mermaid* through a difference in their secondary extensions. This suggestion, which is clearly ingenious, may even take care of cases in which a pair of terms has nonempty extensions, but where it is plain that they have different meanings, such as "creature with a heart" and "creature with a kidney," when there are no creatures with hearts that are not also creatures with kidneys.

On the other hand, it leaves us without a theory of meaning for *pictures,* which we have wanted to include among the vehicles of understanding. Somehow a picture of a unicorn and a picture of a mermaid have different meanings—but what are the secondary extensions with which we can distinguish them semantically? Pictures of pictures of unicorns may differ from pictures of pictures of mermaids, but it is awfully difficult, and somehow a bit unwieldy, to distinguish pictures of pictures from pictures themselves.

Whatever the case, some distinction is needed, some way of representing the fact that terms may have different meanings even if they stand for the same things, and it has seemed obvious to philosophers of language that another dimension must be added to the usual dimension of standing for (or denoting, or designating, or referring), with which the analysis of definition has proceeded since ancient times. A great contribution to our understanding of the issues was made by the logician Gottlob Frege, who argued through the following famous example that meaning could not be simply the same thing as standing for. It is widely accepted that "the Morning Star" stands for the same planet—Venus—as "the Evening Star" stands for. But if that were all there were to the matter, we could not account for why "the Morning Star is the Morning Star" is trivial (both expressions standing for the same planet) while "the Morning Star is the Evening Star" represents a genuine piece of knowledge. It is a real discovery that one and the same thing is indicated by "the Evening Star" and "the Morning Star"—and it is not difficult to find examples that confirm Frege's point.

Frege then proposed that there are two ways to understand significance. One is the way of naming or standing for or designating, which he called, in German, *Bedeutung.* The other he called *Sinn,* or "sense." So each term has two ways of being understood, either through *Sinn* or through *Bedeutung.* The *Bedeutung* of *horse* will then be the class of horses. The *Sinn* of the term will then be the *concept* of horse. It was perhaps because he found the notion of concepts repugnant that Goodman introduced his idea of secondary extensions, for there really is a question of what and where concepts are. Frege supposed they were neither physical things nor mental things but existed in some third realm, remarkably similar to Plato's realm of forms. The thought, then, was that we grasp the concept a term means when we understand it—but Frege never explained what grasping was like, or what it could mean that something neither mental nor material could explain the way we understand words and expressions. Goodman believed that at least pictures are good, clear-cut objects in the real world, and the question of understanding pictures itself something psychology could explain someday in a scientific way.

For the moment it is enough to have simply widened the concept of meaning beyond the mere notion of naming, or *Bedeutung.* And we can now at least say in a general way what the problem with Socrates' theory of definition would come to. We might say that in addition to having the same *Bedeutung*—in addition to there being nothing one term stands for that the other does not—two terms have to be connected in another way—and this may then guarantee, if we can identify it, that there can be no counterinstances. But then, perhaps, the thing to do with definitions is to find out when two terms have the same *Sinn,* making simply circuitous Socrates' effort to secure definitional synonymy through examining that which terms stand for. For, knowing that two terms have the same meaning, we know without having to examine cases that they *must* stand for the same things if they stand for anything at all.

The problem, then, is to find out what this connection really is, if there can be a connection other than through the *Bedeutungen* of terms. Sometimes it was held, by theorists of definition, that the defining expression was to be an *analysis* of the expression to be defined. So let us say that the connection is an analytical connection. What would this be? For this we must turn to the philosophy of Immanuel Kant.

# 17

# Analytic, Synthetic, A priori, A posteriori

THERE IS ANOTHER WAY to look at Cephalus's attempt at a definition of justice. It is that, since we are able with only slight efforts at imagination to conceive of a counterexample, it is plain that "X is an example of justice though X is not an example of returning to someone what belongs to him" is not contradictory. If it were contradictory, we would know in advance—would know, as philosophers say, a priori—that there could be no counterexamples. So one test for the analytical connection might be this: Such a connection exists if the denial of its existence is contradictory. And it might then be said that Plato—or Socrates—only went so far as to show that the denial of the various definitions was never contradictory. In order to establish that a definition in which the defining expression really was an analysis of the expression to be defined, he would have had, beyond that, to establish somehow that the denial of it was contradictory. But this he did not attempt even in his own famous definition of justice; perhaps it was because he was so anxious to use it to build up a picture of the ideal state, a matter to him of some urgency, that he was less interested in whether the definition was as tight as rigor would have demanded.

Kant marked out a class of judgments, or propositions, which he designated as analytical, the test for which was that their denials were contradictory. Hence, if a proposition were analytical, no way could be imagined in which it could be false—just because no way could be imagined in which its denial could be true. As semanticists would say today, an analytical proposition would be true in every possible world and its denial false in every possible world. Imagination is not to be understood as referring to a psychological opinion. People have varying powers of imagination. Someone may so need the love of another person that he is incapable of imagining infidelity on the other's part. Still, infidelity remains a possibility, even if never actualized, just because it is consistent to say, even if false, that the other is unfaithful. Iago lied about Desdemona's promiscuity. But he did not voice a contradiction. That is why jealousy was so great a torment to Othello: Being old and ugly, he could easily imagine the infidelity of his young bride, and he had no way of finding out whether his fears were realistic or not. In truth, such was Desdemona's character that unfaithfulness to a husband was really almost unthinkable and almost contradictory. But it remained, even so, an abstract possibility and in consequence Othello, given *his* character, could never rest in the certitude that she was not. Such certitudes may best be found in mathematics—the positivists believed that all mathematical truths were analytical—or in logic. But it is plain that no proof, no demonstration, could establish the analyticity of Desdemona's chastity. That Desdemona was chaste was a proposition whose denial was consistent or noncontradictory. It remained a possibility, even if not a truth.

Kant had in mind primarily subject-predicate propositions—propositions of the form '*S* is *P*', and his thought was that when a proposition is genuinely analytical, the thought of the predicate is already, somehow, if only vaguely, already there in the subject, so that in making this explicit, we are but clarifying our thought. He specifically describes the analytical propositions as "explicative": They do not contribute to our knowledge but merely clarify what we already know, if less transparently to ourselves. And indeed this was something Socrates would have endorsed. It was not his view that we add to our knowledge through dialectic. He described himself as a midwife, able to deliver only what was already there. He disclaimed any power to impregnate the minds of his discussants. (This is something that should be kept in mind when we consider the "Socratic method" of teaching, which has no value when the primary intention is to instill information.).

Synthetic propositions are, in Kant's unlovely but exact term, "ampliative." The predicate adds something to the subject. "Bachelors are unmarried mature males"—a classroom example—is analytic; it might be used to remind someone that the woman a bachelor lives with cannot be his wife—and the response to this can only have the form, "of course." "Bachelors are unhappy" gives real information, or does so if it is true, but there is no way of finding this out short of serious canvassing of bachelors as to the state of their souls. In order to carry out such an investigation, one would have to know what one meant by *bachelor,* and so science cannot proceed without definition. Still, if all we had to go by were dialectic, we could never increase our knowledge. And this, too, may have been something Plato, who was deeply conservative in many matters, would have acknowledged. He thought that we already have all the knowledge we require in order to navigate the world, the problem being to set it out clearly. He almost certainly believed this knowledge innate, which meant that education for Plato was very peculiar by contrast with our views, which is one of the things that makes the *Republic* a difficult work to accept. Plato resembled the Mandarin Chinese who thought the important thing was to establish a moral-political order, and that there was no guarantee that new knowledge would not upset what one had—so why take the chance? The executioners of the French Revolution are said to have said, in guillotining the great chemist Lavoisier, *La république n'a pas besoin de savants.* And often in history—think of Maoist China—the augmentation of knowledge is regarded as counterrevolutionary.

A chief problem with Kant's formulation—pointed out first, so far as I know, by Quine—is that the notion of contradiction is quite unclear. Indeed, Kant's notion of contradiction precisely takes for granted, rather than clarifies, the notion of analyticity. We have,

Quine allows, a clear idea of formal contradiction. We know that a proposition of the form *P* and not-*P* is necessarily false, and this in consequence of its logical form. Hence we know that *P* or not-*P* is necessarily true, just because *P* and not-*P* is its contradictory. And so any proposition or set of propositions that entails something of the form *P* and not-*P* is contradictory and its denial analytic. But "bachelors are not unmarried mature males" is not formally contradictory, and so the question becomes salient as to how it *is* contradictory. This is not a distinction Kant perceived, to the detriment of his system, and Quine pressed past this objection to the claim that the entire distinction between analytic and synthetic propositions is untenable. I shall examine his alternative views after making just a few further remarks on Kant's philosophical motives, putting the question of the analytical connection aside while I do so.

Kant was actually interested in a four-way distinction, and in fact was not especially interested in analytical propositions, which he regarded as necessary trivialities. But neither was he especially interested in those synthetic propositions whose truth or falsity are to be determined a posteriori rather than a priori—by empirical examination of their subjects. He did recognize that there cannot be analytical a posteriori propositions, but notwithstanding he insisted that there were synthetic a priori propositions—propositions that were informative or at least not trivial, but that even so could be known prior to any investigation of the world. Indeed, he connected the very possibility of philosophy with the possibility of there being synthetic a priori propositions—for in his view, philosophy is not an empirical science; it does not, just as Wittgenstein was later to maintain, increase our knowledge of facts. But it does increase our knowledge, and it does so in a way that does not depend on what we experience in the world, largely because what we experience in the world conforms to what we discover about the structure of experience synthetically, altogether prior to experience.

Kant's discussion is stunning. He first sets out to prove that philosophy is possible by showing that synthetic a priori knowledge is actual. It is, he held, actual in mathematics and geometry. He would have rejected the positivists' claim that mathematics is analytical, for it failed to square with our intuition that mathematics is not trivial—that in fact it is the best example we have of knowledge that is necessary—could not be otherwise—and certain.

His famous example, on the other hand, seems contrived. In 7 + 5 = 12 Kant argues that what we have on the left side of the equation sign is a mere sum, and that 12, the number on the right-hand side, is not "thought" when we merely think the sum of 5 and 7. The equation gives us a thought not contained in its component parts—that they are equal—by contrast with the thought in "all bachelors are mature unmarried males," which merely brings out what is already there and present in the expression *bachelor* itself. So it was not analytical. But neither was it a posteriori, for its truth does not depend on counting what we have when we have a pile of five things and another pile of seven things. If we should count them and get more or less than twelve, we would not conclude that $5 + 7 \neq 12$. We would assume that something happened there, in the world, which we had not noticed. Since the only alternative to analytical was synthetic, and the only alternative to a posteriori was a priori, Kant insisted that 7 + 5 = 12 is synthetic a priori. And, whatever the detail may be, there is a powerful insight here. Mathematics really does not seem either trivial or contingent on the outcome of experience. There seem to be mathematical discoveries and truths that are not mere matters of analysis. But, at least for the mathematics most of us know, our knowledge seemed indemnified against experience: If experience should somehow be inconsistent with it, the spontaneous response is, so much the worse for experience.

And this gives us the model, Kant believed, for philosophical propositions. Consider, "Every cause has an effect." This is clearly trivial, just because having an effect is part of what it means to be a cause. There are no "causes in themselves," to use a witty phrase of Nietzsche's. And this seems so even if we find it difficult to say what the criteria of analyticity are; it just seems a rule of meaning that causes have effects, as it does that wives are married. Consider again, "AIDS is caused by a retrovirus." This is certainly not a matter of meaning but of fact, and it is far from certain that it is true without qualification. Considerable research in immunology remains to be done before we know whether it is true or not. It seems synthetic and vehemently a posteriori. But now consider, "All events have causes." It is not part of the meaning of *event* that it has a cause. But neither does it seem contingent, a matter merely of experience. To say that there are uncaused events is to say that we must acquiesce in those events being unexplainable. This is in violation of a thesis formulated as the Principle of Sufficient Reason by Leibniz, which he believed plays the role in science that the principle of noncontradiction does in logic and mathematics. For whatever happens, there is sufficient reason. Kant's "Every event has a cause" is a version of the Principle of Sufficient Reason in the sense that it defines, in advance, what it means for the universe to be intelligible. Every explanation confirms it, in a sense, but not in the way in which the positive outcome of an experiment confirms a theory. It confirms it by conforming to it, for the Principle of Universal Causation prescribes in advance the very structure of experience.

Kant offers us a theory of the mind as preshaping the experiences it receives, which are processed into preestablished shapes, perhaps as the eye transforms the quanta absorbed by the retina into neural configurations. To find out what the structures of experience are, we must work from within the mind, since we cannot take a position outside the mind to see whether it works a certain way. Were we to take such a position, we would be using, in the examination of the mind, precisely what we went outside to examine—and hence we would not have succeeded in stepping outside. But for just that reason, the mind is not given as part of experience, for then we *would* be outside it, and that, as we saw, is evidently not possible. Hence elaborating the principles by which the mind forestructures experience requires a whole different method from building up a picture of the world—for it concerns the architecture of building pictures, and cannot, then, be part of the picture we build. Philosophy, Kant supposed, is nothing other than identifying the a priori structures of the mind. It is a heroic and profound view of the task of philosophy and really would reinstall philosophy as Queen of the Sciences. But in fact philosophy had never been unthroned. It cannot have been because it would have to preside over its own impeachment, and so it cannot seriously be impeached. It can merely become invisible to itself, which in effect is what Kant taught. All he did was to remove the dust and find a way of holding up a mirror.

# 18

## Totalistic Thought

SOCRATES AND HIS COMPANIONS were not engaged in collaborative lexicography seeking merely to get the rules of meaning as clear as they could. Definition was, in Plato's view, in one respect a method of discovery: To achieve definition of a term was to grasp an essence, the essence, in effect, of the things for which the term stood. So in a way, definition was a method of science if science itself, as Aristotle imagined, was addressed to the essences he believed, as did Plato before him, define the universe. Thus the enterprise engaged in so picturesquely by Socrates in the marketplace of Athens embraced, together with a view of understanding, a view of knowledge and a view of how the world itself must be, if knowledge and understanding are as the dialectic pursuit of definitions suggest them to be. The world outside the cave is constituted of the essences, or forms, that penetrate the world within the cave; and as each essence is unique and independent of each other essence—just as the empiricists were centuries later to suppose that simple properties or simple ideas were unique and independent of one another—it made sense to suppose the definition of a single term could be pursued, without reference to the meanings of other terms in the language, whose meaning must be independent of that of the term under scrutiny. But suppose this view of independent and autonomous meaning is wrong? Suppose words form families, so related that a change in the meaning of one would imply or entail changes in the meanings of the others?

Aristotle suspected something of the sort in once suggesting that all definition might be circular, that we will find ourselves sooner or later using, in the definition of a term *T,* other terms into whose definition *T* enters. So *T* is finally part of its own definition, as though the lexicon of a natural language folded back upon itself, and each term presupposed each other term in a totalistic system of internally related meanings. So instead of a mosaic of basic units of meaning, the dictionary is almost an organic structure of interdependencies. Then, if Plato's view of definition implies a view of the world as a mosaic of primary essences, each in its own space, unaffected by what might occupy the other spaces, a different metaphysic might be implied by the interdependency view of words—namely, one in which each thing is interdependent with each thing and the world itself is a totalistic system of mutually penetrating things. Of course it may be a mistake in either view to reason that the world must hang together as our language hangs together—but this is not a topic I can pursue until much later in this book. The point is that we have the possibility of two quite different views of the nature of understanding, and of reality itself, if these views in fact imply a metaphysics.

Realistically, in any case, one has to use words to clarify words, and one can only fix a meaning if other meanings are taken as fixed. But something quite parallel may be thought to hold in regard to the kinds of sentences that were, according to empiricist or positivist views, to form the foundations of understanding—the simple or basic sentence that is fully verified against a given experience: "Here now red," voiced in the presence of red, for example. Just as Plato supposed the forms independent and noninterpenetrant, so the positivists supposed a kind of atomism for basic sentences: Wittgenstein even used the term "atomic proposition" to refer to propositions that were simple, having no further propositions as components of themselves, hence as being capable of truth no matter what other propositions were true or false. In classical conceptions of axiom systems, it would have been supposed that the axioms themselves are quite independent of one another, in the sense that they are logically unconnected, and that the truth or falsity of each axiom might vary independently of the truth or falsity of the remaining axioms.

This perhaps merits a digression. In the history of axiomatized systems, it was believed that knowledge falls into two classes of sentences—theorems, which are known through logical proofs; and axioms, which cannot be proven within the system but are known in some other way—by some act of simple or direct intuition, perhaps. Perhaps they are self-luminously true, as Plato supposed the idea of the good to be self-luminously meaningful. Asked how one knew the axioms, the temptation would have been to say one just *does* know them—just as Moore was later to say that we just do know what good is, since we clearly cannot know it through anything more fundamental than it, given its simple nature. In order for this view to be plausible, the axioms themselves had to give the appearance of great simplicity. "A straight line is the shortest distance between two points," for example, seemed the kind of sentence one knew intuitively, by some single intuition. It may have been this that later recommended the view that the sentences of mathematics were analytic and mere matters of definition.

Now the famous exemplar of axiom systems, the great geometrical system of Euclid, seemed in fact to rest on fundamental propositions of just this order. Or it did so with the exception of the indispensible Parallel Postulate, which, because of its complexity, seemed insufficiently simple to be known as such, or known by instant understanding, and which accordingly appeared as though it *must* be a theorem and admit of proof:

> That, if a straight line falling on two straight lines make the interior angles on the same side less than two right angles, the two straight lines, if produced indefinitely, meet on that side on which the interior angles are less than two right angles.

Some twenty centuries of effort to prove a proposition that Euclid profoundly recognized as essential to the further elaboration of geometrical truth culminated in the recognition that it was independent and hence unprovable through the remaining Euclidean axioms, inasmuch as it was finally perceived that the *denial* of the Fifth Postulate was consistent with the truth of those axioms. It was shown that no contradiction followed by supposing that—to take the more tractable version of the Fifth Postulate—no lines could be drawn parallel to a given line through a point outside it. Or that indefinitely many such lines could be drawn parallel to a given line. These denials generate geometries very different from Euclid's, and it is known that each is consistent if Euclid's geometry is consistent—that none of them entails a contradiction unless Euclid's geometry does.

Now, the basic observational sentences that positivists made so central to meaningful discourse, and that were believed to constitute the foundations of empirical knowledge as the axioms were believed to constitute the foundations of mathematical knowledge, were believed atomic in this sense: that their truth or falsity in no sense depended on the truth or falsity of the other sentences in the foundation—though of course the truth or falsity of the higher-order sentences, which these verified or falsified, really does depend on them. The belief would be that truth flows upward into the system from its foundations, much as meaning flows into the lexicon of a system through the undefined or primitive terms.

But can we any more suppose there are these little quanta of truth, autonomous and independent, if we deny the corresponding possibility for the terms of a system? If the terms form an interdependent system, must not the sentences, however seemingly basic, also form an interdependent system, so that the entire edifice of beliefs penetrates any single act of verification just because, in some sense, the meaning of the candidate basic sentence presupposes the remainder of the system? Only by holding certain propositions to be true, and then forgetting we have done so, might we then think that we have found a simple, fully verifiable, foundational sort of proposition. But if the propositions form a system, then we might find a situation fully parallel to that which we found with vocabulary, that we may be dealing with something totalistic rather than atomistic, something where the truth or falsity of a given sentence is in hostage to the truth or falsity of the remaining portion of the language, and that a single-minded verification is no more to be had than a single-minded definition of an isolated term.

Part of the breakdown of positivism as a philosophical movement outstanding for its responsiveness to science was the recognition, specifically among those who took science as seriously as the positivists themselves, that the division between theory and observation was nowhere as sharp and absolute as positivism had insisted that it was. Observations are experiences saturated with theory, so that our sensory experience of the world cannot be segregated, as observation, from whole sets of beliefs and attitudes that penetrate the experience so thoroughly that it is as though theory and experience are one. And that means that different theories imply differences in experience, so that the same common retinal basis is consistent with radically divergent experiences, since the question is what the meaning of the experience is—and this is not to be answered without bringing in large segments of theory. The meaning of an experience is a product of the location of the experience in a body of belief, and the entire system, once more, functions totalistically.

The distinction between analytical and synthetic propositions, hence the distinction between matters of fact and matters of meaning—or between a priori and a posteriori knowledge—itself begins to give way under these considerations. Hence the distinction between what is true by definition and what is true by correspondence with experience is itself not something that can simply be determined by some sentence-by-sentence examination. The charge that these distinctions were more a matter of dogma than the philosophical certitude its adherents had believed was due to the logician Quine, who offered a different model altogether from the atomistic and architectonic one tacitly endorsed by the positivists. Quine's was instead a kind of organic model, which treats the system of beliefs that defines a stage of human knowledge as an instrument for the organization of experience—in which, admittedly, different propositions may play different roles. Certain propositions are more pivotal than others in the operation of this system, and these may, just because of that, be regarded as necessary truths—but the term *neces-*

*sary* carries much the same connotations as it might in connection with tools. Some tools are more necessary than others because the functions they subserve are more basic than other functions. For Quine, when a proposition is really deeply embedded in the system, there is a temptation to think of it as an unalterable truth—something like Kant's synthetic a priori propositions. These propositions define intelligibility for those who live by means of the system. Perhaps the principle of universal causation would be of this sort. But sometimes the system does not operate effectively; it does not function smoothly, and adjustments need to be made. And the time may come when we might have to give up on the principle of universal causation—or the principle of the excluded middle in logic—in order that the system should be effective in the only task that matters: the organization and integration of experience. Nothing is sacrosanct, nothing is immune to revision, but there are priorities as to which propositions we are most ready to sacrifice.

It is said, for example, that one basis for resisting the Copernican theory that the sun is stationary relative to the Earth was that it contravenes biblical text. In the Bible there was the commandment, complied with by the Sun, "Sun, stand thou still!" But how could this have been true if the sun were stationary? The command should have been, "Earth, stand thou still"—but if the Bible had wanted to say that, it would have said that. To be sure, we can say the Bible is not authoritative on matters of astronomy, but if we question the Bible in one place, we have given *ourselves* an authority the Bible was supposed to have had, and it may be crucial to the most important thing there is—our salvation, our freedom from original sin—that we credit the Bible thoroughly. Why believe it in one place and doubt it in another? By contrast with our eternal well-being, astronomical theory is pretty trivial. That would have immunized the Bible against revision, but over the years after Copernicus, it became too obvious that refusing to revise biblical teaching induced tensions all across the system of beliefs: Geology, evolution, even archaeology required severe modifications in the way the text was addressed, and Fundamentalism can be maintained only by refusing powerful inputs from the sciences. And yet it can be done.

One can regard all that as the devil's input, as a way of testing faith. There were even those who believed that God had created the world with fossils in it, just to test our faith when they were discovered, so that though the world is exactly as old as the Bible implies, we find ourselves tempted to believe it millions and millions of years old—and we must gamble. But are we prepared to place our souls on the gaming table or not?

In any case, in Quine's view, any proposition can be held constant if it is important enough to hold it constant. There is an element of choice, an inexpungible component of decision, at every point. We do not willingly, in science or religion, surrender certain propositions—but neither *must* we surrender them under the onslaught of experience. For we can always explain experience away if it is important enough for us to do so. Postpositivistic philosophical thought has stressed, against what now is stigmatized as dogma, the extreme flexibility of the system, its radical alterability, its status, almost, as living fiction—the question only being what enables us to function in life. Truth is less a property of a single sentence conferred by an atomic fact than a property of the total system. The property in effect is this: The system works. It enables us to go on. It is true in the way in which a ship is seaworthy. If the ship does not carry us across the waters, we abandon it for another or make repairs. And so with our system of beliefs. The system, as Quine puts it, faces the tribunal of experience collectively, and meaning itself is conferred on experience by what significance it is supposed to have for the total system.

It may, in this view, once more be observed that the distinction between moral language and the language of description weakens. It weakens because the model of holding a single sentence up to experience and determining whether or not it is true has itself weakened as a paradigm for knowledge.

It is difficult to believe that so vast a change in philosophy should have taken place in a matter of a few decades, but many philosophers, myself included, have lived through this change, and have had to come to terms with the question of how much of what passed for philosophy can be retained, since, on the new model of language, everything is seen so differently. For the moment, perhaps, it suffices to draw attention to a set of beliefs that must have been so deeply embedded in philosophical consciousness as to have determined how, from the beginning, philosophy was to be done. It was that thought must be organized in a certain way, the model for which is indeed the axiom system of Euclid, with a stock of basic or primitive terms, connected via definition with the remaining terms of the system; and a stock of basic sentences, sentences that are self-evident truths if one is a rationalist, or that are immediately verified by experience if one is an empiricist. This model has dominated philosophical thought about thought perhaps since the time of Plato, and it is this that has eroded away in recent times under the onslaught of a whole new way of viewing philosophical thought. In view of this new way of thinking, the problems of this chapter will have to be rethought. Perhaps there is no way to salvage them. Their sole use may be to make explicit what it is now important to believe about understanding that cannot easily be defined save against what we must repudiate—and this, in effect, is the philosophical thought of millennia.

# 19

## Geometry and Reality

ALMOST FROM THE BEGINNING of philosophical reflection, geometry seemed the luminous exemplar of knowledge in its highest vocation. The regular geometrical figures seemed precisely to illustrate Plato's thesis regarding ideal forms as being distinct from their exemplifications in the sensory world and perfect in their purity. Every freshman in philosophy is able to grasp the thought that in speaking about circles or triangles, we are not describing the irregular inscriptions made on pieces of paper with compass and rulers—diagrams that, however seemingly sharp, reveal perturbations under magnification and dissolve into paths of chalk or ink particles if the magnification is raised a few degrees. But the triangle and the circle are neither irregular nor material, they are beings of pure abstractness; and the fact that we can grasp the truth that the properties we ascribe to triangles and circles are properties we ascribe to *them,* and that we are able to do this on the basis of degenerate appearances in the degenerate world of sense-perceptions gives a vividness and application to Plato's theory of knowledge. The fact, moreover, that we are able to make application of geometrical truths to human problems—measuring land, navigating a coast, determining heights—is in itself an assurance that the way to find our way about here below is to ascend to the glacial purity of the realm of forms. It virtually promises that the philosopher, like the geometer, should, just because of his abstract intuitions, make the ideal ruler (in the sense of the term that applies both to measurement and to kingship) in the bumpy and irregular realm of human affairs.

With the systematization of geometry in Hellenistic times, where the entire domain of straight and curved lines, open and closed, of planes and surfaces and angles, was regimented into an edifice of astonishing clarity and architecture, the system of Euclid in turn offered a paradigm of how the world must hold together if the Platonic intuitions were sound. And it offered a model that, down to the present, has dominated the minds of thinkers as what must be emulated in the organization of knowledge: axiomatization, in which the entire system sits securely on unshakable foundations, held together by lines of logical force—a kind of cognitive cathedral in which we may find shelter from the seemingly disordered world. The axioms of Euclid seemed, indeed, to offer an example of the power of understanding, isofar as merely to understand the terms tied together in the basic proposition of the system meant to know the propositions to be true. Like the form of good in Plato's beautiful system, which illuminated itself while illuminating everything else (the form of forms must contain itself as an example), the basic postulates, with the exception, as we noted, of the Parallel Postulate were believed to be self-luminous. The idea that understanding entails knowledge as a matter of course and necessity gave a philosophical importance to the faculty of understanding that was enshrined in the central practice of definition.

This dream dissolved, slowly, with the advent of the non-Euclidean geometries. Slowly, because at first they seemed to be merely curiosities, for the world itself seemed Euclidean in its geometrical dimensions, and so only the geometry of Euclid could be true. And yet this had to be troubling were philosophers to have pondered it at any length. For how could the axioms of Euclid's geometry necessitate the geometry of the universe, if understanding indeed entailed knowledge, since the understanding of the non-Euclidean axioms did no such thing? Was there not some distinction between understanding and knowledge that ought to have caused thinkers to wonder where the connection lay, since the non-

Euclidean geometries were coherent and consistent? It seemed, instead, a purely contingent matter that the universe should be Euclidean, no longer a guarantee, since coherent alternatives were thinkable. Kant believed that geometry offered an example of synthetic a priori knowledge, and part, surely, of Kant's position was underwritten by these considerations: At least the Euclidean postulates were not analytic, inasmuch as their denials do not entail contradictions, not even in the rather ill-defined sense of the term Kant enlisted. On the other hand, they did not seem a posteriori, for then one would lose the connection between forms and their sensory exemplifications that Plato enlisted in support of his theory. The fact that nature might not show any perfectly parallel lines was quite consistent with the eternal truths of parallelity in which geometrizing philosophers believed. And so they seemed as though they must be a priori, there being no ready alternative. Hence synthetic and a priori at once, just as Kant said.

If one went a step or two further in the direction of Platonism, one might want to explain the Euclideanness of the world with reference to the forms—the circle, the sphere, the triangle—which penetrated the world as mere appearance, and gave it what rationality it possessed. And this gave in addition a certain dignity to the world, for the basic geometrical figures had a certain moral dimension in men's minds. There was a reason why circular motion seemed the most perfect of motions, why the altar of Apollo would be made in the form of a cube, why the universe itself should be regarded as nested spheres, rotating around the solid Earth. If one of the non-Euclidean geometries were true, not only would the Platonic heavens be populated with very odd bodies indeed, but the very idea would be offensive to the moral sensibilities of those who accepted the morality of mathematical forms. One can get a sense of this by thinking of the disgust Johannes Kepler felt with his discovery that the planets moved in elliptical rather than circular orbits: It seemed somehow not right that this should be true. The physicist Leo James Rainwater won the Nobel Prize with a theory about the atomic nucleus, which required that it have the unedifying form of a cigar.

This was offensive for just the reason ellipses were offensive to Kepler: Even in the twentieth century it seemed as though the nucleus ought to be spherical. Aesthetic and moral factors color our views of how reality ought to be, and when Marcel Duchamp devised a series of yardsticks for various geometries, placing them side by side as if they might represent the world just as well as the familiar straightedge, this was a gesture of surrealist impudence as shocking as his display of a urinal as a work of art.

By that time, however, the thought was becoming more and more acceptable that the geometry of the physical world might be non-Euclidean after all. Or that determining what it was could not any longer be regarded as a matter of human intuition and did not depend on the factors that made it seem obvious that the world was Euclidean, namely our perceptions. It might be true that our perceptions really were Euclidean, and in truth there is empirical psychological evidence that we compute, spontaneously, the angles and lines of our spatial lives with a Euclidean metric, long before we learn about geometry in schools. (A blind three-year-old, in a noted experiment, computed paths in such a way as to give evidence that she was "wired up" to operate along Euclidean lines; and experiments with rats in mazes support the hypothesis that they, too, spontaneously compute space along Euclidean lines.) So *we* may be Euclidean creatures, and our survival as navigators of space, then, argues for physical space being hospitable to our wiring. But this may be true for the relatively small spaces we in fact navigate, and the question of whether the physical world as *such* is Euclidean is another matter altogether. And by the time Duchamp exhibited his funny work, there were doubts. For by then it had begun to seem as though it were a matter of choice. Physics would become very complex indeed if geometry were not Euclidean, so long as the physics was Newtonian. But when it became Einsteinian instead, the reverse seemed true: Physics became complex and unwieldy if physical space in fact *were* Euclidean. If it were non-Euclidean, physics would become much more manageable. And at that point it seemed as though it were a choice. The question of the true geometry could no longer be answered independently of physics, and indeed there appeared to be a choice of geometries, as there was a choice of physics. To hold one's physics constant and vary one's geometry or to hold one's geometry constant and vary one's physics seemed very much matters of choice—and there and then geometry began to be thought of as a matter of convention. When it was so thought of, an immense and powerful tradition crumbled away: Geometry had to lose its metaphysical magic, and by an ironic reversal, the relationship of geometry to physics began to give support to the anti-foundationalist philosophy of postpositivist philosophy. In fact, the new geometricophysical complex seemed precisely to support the view that what we may believe to be fundamental truths are very much matters of different sorts of priority. You can defend Euclideanism forever, if you are prepared to make concessions and adjustments elsewhere in your system. But, for that matter, one can be a flat-earther forever, if you are prepared to make the appropriate concessions elsewhere in that system. Or you can believe in angels or Hindu deities.

The holistic or totalistic character of our system of beliefs is underlined by the newly appreciated relationship of geometry to the rest of the system. Sometimes it has been held that one of the problems in there being a true science of the human mind is that the mind's contents hold together in a holistic way. A person can be supposed to believe anything if we are prepared also to suppose he believes whatever else might be required for him rationally to do so. A man might, to use an example John Dewey employed, believe he is dead. You prick his fingers to show that he bleeds, and he simply says that this shows that dead men bleed. A man puts a letter in a mailbox, and we spontaneously assume that he means for the letter to be sent on to its destination. But he is a stranger who believes our mailboxes to be disposal bins, and he is merely trying to get rid of the pieces of paper he has put stamps on because he assumes that this is a tax on garbage. Such considerations have been thought compelling against the hope of a behaviorist account of human psychology, in that what we do outwardly may take any number of descriptions depending on what we believe and what we want—so that the bare behavioral gesture is compatible with any number of descriptions because there may be any number of explanations, each incompatible with the other, and no certainty as to which is right.

But as a differentiating criterion for the structure of mind, this holistic dimension fails, for it is paralleled by the corresponding view that any proposition regarding the world can be held true providing we are prepared to make adjustments and concessions somewhere else. Geometry can be Euclidean if we insist, providing we are flexible about physics or find some way of explaining things away that allows us to maintain a degree of consistency across the system of our total set of beliefs. It was Quine, once more, who insisted that our beliefs face what he termed "the tribunal of experience" in a collective way; and it is then possible for us to make any of a perhaps indefinitely large number of adjustments in the face of experience, since the main thing is to keep the system going. How curious that this should vindicate the way in which Plato's cave dwellers operated: forming hypotheses, making guesses, patching up. The anthropologist Lévi-Strauss characterized the operations of primitive mentalities in terms of *bricolage*—a French word that means, more or less, "tinkering." But the difference between primitive minds and sophisticated minds—if Quine is right—lies only in the primitiveness or sophistication of the tools: there is no escaping *bricolage.* And the inspiring hope in a knowledge immune to change and revision, of which geometry had seemed to offer the best example, gave way in the minds of contemporary philosophers to a far messier conception of things. It was a concept perhaps as repugnant to a Platonic sensibility as elliptical orbits were to a circle worshiper like Kepler.

Philosophy itself is of a piece. You cannot address a part of it without addressing the rest. Philosophical knowledge is of a piece with the rest of knowledge in that if you are going to hold to a given philosophical belief, considerations of consistency will compel you to adjust in other places. We have already seen our concept of understanding take us from terms to propositions to total systems of propositions in search of a unit, and then to find that understanding itself is a more disordered, chancier, more complex matter than the early paradigms in the theory of definition appeared to promise. And we found, beyond that, that questions of understanding could not be segregated from questions of knowledge. But if this is true, then we had better ask what knowledge any longer means if even geometry is a part of the mechanism rather than a shining model. Predictably, the concept of knowledge has been eroded by the decline of the definitional paradigm of understanding, and I now feel it is time to tell that part of the story.

# PART III

# Knowledge

# 20

## *The Analysis of Knowledge*

I EARLIER OBSERVED THAT there is a structure of controversy regarding the analysis of knowledge very like that which concerns the analysis of good. And though the suggestion that "I know that P" has a performative dimension, and that in using it the speaker in effect gives his word that P is true, has drawn philosophical attention to a dimension of linguistic behavior up to then very largely neglected, it still leaves open the possibility that the speaker is also describing himself, just as he would be describing another person were he to say that *that* person knows that P. And the question then is, What makes such a description true? What are we saying about another, or for that matter about ourselves, when we ascribe knowledge? When Austin wrote, in effect, that in saying "I know that P," I am not saying that I have accomplished some special cognitive feat on the same scale as merely *believing* that P, but at the very top of that scale, he may have been drawing attention to the possibility that there *is* no introspective difference between knowing and believing. The difference, from the point of view of introspection, may be nothing at all like the difference between hating and loving, anguish and ecstasy, or fear and the feeling of security, which we can all easily enough tell apart. Rather, the difference between knowledge and belief may be external to any psychological state.

In one of the earliest efforts at the analysis of knowledge, the *Theaetetus* of Plato, Socrates and his fellow conversationalists come to the view that knowledge consists of true belief plus some other condition, which is not successfully identified in the dialogue. But consider simply the first two components of the analysis—that knowledge, at the very least, is true belief (or 'opinion'). What we can at most determine by introspection is that we in fact believe that P. Whether P is true is quite external to the fact that we have the belief, and certainly nothing internal to our psychological condition will distinguish true beliefs from false ones, any more than anything internal to their inscription on a piece of paper will enable us to discriminate true sentences from false ones. True sentences like false ones are differentiated by circumstances outside the fact that they are sentences: Truth and falsity are matters of success or failure in having the world support what is said. You cannot tell from the sentence, "The battle of Hastings occurred in 1066," whether or not it is true. Its truth or falsity is altogether a matter of historical fact. And so it is with the *belief* that the battle of Hastings took place in A.D. 1066. Of course, what makes a belief true may itself lie within the scope of introspection. I may believe that I love my wife. And, just possibly, if love itself is a psychological state accessible to introspection, I can verify this belief about myself by seeing whether in fact I do love my wife. Still, this is a distinct piece of introspection from that through which I know that I believe I love her. Belief is one state, love another. But in any case, if belief is the psychological component in knowledge, then there may very well be no way of telling whether, on the basis of that psychological component, it is knowledge or belief. As we shall see, the indiscriminability between knowledge and belief is what generates a great deal of what has obsessed philosophers down the centuries in their quest for cognitive certitude.

The standard analysis of knowledge, at least of what is called propositional knowledge, usually consists of three components, most of which are not matters of contest, plus further components on which there is very little consensus. The usual view is that knowledge is had when one holds a true belief, and is justified in holding it. So there is a psychological component (belief), a semantic component (truth), and then a justificatory component that makes it appear as though there were an *ethics* of belief—that is, a question of what a person ought or ought not to believe, very much as there are actions a person ought or ought not to perform. Descartes, for example, laid down some very severe conditions on justification, insisting that one ought not to believe a proposition— hence cannot be said to know that proposition to be true—if there are any grounds for doubting it, so that only those propositions are fit objects of knowledge that are immune to rational doubt. This, to be sure, may then restrict the propositions that represent knowledge very narrowly indeed—so narrowly that one may suppose it possible that there is no knowledge at all, since nothing is immune to doubt. And this possibility possessed Descartes, whose great work, the *Meditations,* wrestles with the specter of total skepticism, from which the author emerges triumphant, displaying some crucial examples of knowledge he feels to be unshakable. These unshakably secure pieces of knowledge are then to serve as foundations for the edifice of beliefs that it was Descartes's mission to construct, along lines of splendid epistemological architecture.

If one so tightens the concept of justification that one is unjustified, hence ought not to believe such propositions as those in connection with which doubt is unreasonable or even incoherent, then perhaps there is no further condition beyond justified true belief in the analysis of knowledge. Further conditions arise only when the Cartesian criterion of justification is then relaxed. For even if we accept, as few philosophers since him have done, those few triumphant examples of propositions immune to doubt, Descartes's vision of knowledge may be so constrained that much of what we would like to suppose we know is consigned, at best, to the domain of opinion. But in order to enfranchise more of our beliefs in a wider circle, to expand the range of what is or can be known, we find we must meet some other conditions to compensate for the weakened version of justification that is to enable us to make the expansion.

Consider an example. Someone is justified in believing a true proposition, and yet we would hesitate to ascribe knowledge to him in the following well-known case. He glances at a clock, sees that it says nine o'clock, and believes that it really is nine o'clock, which in fact it is. Such a person is justified in the belief because it is precisely with respect to glancing at clocks—or phoning to find out the time—that we do suppose ourselves in possession of the relevant evidence in such matters. How else would we be justified? If the clock were fine, there is little doubt that we might say the person knew that it was nine o'clock. It happens that the clock is not fine, however: It is broken, but, like every broken clock, it "tells the right time," so far as outward appearance is concerned, twice a day. The deceived person glanced at the clock just when in fact the time really was nine o'clock. So his belief was true as a matter of accident. It is easy to generate countless such examples. There is a story by Sartre in which a prisoner, meaning to deceive his interrogators as to the whereabouts of someone they are seeking, deliberately lies. It just happens that the person he seeks to protect is where he says he is. The speaker intended to lie, but the world tripped him up, and what came from his mouth was true instead. His captors acted on his words, which they believed true and were justified in believing true. They were justified because a man in the prisoner's situation put up his body and his life as collateral. They knew, and assumed he knew, that if caught in a lie he would die only after terrible torture. So they felt they could act on his words, which were true—but did they *know* where the sought-for partisan in fact was, even though they found him where they (rightly) believed they would? Few of us would say they did.

This gap in the standard analysis of knowledge was discovered by Edmund Gettier, and the problem of closing it is known as the Gettier Problem. One way, certainly, of closing it is to say that a person has knowledge when he is justified in holding a belief that is *nonaccidentally* true. It should not, we feel, be a matter of sheer good luck if we are to have knowledge. If it is knowledge, it should be somehow guaranteed by the structure of reality and our relationship to it. And it is luck that the nonaccidentality condition is meant to exclude. If by "not a matter of accident" one means that it is "a matter of necessity," then there is a question of whether we have got far beyond Descartes after all. For perhaps necessity simply means that doubt is incoherent, or it at least gives a reason why there is no room for doubt. And do we then know such things as what time it is, since our evidence in such matters is such that, everything appearing the same, we can as easily be wrong as right?

For consider the consequences of construing the notion of necessity, or nonaccidentality, in some way that does not quite entail the Cartesian criterion. For example, some philosophers have found plausible and attractive a causal theory of knowledge, in which knowledge is had when one is caused to believe a proposition *P* by the very thing that makes P true. Suppose, for example, I believe that it is raining, as it is, and that my so believing is caused by the rain to which the belief refers. This is a very nice model of knowledge, at least for a wide class of propositions, in that it involves three components and three relationships, all of great philosophical importance:

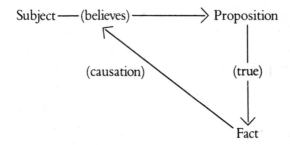

In this analysis belief is a relationship between a subject and a proposition; truth, a relationship between a proposition and a fact; causation, a relationship between a fact and a subject. When all the relationships are satisfied, then there is knowledge. Or at least there is a sufficient condition for there to be knowledge. Or at least for empirical knowledge. Perhaps not all kinds of knowledge quite fit this model—mathematical knowledge may fail in many ways to fit it—but let us concentrate on those cases that do appear to fit it.

The difficulty with this wholly natural model is that causality, too, has its treacheries, and it is not difficult to construct examples quite as flawed by accidentality, even when the causal condition is satisfied, as the somewhat more vulnerable examples considered above. Suppose I believe it is raining because there is a pitter-patter sound outdoors, a usual piece of evidence for rain, largely because the rain causes that pitter-patter sound. Now let's introduce some crazy possibilities. Unbeknownst to me, a lot of insulation has been placed on my roof, which deadens the sound that rain makes. But the wetness short-circuits a wire, activating a tape recorder that just happens to contain a tape recording of the sound of rain on the roof someone made as a gift she intends to give me, knowing I find the sound soothing. So the rain causes the sound on the basis of which I believe it to be raining, as it is. Do I know it is raining even though all the conditions are met, including the causal condition? Few would say I do know, just because the causal route is so improbable and—well—accidental. So, whichever route we take, the same question arises of excluding nonaccidentality from the justification of belief if it is to be knowledge.

Each of the components invoked to this point is a philosophical concept, whose analysis is exceedingly intricate and predictably controversial: truth, justification, nonaccidentality, causation, belief, even the nature of those subjects capable of knowledge, hence capable of believing propositions and being caused to believe them by those facts that make the propositions true. It is, for that matter, exceedingly difficult to think of a concept of any philosophical importance that does not figure, directly or indirectly, in the analysis of knowledge. Small wonder, then, that knowledge should have announced itself, at the very beginning of philosophical speculation, as a topic of the greatest moment. And small wonder that one might suppose that if we understood, philosophically, the nature of knowledge, we would understand everything else in philosophy. The analysis of knowledge is as good an example as one can find of the claim that to understand anything in philosophy is to understand everything, and that all philosophical questions have to be answered at once.

It would, of course, misrepresent those great thinkers who undertook a philosophy of knowledge to suppose that they had a disinterested concern with getting conceptual clarity. For Plato, knowledge offered the possibility of security in a world pounded by the surf of change. Knowledge, in putting us in touch with truth, gave us something that could not be otherwise, a neccessity of some sort, and hence bedrock for the erection of a stable social order. Descartes, too, was interested in erecting an edifice of scientific cognition that would stand forever, a piece of knowledge impervious to time and change. He was himself a scientist, a cosmologist, physicist, geometer, physiologist, and he thought science needed such foundations as he sought to provide. As we saw in the last chapter, a very different vision of science is currently in favor, one that dispenses with foundations altogether, and that is subject to adjustments and concessions and priorities—an almost political vision of science by contrast with the stable vision of politics Plato felt so desperately required, one in which trade-offs and temporary coalitions hold the fabric of our beliefs together in some coherent way. I suppose it is true that as we subscribe to the totalistic view of science outlined above, the concept of knowledge becomes decreasingly important except as a philosophical problem: We have learned to live with uncertainty and probability and relativities of every order.

And yet this surely misrepresents some deeply human need, to have the truth where the truth may be had in matters that concern us in our human dimension. It is impossible not to sympathize with the narrator in *Remembrance of Things Past* in his need to know the degree to which a beloved woman loves him back, whether she is faithless or not. People need to know who their parents really are; we all want and need to know what really happened at certain dark moments in history. One wants to know whether the accused is guilty of the crime, and in what degree he is guilty if guilty at all. We want to know whether we will get over the disease that is weakening us; we need to know whether the tumor is benign or not. There are circumstances in human existence that cry out for knowledge, and against which the easy relativism of the philosopher appears almost cruel. Perhaps at just these junctures where knowledge is so much a matter of interest, the very possibility of knowledge is excluded. But I offer them in order to remind ourselves that knowledge is not a mere philosophical and abstract matter but one of great urgency, and that when one wants knowledge nothing else will satisfy.

So let us begin our discussion of this concept. And inasmuch as we observed that Descartes offered us a very severe criterion for the possession of knowledge, we might begin with his views. We may, finding ourself in possession of knowledge that is such by virtue of meeting his tests, find that we have very little, and so may wish to see how central to the acquisition of knowledge Descartes's criteria can be. Still, if we cannot get even that little bit with the strongest imaginable criterion, it is hardly to be hoped that we can do so with the weaker criteria that give rise to the Gettier Problem.

# 21

# Doubt, Dream, and Demon

DESCARTES'S PROCEDURE IN HIS QUEST FOR CERTAINTY—his search for foundations for knowledge—was to insist that if a proposition or kind of proposition could rationally be doubted, then he would treat it very much as though it were simply false. That is, if—given the grounds or kind of grounds which justify one in believing a proposition or kind of proposition—a proposition could still be false, then those grounds do not guarantee truth. And for purposes of his inquiry, it might *just as well* be false. For example, a good many of the propositions we feel ourselves justified in believing are grounded in sense-experience. Indeed, for most of those propositions there really is or can be no ground other than that one has seen or felt or tasted something—or that those whose testimony one accepts have themselves seen or felt or tasted something. It takes little reflection to come to the conclusion that most of our beliefs about the world are of this sort, and, if the logical positivists are to be believed, the entirety of meaningful (nonanalytical) propositions consists exactly of such propositions. Descartes observes that since the senses can deceive us, it is possible, for any given proposition of this order, that it is false. Truth does not flow from our grounds to our beliefs in such a way as to exclude the possibility of falsehood—we do not have evidential superconductors and consistently with his determination to consider false whatever *can* be false relative to our best evidence, this whole class of propositions is, on the basis of this single consideration, ruled out as candidates for the role of foundations for our edifice of beliefs.

It is of course not required that our senses have ever deceived us, though very few, I should conjecture, can have gone through life without having made some misperception or other. And Descartes's point is that we can never fully trust anything that could in principle mislead us on some occasion. This would be a disastrous policy to adopt in the real world, for we are simply required to take risks, and surely the senses have been guides to reality at so many junctures of life that we could scarcely move a step were we to adopt Descartes's procedure for the practical purposes of existence. It is similarly true that other persons are capable of misleading us, even if they do not mean to lie. For much of what they know is grounded in sense-experience or in memory, which is hardly more trustworthy. Yet were we to abandon our trust in human testimony on grounds of this sort of epistemic paranoia, we scarcely could function in life. But Descartes is not at all recommending that we do adopt these principles in life. In life we are obliged to take risks, to act on less than theoretically certain grounds, to deal in probabilities, to exist statistically. But for purposes of epistemological research, what passes for the best we have in life falls short of what we require in theory. So, strictly speaking, one ought to doubt these propositions, even if in fact it would be disastrous to do so. Moreover, it may be psychologically impossible to doubt much of what we believe. We have very little direct power over what we are to believe and what we are to doubt. Locke would say that there is something almost blasphemous in denying what our senses furnish us with, inasmuch as we were given our senses in order to arrive at the beliefs it is useful for us to have. Descartes is not indifferent to such theological considerations. But they concern the essentially flawed nature of man, which itself is a theological theorem. We really *are* defective beings, and it requires, in his view as in the view of the religion to which he subscribed, a miraculous intervention to redeem us from our errors. The question is whether, in theory, we can make ourselves better, and in the present context this means finding out whether we can shun the very possibility of error and find the straight path to cognitive security. And for purposes of philosophical meditation, this means jettisoning as worthless whatever fails to meet the most exacting criteria. Once more, nothing may meet them. But it would be useful to know even this.

It is instructive to follow Descartes's reasoning a few steps further. It may be granted that there are cases where the senses deceive us, but it must also be insisted that the only way in which we ever discover this is through the senses themselves. In view of this, the very proposition that the senses deceive us itself rests on the kind of evidence it calls into question, and if it is to be taken as authoritative, it instantly dissolves its own authority. And the usual process is as follows. We find ourselves believing or inclining to believe a certain proposition on the basis of somewhat defective experience— the light is poor, perhaps, or the circumstances of perception less than optimal. But then we check to see if there is in fact a person outside the window or if it is only a shadow; to see if the noises are made by an intruder or only due to the settling of the structure. And then, surely, we know. It would be bizarre, it would be a parody of circumspection, to say, Well, you cannot be sure, you cannot be too certain. A man who continued to search for a possible intruder, having probed every corner and ascertained that the floor was creaking, would approach the borders of neurosis. That is not what Descartes is urging us to do, to take the neurotic, as it were, as our model. What he *does* do, however, is move in an absolutely different direction, making the problem of certainty at once philosophical and possibly insoluble. He says, in effect, this: Let your experience be as vivid and clear as it is possible for experience to be, so that there cannot be the slightest grounds for further doubt that the object of experience is as you sense it to be. The light is clear, one is in good sensory form, one has made the trials to the point where there is no further room for serious confirmation. One is having just the experience one uses for settling matters of perceptual doubt. One is having the *optimal perceptual experience.* At just this point one must recognize that one's experience could be just this vivid and yet nothing in the world need correspond to it—because one is dreaming. And the question of how I find out I am not dreaming is not of a piece with the question of how I found out whether my senses are to be trusted in a given instance. In the present case I have *settled* that. What I cannot have settled by any such procedures is that I am *sensing*. Any further investigations along those lines will simply beg the question.

Of course, we do have dream experiences that are fuzzy and unclear, incoherent and extravagant, and that contrast with waking experience in that way. Descartes is saying that it is possible to have experiences while dreaming that cannot be told apart on internal grounds from the experiences we have when we are awake. Imagine the experience of being locked in a passionate embrace with someone, feeling her flesh against your own flesh, knowing her taste, her characteristic odor, the sound of her voice, the sheer thrill and ecstasy of sexual contact. And now imagine dreaming this. Perhaps any of us have had such erotic dreams, not to be told apart from the experiences of making love when in fact making it. And now we ask ourselves which experience it actually is on a given occasion. Looking for a familiar mole or birthmark, seeking for a further fragrance only protracts the problem, for I may be dreaming I have found these endearing entities.

With this move, something astonishing has happened. Experience has just been neutralized for purposes of knowledge, put completely out of play. Suddenly it is as though our experience were some absolutely neutral screen *between* ourselves and reality, so that the truth of our experiences—or their falsity—is altogether a matter of something external to the experiences themselves. Suddenly, in fact, our experiences acquire some of the features of sentences, whose meaning does not determine their truth, so that we can understand a sentence without knowing whether or not it is true, just as, now, we can understand that we are having this or that experience without knowing whether, beyond this fact, anything is really happening. The mind becomes like a private theater, on whose screen experiences transpire that may or may not answer to something outside the theater. Suddenly, finally, experiences get to be for Descartes what shadows or appearances got to be for Plato. And the self becomes a sort of cave from which it now becomes a problem to issue. And at this point it is clear that the incidental possibility of dream *is* merely incidental to the neutralization. Other, equally disrupting scenarios may be imagined.

Philosophers, for example, have imagined the possibility of a brain in a vat. The brain, much like an organ of someone killed in an accident—a kidney, a liver, a heart—is kept vital by being suspended in some sort of soup, as if like the more customary organs, awaiting a recipient. Suppose we knew enough about brains to apply mild electrical stimulation, so that we could furnish it, as it were, with "experiences." Perhaps the brain belonged to a colleague, killed in an automobile accident, and we decide to furnish him with the experiences he would have had had life allowed him to pursue his ambitions: We write the scenario that enables him to return to consciousness, to think he has had a narrow escape, to return to the laboratory, make the discoveries that bring him many rewards and much recognition—the Nobel Prize perhaps!—and to lead, as well, a rich emotional life: to love and marry the partner of his dreams, to have his children, to see them grow, and at last to die a meaningful death, saying his last words to weeping friends and mourning family. And having done this, we switch the current off. It is only a brain on which we have evoked various electrical potentials. Yet from "inside," as it were, it is just as it would have been had the owner of the brain undergone the experiences instead. So the experiences themselves carry no guarantee of their authenticity and are, once again, neutral as to whether anything is really happening or not. Once more, it is like being enclosed within a cave, spectator to experiences that *may* be authentic but then again may not be, with no internal criterion available in principle to determine between what are now seen as competing incompatible hypotheses. And at this point it is perfectly clear that there is almost nothing experience justifies us in believing.

Descartes himself offers an equally extravagant scenario to much the same consequence. He imagines the possibility of a demon, powerfully subversive of his cognitive ambitions and malign enough to induce false beliefs at every point at which Descartes supposes himself possessed of true beliefs. Once more, the question of justification is put in jeopardy. But this is because the very principles Descartes would appeal to in justification of any beliefs at all are themselves subject to the demon's malign interventions. This is not so much to imagine grounds for doubt but to imagine that grounds for doubt can be imagined. All tethers to the ground of belief—all connections to the world—have been severed, and Descartes floats, loose and unanchored like a balloon, in the drifts and currents of unresolvable doubt. How indeed is he to cast anchor when the very rope with which he might do it is itself a figment, a fiction he is induced to believe real?

It is difficult to imagine a more severe impasse than this. Descartes has so construed his situation that it has to seem the fated and unique result is a total skepticism. There is, really, nothing he is justified in believing, at least by the criteria he has imposed on his beliefs, since each belief can, consistently with his having it, be false. Hence no belief is of a kind to serve as foundational in the structure of knowledge. But the defects of the foundation are transmitted to the structure itself, which is vulnerable and insecure. To be sure, when he puts aside his meditation, and takes life up again, he will act, as he cannot help but act, in the light of beliefs he cannot help but hold. But his ambitions, of reconstructing his beliefs upon unshakable foundations, will have been defeated. It is the best that he can do, the best that anyone can do, and, like the rest of us, he must learn to live within his cognitive means. In a certain sense, the meditations leave everything as it was. He has the beliefs he had before he began. It is only that he now appreciates the intense limitations his investigations have revealed. It would be insane to allow these limits to affect his conduct in practical life. But it would be arrogant not to recognize what a flawed and limited creature he is. Unless, of course, he can find a way of extricating himself from the impasse, or even draw from the very structure of the impasse the conditions for escaping it.

And this is what Descartes undertakes to do. It is not just that he escapes, so to speak, from the jaws of total doubt. The certitudes he arrives at require that he have had that total doubt. That doubt scours clean away beliefs he might have thought he could count on. But in the act of scouring itself, he finds a saving truth.

# 22

## *Thinking and Certainty*

SUPPOSE ONE SERIOUSLY WORRIES whether one is a brain in a vat, or that one is dreaming, or that a malign demon constantly subverts one's beliefs so that they will always be false. Can any belief survive these severe tests? Descartes's answer is that certain things must be true of someone who is mistaken; specifically, that person must *affirm* something. One can always avoid error by refusing to affirm—to the degree that this is possible, disengaging oneself from experience in such a way that experiences occur without our endorsing any of them as more than what they present themselves as being: merely as experiences that one can describe to oneself without going further and saying, of any of them, that they refer to or are caused by something outside themselves. Of my experiences I offer no explanations and seek for no references; I treat them, so to speak, in absolute terms. I restrict myself to whatever is consistent with any explanation whatever of what I am experiencing, neutral, that is to say, as to whether it is caused by what I would spontaneously have believed it was an experience of, or caused by something I ate, or by some mad scientist treating my brain—me—as a kind of organ on which he plays in such a way as to induce experiences free of ulterior reference. I put it all in brackets and put myself at a distance from it, across which I merely survey it as a spectator, as if it had nothing especially to do with me. And as long as I maintain this posture of utter and willed neutrality, I cannot be mistaken about anything. Neither can I achieve any truths, so it is, for someone bent on knowledge, not an especially advantageous position. It is advantageous only for someone instead bent on avoiding error.

Now two propositions concerning myself fall out of this exercise. The first is that I am a being that has experiences of this sort, which Descartes calls ideas. Each of the strange possibilities he considers is available only in regard to a being that has ideas. It would not make a very interesting skepticism to ask: Suppose I were a stone, or a carrot, or a snail, unless, consistently with this, I were a stone with ideas, an experiencing carrot, a dreaming snail. The second is that I am a being capable of acting in a certain way with regard to these ideas. I can, for example, affirm them as true, or deny them as false, or refuse to do either of these things. It is as though the space between the experiences and the being that has the experiences were a kind of space in which these kinds of actions can take place. Now only if two conditions are satisfied can there be a mistake. There must be an idea, and there must be an affirmation. I must say, as it were, that the idea really is caused by what I would spontaneously say it was of—that I really am, for example, experiencing a dog. So, on the hypothesis that I am always mistaken, then I must always be affirming some idea. Now, Descartes uses the word *thought* in such a way that thinking consists of performing some sort of action on an idea. I can, in the simplest case, simply affirm the idea, asserting that it is true. So, on the hypothesis that I am always mistaken, I must always be affirming or, in Descartes's specific usage, I am always thinking. So unless I were a thinking being I could not be in error. So I know at least one truth that emerges from the most damaging of skepticisms: that I am a thinking being, namely a being that has ideas and acts upon them. This is a truth that is presupposed by the very sort of meditation Descartes is undertaking, namely that he is the kind of being that has the qualities without which such a meditation could not take place. It is a truth about ourselves as well, so far as we comeditate with Descartes. Whether a brain in a vat, a dreaming stone, a dreaming person, or a person who is awake as I would believe myself to be, staring at a fire and wondering what it would mean for it to be but an illusion, I am a thinking being, an *ens cogitans*.

This proposition about himself, Descartes supposes, cannot coherently be doubted, just because doubting is itself a mode of thought, and so the doubt requires for its execution precisely what it means to call into question. So it cannot be called into question; it is self-validating in the respect that its denial is self-stultifying. Note that this consequence follows only for someone actually seeking to call into doubt the claim that he is thinking—a proposition at once about himself, as an agent, and about an idea, on which he performs the action of affirmation. It is a kind of second-order act, a thought about thought, and accordingly a thought about the person who is thinking by that person as such. "Descartes is thinking" is not an analytical truth. For it is possible that Descartes is not thinking; namely, Descartes is simply having an experience. Its denial is not self-contradictory. It is an unusual proposition in that its denial is incompatible with its own content, a bit like saying, "I am saying nothing." In saying that one is saying nothing one is saying something, namely that.

Now it is not simply that whoever executes this meditation is a thinking being. There may be thinking beings that cannot execute this sort of meditation at all. What Descartes has shown, if he has shown it, is that he is a being thinking about thinking, a being whose own states are objects for himself, a being that is self-reflective. And indeed, this is the only proposition that really is self-validating. Most persons, including Descartes himself before he undertook this meditation, are thinking beings all the time. But they are not *res cogitans* in Descartes's sense because they are not especially reflective on their conditions. Life could go on perfectly well without their achieving this sort of discovery, without their doing philosophy, as it were. And in a way it would be true of them that they are thinking beings. But calling them such would not be self-validating nor its denial self-stultifying. It is only when I call myself a thinking being that these extra conditions emerge—not from the fact that I think so much as from the fact that I think about my own condition as a thinking being.

What Descartes finally shows is that he is a philosopher. And it would have been false that he was a philosopher before he undertook this meditation or that others are philosophers just because they think, unless they themselves take on the meditative task. The "proof" that he is the kind of thinking being that he is is only one a philosopher can give and consists of doing philosophy. As a general statement about human nature, it is of course false.

And at this point some very strange results begin to appear. If "I think" or "I am a thinking being" really is an indubitable proposition, and so qualifies as foundational for all our beliefs, philosophy itself must be foundational for all our beliefs, and in this way really is "Queen of the Sciences." On the other hand, if life goes on quite adequately without it, then the place or role of philosophy becomes quite obscure. It seems to be everything and to be nothing, depending on whether I am executing a meditation on first principles or not.

There is a further consideration. If thinking that I think is indeed foundational for all our beliefs, I cannot know anything with certainty unless I do so within the framework of a Cartesian meditation. I cannot know anything with certainty unless I know what my nature is—unless I know about myself that I am a thinking being. Since what Descartes is doing is building a theory of knowledge, the consequence is that I cannot know anything unless I have a theory of knowledge. And this again makes the philosopher indispensable for whatever there is by way of knowledge in the world. But can this seriously be maintained? Must the scientist master philosophy before he can be said to have mastered anything at all?

Descartes himself was a scientist, and having developed an optics, a geometry, a physics, and a cosmology, for which his evidence was whatever it was, he perhaps felt it urgent to then find some way of showing that the evidence was itself justified, and justified in such a way that his science could not be vulnerable because of shaky foundations. The task accordingly was to secure the foundations through propositions in connection with which doubt was incoherent. So he conceived of the kind of exercise he carried through in the *Meditations* to be the keystone of his entire system, and viewed his science as grounded in his philosophy. Kant argued that the *cogito*—the "I think"—of which Descartes made so much was not an indubitable proposition but something that accompanies whatever proposition one asserts. And I suppose it could similarly be argued that philosophy, as construed by Descartes, is not so much a science as something that accompanies whatever science there is, guaranteeing it in whatever way "I think" guarantees thought, needing no guarantee of its own. So perhaps philosophy would be part of whatever scientific curriculum there was, and in addition to learning what evidence in fact justifies the theories one masters in mastering a discipline, one would have to learn what it takes to secure the evidence. Philosophy then would be an indispensable part of every science.

But against what contingencies of evidential overthrow could such stratagems indemnify the scientist? Descartes was as interested in security and solidity—in eternity and immortality—as Plato was in constructing the Republic, where again the main problem was to secure the foundations against political change and overthrow. And Descartes's scientific contributions have, in some cases, withstood the test of time remarkably well. At least part of his optics is received truth, and his geometry remains as part of received mathematics. His cosmology is perhaps best regarded as a curiosity, overthrown (as it turned out) by Newton, though science is so subject to alteration that it can at least be imagined that someday someone will find in his theory of vortices the basis of a superior vision of the constitution of the universe. His physiology is likely to have been too crude and mechanistic to have survived. In any case, the tests passed and failed have little to do with the test made central to the *Meditations,* namely to find some way of circumventing the bizarre possibilities of being brains in vats or vivid dreamers or victims of malign demons. These are possibilities that arise only against the thought that experience could be exactly as it is only radically different: exactly as it is though the world for which it is to be regarded as evidential varies totally, and is altogether underdetermined by the testimony we have. The stratagem at best works for certain very remarkable illusions. And how important is it really for science to fend off such possibilities? It is not that illusion itself does not take place. But how important is it that scientists should guard especially against it? We can imagine a pair of scientists discussing a novel theory, discussing the evidence for it, reviewing the experiments that have tested it: Let us imagine there are many tests, and that the theory has prevailed over the effort to falsify it totally. And now one of them says well, suppose we are victims of an illusion. This could be said. It really is possible to imagine that agents of an alien power have drugged us, causing us to believe things that have no basis in truth. Or that some mad figure out of James Bond, bent on conquering the world, has hypnotized us to believe what we believe. But this cannot be a serious part of scientific probity. We have instead taken a sharp turn in another direction, given over discussing the proofs that pertain to science, begun another kind of discussion altogether.

And what would it mean for one of us to say, Let the enemy do its worst, let the mad doctor do his utmost—at least we can think and cannot be wrong in thinking this! It would mean very little, it would mean nothing at all so far as publishing in the *Physical Review* or in *Nature* or in *Science* is concerned. And that is how it is with Descartes's theory of knowledge. The problems it seems to solve are not, just as the positivists long ago insisted, real problems. They are problems that begin when real problems have been carried as far as we can carry them. And even if we prevail, as Descartes supposed he did, the problem of testing our theories would remain. Those theories, being scientific, would have to be tested and probed in ways having nothing to do with the bare indubitability of our thinking essence. The foundation may be unshakable. But the structures of science may have to be rebuilt even so. The certainty of the foundation is not in any respect whatever transmitted upward to the structures we are intending to erect on it.

What is true of Descartes is true by and large of the theory of knowledge as such, construed as a philosophical discipline.

# 23

## Internalism and Externalism

A GREAT MANY CREATURES—human beings certainly, and a great many animals almost as certainly—behave as they do because they perceive the world as they do. And some of the features of the concept of knowledge must apply to a great many of the actions we explain with reference to the way in which a person or an animal represents the surrounding environment and its own situation within it. Thus certain features of the analysis of knowledge with which we began our discussion must have a place in explaining such behavior. The person or animal is caused to have a belief by whatever makes the belief in question true. Thus a frog extrudes its tongue because it is caused to believe that an insect is flying before it by the flying of the insect: So the frog has a true belief caused to be there in its representational system by whatever makes it true. Of course errors are imaginable. The frog may extrude its tongue when an experimentor, like a Cartesian evil genius, simulates a pattern similar to what would be explained with reference to a bug in flight. The dog believes his master is outside the door because we fool him into believing this by playing a tape of the master's voice. But these illusions and errors based on them would be impossible if the model of knowledge we are using were not applicable: There could be no false beliefs if there were not beliefs, and no errors or illusions save within the framework defined by the model of knowledge.

On the other hand, the propensity to form beliefs at all must be connected in some sense with a certain evolutionary success: We believe what we believe because beliefs have a certain survival value. And indeed, the fact that there are creatures whose survival depends on correct representation means that the power to represent must play a role not less powerful than that played by the power to reproduce or metabolize. So knowledge has a kind of biological dimension and the theory of knowledge accordingly has a scientific as well as a philosophical side. Some thinkers have sought to "naturalize" epistemology, seeing its problems as very largely those of explaining the conduct of creatures that have certain powers of representation in their repertoires of strategy for survival. Granting the constant possibility of error, just think of how often we must be right, so far as representing our situations is concerned, in such routine matters as driving to the market, or even walking to the market, with the countless stimulations these projects involve and the countless changes in representation these stimuli induce.

Of course, much of this takes place without any reflection on our parts—without, for that matter, any serious intervention in the processes of representation that involve "thinking" in the sense in which Descartes used that expression. If the frog and the dog know, if we know when we behave in the light of successful representation, we know very little about the processes of knowledge, most of which in our case and all of which in the cases of the dog or frog take place beneath the threshold of self-consciousness. For Descartes, knowledge of knowledge was what played the central role in his speculations, and it is far from clear that were we to have knowledge of knowledge where our own cognitive procedures become, as it were, objects for ourselves, we would have anything like the survival successes we in fact may be supposed, on the evidence of evolution, to possess. We might be vastly reduced in our effectiveness under reflection, and it is accordingly understandable that Descartes only undertook his meditations in an atmosphere in which practical decisions were not required: He depicts himself as snowbound, shut up in a cabin as, metaphorically, he finds himself shut up within himself. And in this protective atmosphere, sheltered from the external world, he can afford the luxury of philosophical reflection and pay attention to what takes place within his mind when he thinks. Nietzsche, many years later, argued that most mental processes take place without any accompanying consciousness, and he went on to raise the question of the survival value that consciousness might have, given that it could play a very reduced a role in the ordinary transactions of mental life—representing, feeling, remembering, desiring. For Nietzsche, the human being has a mental life only rarely and peripherally illuminated by self-consciousness. For Descartes, on the other hand, consciousness is what human beings *are*—whatever takes place takes place in the light of consciousness. And to be human is essentially to reflect on one's defining mental life at every moment. In Nietzsche, almost everything takes place outside the inner spotlight of conscious reflection. For Descartes there is a severe doubt whether anything takes place at all outside consciousness. Nietzsche, in a way, is an externalist about knowledge: Knowledge describes the way creatures of a certain sort represent the world. Descartes, by extreme contrast, is an internalist. Knowledge, for him, is something that must be sought for from within consciousness and from among its presuppositions.

It is impossible to emphasize too heavily the sheer incommensurability of an externalist and an internalist approach to knowledge, even if the analysis of knowledge, up to a certain point, should be something both parties agree to. Both parties accept that knowledge is a true belief justified through being caused by what makes it true. For the externalist nothing further needs to be said. For the internalist everything remains to be said, for the question is how we are to tell, from a reflective consciousness of our beliefs, which if any of them is true. For the externalist there is no problem and for the internalist, unless something remarkable takes place, there is no solution. The externalist perceives us as in a world that rains stimuli on us. The internalist finds the very existence of what the externalist takes for granted the deepest problem there is, namely whether there is a world external to ourselves to whose existence our beliefs can testify.

Internalism has furnished the agenda for the theory of knowledge as it has been practiced by philosophers ever since Descartes. For the classical epistemologist, externalism is not of the slightest help: It does not solve a single problem but only changes the subject. Internalism, nevertheless, is extremely instructive. It brings certain structural features of the nature of representation to the surface, and in view of the degree to which the entire history of philosophy is framed in terms of these structural features, it is greatly worth our while to follow Descartes as he seeks, by procedures of pure ratiocination, to think through our beliefs to their causes, and hence to the existence of things outside ourselves that explain why we represent them as we do. It is an altogether audacious enterprise, no less so because of the fact that it is impossible. The skepticisms to which internalism gives rise are altogether irresoluble. But let us return to Descartes and the corner into which he has argued himself.

# 24

## *The Ontological Argument*

SUPPOSE IT WERE TO OCCUR to a librarian that an Evil Genius might have filled the shelves of the history section with books that purport to tell their readers what actually happened in the past, but that in fact are fictions through and through. Or the librarian at least feels that something like this could have happened. And so he—or she—decides to find out, by examining the books, whether they are in fact history or fiction. The problem is that a book can contain just the sentences it contains, tell just the story it does tell, whether or not there is anything external to the book of which the book is true. And the librarian asks whether this is neccessarily the case or whether there might be some internal criterion, on the basis of which one can infer to an external reality, a real past, the story of which the book itself narrates. Sometimes, for example, it is thought that very plain language is a mark of truth: There was a time when the simplicity of language in the New Testament was appealed to as evidence of its truth. But of course one can write a novel in just such plain language in order to induce a belief in its veracity, as in the *Narrative of Arthur Gordon Pym,* by Edgar Allan Poe. Or the book may contain some such statement as, "Everything I am about to say is true, so help me God." But that is no more a guarantee of truth than the disclaimer used in works of fiction, "Any resemblance to actual characters living or dead is purely coincidental," is a guarantee of creative imagination. And, as with dreams, any mark internal to the story, which is then taken as a mark of an external correspondence, can simply be imagined to have been put there by the Evil Genius to induce such an inference. So the question is whether something can be found that, much in the way that the Evil Genius cannot cause me to be in falsehood when I believe I am thinking, the Evil Genius is impotent to cause me to be wrong when I believe I am right about some external matter. Can there be, as it were, a book from the very understanding of which its truth somehow follows—a book that cannot be read with understanding against the possibility that it is false? Can there be a self-validating book?

Let us somewhat widen the example by imagining that the Evil Genius has enclosed us in a vast library, and that we are challenged to seek among all the books for some special volume that will instruct us that there is a world outside the library. This is almost exactly the situation in which Descartes imagines himself: He is locked, metaphysically speaking, in the world of his experiences or his "ideas," as he puts it, and though he has deduced certain facts about himself from this situation—that he exists and is a thinking thing—there remains the possibility that he might be just as he is, in possession of just the same ideas, but beyond this there is nothing, however pressing may be the conviction that the ideas, many of them, answer to a corresponding reality. I find it difficult to believe that I am only dreaming that I am typing on a typewriter, for there is the sense of moving my fingers against resistant keys and letters forming on palpable paper. But it was just such ideas as these that Descartes convinced himself could be dreams, without substance, and utterly deceptive. So his question, then, is whether there is not some idea that cannot be doubted, an idea from the very possession of which its truth somehow flows forth, hence an idea I could not possess if it were false. Descartes pretends to find such an idea, namely the idea of God, and it is striking that the idea of God rescues him from darkness very much as God himself rescues him, theologically, from error. He finds that the idea of God is precisely that self-validating idea that cannot be had if it is false, and so it *must* be a true idea: God must exist, and there is, accordingly, a reality outside himself and his ideas. It would be as though the librarian were to find a volume that could not be in the library if it were false. Hence even if placed in the library by the Evil Genius, the Evil Genius is necessarily in service to a higher power, and he will have put in the library a volume that is the key to appreciating his own limits and hence the limits of deception.

Descartes's reasoning draws very heavily on a famous argument of medieval philosophy, invented by Saint Anselm and known as the Ontological Argument. The Ontological Argument seeks exactly to proceed from the idea of God to the existence of God, and does so more or less as follows: Let us first make sure what it is whose existence we are denying when, if we are skeptical about the existence of God, we deny or, less dogmatically, simply doubt the existence of God. Are we certain it is *God* whose existence we doubt or deny? What is it that we understand by *God?* One might, for instance, have in mind a whiskery benign presence in a sort of robe, much as God is pictured on the Sistine ceiling. Well, God *may* look like that, but that he *should* look like that is surely something that can coherently be doubted or denied: There is nothing contradictory in saying that a whiskery being in a blue bathrobe does not exist. But that would be like denying the text on the basis of an illustration. God, as depicted by Michelangelo, is a determinate, definite being, existing in the same space with Adam. But it is far from clear that this could be a picture of God as God really is, just because it is far from clear that God could have a determinate form. God, rather, is a being limited by nothing, an infinite being, a being than which a greater is inconceivable. And I suppose it might be easy enough to picture a being greater than what we see in Michelangelo's representation—someone younger or stronger, or who takes up the whole ceiling. Indeed, to worship a whiskery being in a blue bathrobe is hardly more dignified than worshiping a golden calf. It is idolatry, which is worship of a finite thing. If we conceive of God as a finite being, then we have not really conceived of *God.*

So let it be granted that God is a being than which a greater is inconceivable. Then, Anselm argues, and Descartes argues similarly in the *Fifth Meditation,* that God must exist. For suppose we conceive of him as we do but as *not* existing. Then we have not conceived of a being greater than whom none can be conceived, for we can conceive of a being just like the one we have conceived of, only *this* one *exists.* For suppose God does not exist. Then this must be because of something external to God which prevents God from existing, and this is inconsistent with God being conceived of as limited by nothing outside himself. But suppose it were the case that God exists, but in such a way that it were possible for him not to exist, even if he is not dependent on anything outside himself for his existence? Then it would certainly be possible to conceive of a greater being than *that,* namely one that exists *necessarily,* that cannot be conceived not to exist, whose nonexistence is impossible. But this, if indeed God, cannot then be thought of as not existing. Hence if we claim to have conceived of God as not existing we have not after all conceived of God. And we must begin all over.

The idea of God, then, is the idea of a being that exists necessarily, a being whose existence is necessitated by the nature we are required to conceive of as God's when we have succeeded in conceiving of God. As Saint Thomas said, God's existence is one with God's essence: *Suum esse est sua essentia.* And this calls for some rather careful comment. We had better, before acquiescing in the Onto-logical Argument, come to terms with what the notions of essence and existence come to.

They come roughly to this: The *essence* of something would have been more or less the *definition* of that thing, namely the properties necessary and sufficient to be a thing of the kind defined. And here we are back on familiar territory, in the topic of definition of which so much of the historical substance of philosophical thought is constituted. As we saw, science was conceived of by the ancients as concerned with essences, which meant that the search for definition was never merely a lexical matter but really something much more profound: a quest for what made things of a given kind things of that kind. If being rational animals is of the essence of being human, then we understand what it is to be human when we grasp that essence. In a way, understanding and knowledge are one in such a view: To know is to know *what* something essentially consists of. To understand *triangle* is to know what it is to be a triangle, which is knowing what properties are necessary and sufficient for trian-gularity. Nothing could be a triangle that had more or less than three angles. But color is not part of the essence of triangles, though as a matter of accident, as the medievals would say, this or that triangle should be blue or pink. And in particular, it was a matter of accident that there should *be* triangles, or that triangles should exist. For their existence is not part of their essence. No more is it part of our essence. If we are essentially rational animals then it is, in a sense not unlike that which Kant invoked in his discussions of analyticity, self-contradictory to deny that men are rational. It might be false but not contradictory to deny that men exist, on the other hand, for even if men do exist, existence is not part of their essence as rationality is. Existence is an altogether external and accidental matter with human beings. Jean-Paul Sartre cleverly ar-gued, in this tradition, that there is no human essence; he argued that we have an existence but not an essence. Existentialism is the view that the human being is pure accident in a kind of way, that we are free just through the fact that we are not necessitated in any way. But the point remains the same: The existence of anything whatever is not part of the essence of that thing. It is always a contingent matter whether things of a certain kind exist. Or, in Kant's idiom, the proposition that this or that exists is always synthetic and never analytic. If it were analytic, the existence in question would be necessary and existence would then be essential—as Saint Anselm and Saint Thomas said it was in the case of God. "God does not exist" is uniquely contradictory because "God exists" is uniquely analytic. It is analytic because, in thinking the subject, as Kant would say, we think the predicate as well.

In the great epistemological epic transacted in the pages of Des-cartes's *Meditations,* good trumps evil. God's goodness is as much a necessitated part of God's essence as his existence, and once it is shown as a necessary consequence simply of possessing the concept of God that God exists, Descartes concludes that it is inconsistent with divine goodness to allow him to languish in the desire to know. Much in the manner, more compelling in the seventeenth century than now, in which Locke argued that it is inconsistent that

God should have given us senses and then made them unreliable and unfit for cognitive use, Descartes contends that if we are circumspect in not abusing our cognitive endowment, we may achieve as much certainty as is commensurate with our station in the universe. It has been an item of standard criticism that Descartes's argumentation is circular: He first proves the existence of God and then appeals to the goodness of God to indemnify his proof against error. But of course there really is no circle. The strategy of the *Meditations* is this: The Evil Genius raises a question of whether we have knowledge, given that we have understanding. We know what our ideas mean throughout the dark period of cognitive doubt; it is not as though our language somehow cannot be trusted; it is not as though the *Meditations* were gibberish. So we in effect know what it would be for our ideas to be true; what we do not know is whether they are true. But then the idea of God gives us a case in which understanding entails knowledge: We could not claim to know what *God* means and at the same time harbor doubts as to whether God *is*. So the ontological argument easily slips past the embargo on knowledge raised by the Evil Genius. But once that blockade is run, the Evil Genius is simply vanquished. We are assured that if we proceed with due circumspection, we can have such knowledge as we require. There will still be doubts. But they will not be the radical doubts of the sort supposed so paralyzing by the Dream Argument or its cognates. Radical doubt can be relieved only by radical measures. But the ordinary doubts that arise in the normal adventures of life, the doubts we have in poor light or dim circumstances, or because we are too impulsive in drawing inferences, are removed or removable, so far as they can be removed, by the simple remedies of elementary cognitive caution. Perhaps we are always less than certain in the sense of certainty that is needed to overcome radical doubt. But then that kind of certainty has no place in the normal pursuits of ordinary life.

The *Meditations* end with the world restored—an imperfect world, fraught with dangers and obscurities, but one in which we are assured of what we need to navigate its treacheries. We have broken through the screen of ideas, and the Ontological Argument is like the answer to a logical prayer. Anselm himself saw it in exactly those terms. He *believed* in God. But he wanted some way of giving rational support to his belief, of justifying the belief in a perfect being, a being greater than which none was thinkable. And he was graced with the recognition that the very definition of God compelled assent to his existence. Alas for all the good news it promises, there is a flaw in that argument of rather deep consequence for philosophy.

# 25

## *The Notion of Existence*

THE ONTOLOGICAL ARGUMENT, whatever its defects, connects in a single logical operation the three tasks of philosophy: It goes from the analysis of understanding to an uncontestable epistemological certitude to a necessary characterization of how the world must be, given that understanding and knowledge are as it requires. And since, after all, the concept of understanding—of achieving a definition through identifying the properties essential to membership under a given concept—has been standard in philosophy from its beginnings in the dialogues of Plato, the Ontological Argument would have seemed an inescapable consequence of philosophical practice. To understand, in its case, is to know, and to know is to recognize the existence of a being necessary in whatever world there is—a being whose nonexistence is unthinkable. So the Ontological Argument furnishes a model for a certain kind of philosophy—rationalism—which seeks, from our concepts, to excogitate first the existence and then the nature of the real world: to specify how the world must be through an irresistible exercise of pure ratiocination. It was Kant, in his *Critique of Pure Reason,* who identified the fatal flaw in this argument, and with it the hopes that we could, by means of reason alone, navigate the straits between concept and reality. His contention was that existence is not a property, hence not an essential property, and that a fundamental error has been committed in treating *exists* as though it were an ordinary predicate like *blue* or *round.*

Kant's argument is that existence is not among the properties that belong to a concept or that form the concept of something. Let us take the concept of unicorns, and list the essential properties any X must have in order to be a unicorn. It must be a white quadruped with a single horn protruding from its forehead, savage in its nature but tractable to female virgins, in whose presence it becomes docile. Having defined *unicorn* thus, or having at least sketched the main components in the concept of unicorns, there remains the question of whether unicorns exist. Suppose as a matter of zoological fact that they do. There is nothing impossible about unicorns, and worlds may be imagined in which they exist. The medievals doubtless believed the actual world to be unicorn rich. Still, for just the reason that it is also possible that there are no unicorns, *existence* is not part of the concept. It does not enrich the concept of unicorns to say that unicorns exist; what it *does* do is to say that the concept has instances in the real world, or that the concept is not empty.

"Unicorns have a single horn" is analytical. "Unicorns thrive on thistles" is synthetic, inasmuch as their dietary peculiarities are not part of the concept of unicorns and could be found out only by examining unicorns and finding out what they like to eat. "Unicorns exist" is a curious proposition, since it is not really about unicorns at all. What it is about is the concept of unicorns, or perhaps about the word *unicorn*. And what it says is that the concept is not empty or that the word stands for something. *Existence* is one of those words that concerns the relationship between representation and reality. It does not specify a further feature of the representation. Nor does it specify a further property of the real world. It simply says that the representation has something in the real world that corresponds to it. Grammar notwithstanding, there is a great difference between "Unicorns graze"—which is about unicorns—and "Unicorns exist," which is not about unicorns at all but about *unicorn* as a concept or term.

Kant used a somewhat unfortunate example, saying that there was no difference between a hundred real units of currency and a hundred imaginary ones. What he meant was that the concept of a hundred dollars was the same, whether it was instantiated or not.

Its being instantiated by actual dollars did not follow from the concept. It had rather to do with a proper coordination between concept and reality. Someone who says, "I have a hundred dollars but they don't exist," is not abusing the concept of a hundred dollars. He is rather abusing the concept of having. You cannot have what isn't. There is a connection between having and being. But a man who says, "I have a hundred existent dollars" is saying something peculiar for just the reason that someone is saying something peculiar with, "I have a hundred nonexistent dollars." It is not as though the first says he has a hundred gold dollars and the second says he has a hundred silver dollars. "Existent dollars" is not a species like "gold dollars." If someone says he has a hundred gold dollars and a hundred silver dollars, it would be fair to say that he has two hundred dollars. But someone who says that he has a hundred existent dollars and a hundred nonexistent dollars still has only a hundred dollars. Existence is not a property. Or, as Kant said, "Existence is not a predicate." He meant, of course, that we are not predicating the existence of unicorns (or whatever) when we say that unicorns (or whatever) exist. What we *are* doing, rather, is predicating, of the word or concept *unicorn,* the semantical property of having instances.

*Existence* is one of an important class of terms, like *true,* which makes reference to a certain fortunate relationship between representation and reality. A true sentence is not a special kind of sentence, as an English sentence is: It is, rather, a sentence whose conditions for truth are satisfied. An existent unicorn is not a special kind of unicorn, as (say) a lame unicorn is. It is not even a sensible conjunction of terms. *Existent* does not apply to things but to the relationship between things and concepts, when the concept has things falling under it. So the quest for the nature of existence, which sounds portentous and important, is not a quest for some deep underlying property that all real things have in common and in virtue of which they are real. And this is pretty much what might be expected of the standard traditional project of seeking to specify essences through definitions. It was widely understood that there is never a contradiction in denying the existence of anything, that

"Honest men do not exist" is never contradictory—like "Honest men lie" only false in case there are men who are honest. But, then, this must be as much true of the concept of God as of any concept. "God exists" says that the concept of God is not empty, that it has an instance. But for just that reason existence is not part of that concept. It might be a violation of the concept to say that God is evil or that God is impotent. But "God does not exist" does not in that sense violate the concept, though it may be false in case *God* is nonempty. It is of course open to defenders of the Ontological Argument to say that existence is in that one case a part of the concept, but this then makes it difficult to know what the term means, for it has been defined through practice as concerning the relationship between a concept and reality, and not as part of a concept. So it is a self-defeating strategy to incorporate it as part of the concept: For then we would no longer know what it meant or what we would be saying in saying that God is.

There are doubtless concepts from whose very meaning it follows that they have instances. But none of them quite does what Descartes required the concept of God to do. Thus the concept of concept exemplifies itself, for reasons comparable to those from which it follows that *word* is a word. There would be something oddly self-stultifying were someone to wonder whether there were any words, for the very expression of the doubt should serve to allay it. *Sound* is self-instantiating when uttered. *Mark* is self-instantiating when inscribed, as is *inscription*. And in the special way in which he used the term, *idea* may be self-instantiating in Descartes's philosophy. Less, but not a lot less, trivially, an argument can be made that *I* neccessarily refers to whoever uses it, so that by a rule of language, the speaker who uses *I* correctly must exist. So Descartes's existence follows from the correct use of any sentence using the first-person singular pronoun, whatever the sentence may say— even if it says "I don't exist." And, indeed, "I don't exist" is self-stultifying whenever spoken, asserted, or thought. It is in this regard that his own existence is a matter of proof.

But that is as much as can be said. The Ontological Argument fails through a grammatical mirage, in which existence is misperceived as a property. When this failure is noted, the close connection between understanding, knowledge, and the nature of reality is broken, and a certain hope for philosophy is dashed. And Descartes is back where he started. Having walled himself in conceptually, knowing only the contents of his own mind, there is no way out. He must, in the words of Bishop Berkeley, "sit down in a forlorn skepticism."

# 26

## *Representationalism and Idealism*

*I*T MIGHT AT THIS POINT be valuable to describe what exactly it was that the goodness of God was meant to underwrite in Descartes's picture of knowledge, and hence what is left unjustified if the Ontological Argument fails. Here is Descartes's picture of his epistemological situation. It possesses, as we shall see, pretty much the same array of components and relations that we encountered in our initial analysis of knowledge. First there is Descartes himself, as subject, who monitors the ideas that present themselves to him. Then, if everything is in good working order, there is something external to the ideas, of which the ideas are true. Descartes often conceived of the ideas as pictures, which correspond to their objects through the relationship of resemblance. And then there is the relationship of these objects to Descartes himself, causing him to have the idea in question. Three components—a subject, an idea, and an object—and three relationships—between subject and idea, between idea and object, and finally between object and subject. Since the objects are those externals that constitute the world, we may say that in this picture Descartes is—*we* are, since we are subjects— separated from the world by our ideas. Or, more optimistically, our access to the world is mediated by our ideas. This is an example of what is called a representationalist theory of cognition, and in many cases it has a certain claim to even a scientific credibility, say in the

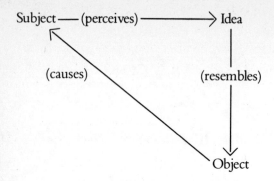

case of color perception. We believe that photons are reflected—or refracted—from external objects, causing us to perceive colors; and if we identify colors with ideas, in Descartes's peculiar use of that term, then one might say that the photons cause us to perceive colors, and that the colors we perceive "correspond" to the objects that reflect them. And there is a serious question whether the colors we perceive resemble the colors of objects, or if in fact colors are altogether within us, and that the world, objectively and scientifically, is strictly colorless. In the seventeenth century, it was an advanced view of things that the mechanical universe had neither colors nor textures nor tastes—that these "secondary qualities," as they would have been designated, were housed in sensate beings like ourselves, and though caused by mechanical actions of external objects on the sensory surfaces of sensate beings, resembled the real world not at all: The real world, defined through the primary qualities of mass or shape or, in Descartes's system, of extension, had none of the qualities that endear the world to us when we believe we are sensing the redness of the rose or the pinkness of the sunset or the blue of the sky. It was because science seemed to strip the universe of all this that science and poetry seemed to be at odds, so much so that the poet Keats once drank to the damnation of Isaac Newton for having destroyed the rainbow. In any case, science itself seems to underwrite a sort of representationalist theory of perception: Perceived colors "represent" an activity at the physical surface of things without in any obvious sense resembling that activity, certainly not if in fact there are no colors in the world. Galileo, who introduced the distinction between primary and secondary qualities, once asked slyly if the persons who believed in the external location of colors would be prepared to locate tickling in the feather that, when drawn across the soles of one's bare feet, elicits an intolerable sensation? We shall find this argumentation very powerful indeed in the polemic against representationalism, or at least in that form of representationalism that includes a resemblance relationship between idea and object. Descartes himself, in other writings, was uncertain of resemblance in any case: He wondered, for example, why the ideas he was prepared to assume were caused by the objects they represented had to resemble their causes any more than do the words in a book that represent, when true, whatever the book describes.

Now, the question that concerned Descartes was how, from his ideas, he was to infer with certitude that there was an object, corresponding to and causing him to have the idea. There were no interesting doubts in his mind as to his ability to characterize what appeared to his mind, or to him. It was the transit from these appearances to their objects and causes that raised the problems. It is easy to see that the beauty of the idea of God, for this system, was that simply having the idea of God entailed that God existed and that God caused in his creatures (us) the idea of him that we have. And then God was to guarantee that we were not systematically wrong with the other ideas that mediate between the world and us. Up to now, Descartes argued, he had believed, by "a rash impulse of nature," that his ideas resembled their causes. And after "proving" the existence of God, this rash impulse was replaced with a rational faith. Still, it remained a representationalist structure with which he was dealing, and it remained a matter of faith, whether blind or rational, that there should be a world of objects "out there" answering to and causing in us our representations of it. And once the Ontological Argument fails, all that is left is the blind faith. Descartes realizes that it is quite possible that the ideas he has could be caused other than by the objects he blindly believes correspond to them. In the *Third Meditation* he realizes that it is thinkable that the causes of his ideas all lie within him. He grants, as it were, that there may be no external objects, only the internal ideas, and that for all cognitive purposes, he may be internally indistinguishable from the brain in the vat. And now, his best effort come to naught, his tethers to the external world are severed. To be sure, there remains the blind faith, and one might, in the spirit of such philosophies, argue that God would not have given us such an overwhelming propensity to trust our senses had he meant us to go empty-handed from the board of knowledge. But now the belief in God is itself a matter of blind faith rather than reason. And for someone who had embarked on the project of reconstituting the entirety of his beliefs on rational foundations, this was a total defeat. Hence the forlorn skepticism.

It is at this point that a theory presents itself in the history of philosophy that calls radically into question the entire architecture of representationalism. The theory, fittingly called idealism, erases the external object, and hence erases two of the relationships that enter into the representationalist picture, that of an external correspondence between idea and object, and that of causality from object to subject. There is only the relationship between subject and idea—one relationship and two components. This theory is due to the great Irish philosopher George Berkeley. In Berkeley's theory, there are only two kinds of things—ideas, which are objects of consciousness, and consciousness itself, which Berkeley regards as a state of what he terms spirit. Ideas are had by spirits and spirits have ideas, and beyond this there is nothing. And certainly there is nothing between which and our ideas a question of discrepancy can arise. The world just is, as Schopenhauer, himself a kind of idealist, was later to say, my idea.

Part of Berkeley's philosophy involved a certain radical empiricism, almost a verificationism. He asked, in effect, what idea we could intelligibly consign to that "external" object we are so anxious to connect with. Locke, who thought representationalism by and large true, went so far as to think of *comparing* our idea of the object with the object itself—much as we identify someone, a criminal, say, by comparing our photograph of him with him. But this, clearly, is not available on the present theory. Perception itself consists in having a representation of the object X. Now we are to compare the perception—call it R—with X itself. But surely we must perceive X in order to do this. That means we must have a representation; call it R'. All we can in fact then be doing is comparing R with R'. Ideas, Berkeley wrote, can only be compared with other ideas. And since X itself is not an idea, reference to it is meaningless. It is useless philosophical baggage. Whatever is meaningful can be expressed in terms of ideas. But X is something outside our ideas altogether, meant to explain our having them. Since we can form no idea of X other than the ideas X is supposed to explain, X is either meaningless or simply consists in the ideas we have of it. With this, X is absorbed into our set of ideas and, as there is nothing outside to fret about, the problem of the external world is solved. There *is* no external world, nor, for that matter, is there an internal world either. There are just the ideas and we who have them.

The term *idea* at this point is becoming somewhat unwieldy. One cannot read the history of philosophy from Descartes on without encountering it, and until the advent of behaviorism perhaps no term was more frequently or variously used by philosophers and psychologists. For Hume, an idea was a copy of an impression, but for Berkeley the term *idea* was perhaps synonymous with impression. After Hume, the term was used for perhaps every mental content not itself an impression. Thus, in the nineteenth century, our ideas would constitute the history of our associations: If two impressions co-occurred, their corresponding ideas would henceforward be associated. In Freud, ideas carried a certain affective charge that went in every case some distance in the explanation of our behavior, especially since, in Freud's picture of the mind, neuroses were caused by ideas that had acquired certain complex emotional associations in the course of the individual's psychological history. But in Berkeley, the term might better have been *appearance*. To perceive an apple, for example, is exactly for the apple to appear to one, and for Berkeley an apple is nothing other than the sum of its appearances to the various senses. Descartes's obsession was whether there was an apple beyond and ulterior to what appeared to the mind—and it was this "beyond," this X, as we saw, that Berkeley stigmatized as a meaningless notion. Meaningless because all we know about the apple is what appears, and if there is something, an X that makes no appearances in its own right—well, this would be simply an empty superstition. What there is is what we perceive, and beyond that—nothing. So the object dissolves into the class of its appearances.

There is, to be sure, a temptation to say that it is the object, the apple, the X, which appears, as though there were something beyond the appearances and separate from them. But Berkeley, I think, would have endorsed the thought that it is here that we may be misled by an artifact of grammar, the subject-predicate form of sentences, which seems to require, in such sentences as "The apple is red," a subject on the one side and a predicate on the other. But if the apple just is the set of its appearances, that sentence should perhaps be translated or paraphrased "There is a red apple-appearance" or even "I am appeared to red-applely" or something equally circumspect and barbaric. The idea that there must be a thing, outside and separate from its appearances, that *does* the appearing was regarded later, by Nietzsche, as a grammatical superstition, as if (to use his example) the lightning was one thing and its flashing another, when in truth, Nietzsche held, the lightning just *is* the flashing. Berkeley's views on language were primitive alongside Nietzsche's, but his philosophy was not remarkably different: For him, too, the apple was not one thing and its appearing red another: The apple just was the appearing red, and whatever else the apple might consist of would be its other appearings—for example, its appearing round, its appearing tart, and so (infinitely) on.

Two consequences follow from this analysis. The first is that the subject is implictly defined as something to which things appear, for there are no appearances that are not appearances *to* something. The second and more characteristically Berkeleyan thought is that there are no appearances that are not appearances to some subject at a given time: no unsensed appearances, as it were, like the flower in the desert wasting its fragrance on the desert air. For Berkeley, to be is to be perceived, and since the essence of things is simply their appearances, one cannot be appeared to and at the same time have doubt as to whether what appears exists. Its existence *is* its being perceived by someone.

Berkeley's argumentation on this point is characteristically ingenious. He advances a thesis that whatever is true, perceptually speaking, of a given degree of a certain quality must be true of every degree of that quality. If warmth, for example, is felt when it is comfortable, it is felt, equally as much, when it is uncomfortable. But when warmth is extremely uncomfortable, then it is painful. And pain is certainly not something in the object, for reasons of a piece with those that led Galileo to insist, as is obvious, that tickling is not in the object. But if pain is not elsewhere than in the sufferer, and again, if pain is simply a very high degree of warmth, then a lower degree of warmth is in the beholder as well, since it is inconsistent to say one thing for one degree of heat and another for another. To be sure, there is the inclination to think that the warmth is in the body said to be warm, and that it would be warm whether we were there with our thermosensors or not. But we would not say that the body "out there" emitted pain whether anyone felt it or not—and so, systematically and by degrees, Berkeley got the entire object lodged in the perceptual system of the subject. The difference between Berkeley and those who, in what they believed to be the spirit of science, subscribed to a distinction between primary and secondary qualities, which they were prepared to house in the perceptual system since they could see no way in which they could be housed anywhere else in the universe, was that Berkeley allowed no distinction between primary and secondary qualities. The so-called primary qualities were themselves as much appearances as the colors and smells of ordinary objects. The world, reduced to its appearances, was all of a piece.

Berkeley's system entails an immediate view of science, namely that science organizes appearances, or, in more recent terminology, our experiences. The laws of science do not refer to a reality behind our experiences, an abstract world of objective forces, but to the experiences themselves. A law is simply a rule for predicting experiences. Berkeley's view of science is exactly that later subscribed to by the logical positivists, for whom the entire edifice of science was reduced to its observational base: Science was finally about our experiences and nothing else. And though the postivists had an extreme distaste for metaphysics, it is striking that their views were of a piece with Berkeley's, and with a version of what Berkeley would have thought of as idealism. The only reality of which we can conceive, hence the only reality we have any legitimate right to believe in, is the world as a system of experiences. The positivists did not arrive at their position through the kind of analysis and argumentation that Berkeley invented. But the results were hardly distinguishable.

It is altogether striking that, in meeting the problem of skepticism in Descartes, Berkeley was constrained to put forward a total metaphysics, a theory of what there is. It is instructive that the effort to keep the theory of knowledge segregated from a theory of the world seems consistently frustrated when we address the classical philosophers. And perhaps we should pause to underline the lesson this implies. There are no isolated moves in philosophy. Every move activates an entire system, so that the slightest contribution to the theory of understanding commits one to a theory of knowledge and finally of the world. And the same could be said wherever one begins, whether in the theory of knowledge or in metaphysics. The answer to any question in philosophy engenders answers to every question. And if two philosophers disagree deeply on any given question, the disagreements radiate outward to the very boundaries of philosophical thought.

There will be further occasion to discuss these systematic matters, but we might simply pause at this point to sketch the picture of the world according to Berkeley. The term *idealism,* which we have used to characterize his position, inherits some of the ambiguity of the word *idea* itself, and it is curious that Plato and Berkeley should be identified with the same label. For Plato the senses were altogether defective and reality itself something that could only be grasped through the intellect. Reality was composed of "ideas," but Platonic ideas are abstract forms that exist outside the realm of human experiences, which are of an inferior reality—that of appearances. For Berkeley, appearances are all there is. Even a Platonic form, to be intelligible, must be defined in terms of the appearances Plato would have supposed it contrasted with. For Berkeley there is no world outside the cave in which Plato held that we are imprisoned unless and until delivered by philosophy. Hence there is no cave either, for the distinction between inside and outside dissolves when outside is defined in terms of inside. And this must have been a singularly liberating thought for Berkeley and for his readers. There is only one world, *this* one, on which all our hopes must be directed. In a sense, this too is a deliverance by a philosopher, but hardly the sort of deliverance Plato envisioned. For Plato, the philosopher was to lead us outside, through the wall that segregates us from reality. For Berkeley the wall was an illusion. We are where we are: There is no other place to go. There is only the world we experience as quite ordinary persons. The rest is myth. Ordinary individuals never have problems of the sort that make philosophy possible. But that is not a defect in the commonsense view of things. If anything, it is a deep defect of philosophy.

# 27

## Idealism, Realism, and Phenomenalism

VIEWED AS A LOGICAL EXERCISE, Berkeley's system of philosophy has manifest advantages. It solves the problem of skepticism regarding the external world by refusing to allow any meaning to a world external to our sensations. And it solves the problem of what we might term alienation from reality, in the sense that we are no longer allowed, in the Platonic manner, to compare what we immediately know invidiously with the real world that contrasts with mere appearance—for appearance and reality now are one, and beyond them nothing. But there are some grave and nagging problems. For one, it really does seem like a logical exercise and seems flagrantly in violation of common sense, which Berkeley prided himself on having preserved. It simply sticks in the craw to say that the world is but a set of appearances. That is virtually like saying that it has the substance of a dream; and even if Berkeley might then challenge us to say what we regard as missing, we feel that there *is* something missing, even if we also recognize that it is hard to say precisely *what,* especially in terms that would satisfy Berkeley's exigent theory of meaning. Perhaps part of what seems problematic can be formulated on the back of a problem notorious in Berkeley—as notorious as was his solution of it. This concerns the existence of objects when they do not appear, or their continued existence between appearances. It is one thing to say that to be is just to be perceived. But what happens when an object is not perceived—does it stop existing? I turn the light out and leave the kitchen, to settle in my study to read. Is there still a kitchen? To be sure, there will be legions of roaches to whom the kitchen appears, in whatever way the world can be conceived according to the cockroach. But it is doubtful if the cockroach's world is mine. My kitchen has gleaming surfaces and attractive cupboards. The roach's kitchen is doubtless a dark, damp world of tastes. So the question is whether my kitchen exists when I am outside it. Of course I believe it does. But with what right can I justify myself in the belief if I accept Berkeley's theses? This is the official version of the legendary question about the tree falling in the forest with no one there to see or hear it, which is everyone's first intimation of a philosophical question.

This problem inevitably gives rise to another position in the philosophy of knowledge altogether, namely that we experience objects directly, and that they are more or less as they seem but cannot be reduced to mere seemings: The seemings, or aspects, are anchored to a continuing object. Called commonsense (or naive) realism, this attractive position is, in a sense, the mirror image of Berkeleyan idealism. Consider the representationalist theory diagrammed a few sections back. It contained three components and three relationships. Berkeley erased one component—the external object—and hence erased two relationships. By absorbing the object to a set of appearances, the relationship of external resemblance disappears, as does the causal relationship between the external object and the subject. Commonsense realism, as it were, assimilates appearances to the *object.* So our relationship to the object is direct and not mediated by a representation. Hence the relationship between representation and object evaporates. Perhaps there is a causal relationship: The object, being as it is, causes us to apprehend it directly (see diagram, next page). From the perspective of economizing, both these positions have advantages over representationalism, and on that ground will be preferred to it,

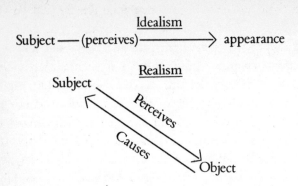

providing there are no disadvantages. But Berkeley's system has the disadvantage, until we can see how to deal with it, of being unable to account for continued existence between appearances. The nice thing about commonsense realism, by contrast, is that realism just means that objects are there, whatever we think and whatever our experiences. In a way, the realist takes a sort of God's-eye view of the real world and defines reality as how the world would be if there were no sentient creatures in it. But, as we shall see, Berkeley too is going to take a kind of God's-eye view of the world, and come up with a solution not terribly different from that of the realist.

It might be thought that the representationalist may accept the realist's account of continuous existence of real objects since, after all, the representationalist has a place in his scheme for real objects: The real object is that to which our representations correspond when our perceptions of them are correct. But this, in a way, is to take an externalist's view of the matter, to look at the perceptual situation from the side, where we can judge the adequacy of the subject's representation. It was precisely by taking, almost uncritically, the externalist's view that Locke talked about comparing our representations—our "ideas"—with the external objects to see if the latter were correct. And Berkeley's famous criticism of Locke was precisely that he took an externalist view of an inescapably internalist position, from which an idea could be compared only with another idea, and from which no sense could be attached to an external object.

In any case, from an internalist perspective, continuity is clearly not something given in experience, for otherwise there would not be the question of continued existence between appearances: There is, so to speak, no appearance of continuity to account for the continuity of appearances. This, in a way, was recognized as early as Descartes. There is a beautiful analysis in the *Meditations* when he observes a piece of wax. It has a certain number of qualities at a given moment, waxy in feel, redolent with the smell of honey, sweet to the taste, marginally translucent, solid. He looks away but, as the wax was left close to the fire, when he looks at it again, it has lost all those properties and gained others instead: It is molten, no longer feels or looks as it did, and so on; it is as though it had changed appearances. And yet, as beneath a change of clothing we acknowledge the identity of the individual, so we *judge* that it is the same object, now under one set of descriptions, now under another. Descartes recognized that we do not *experience* the sameness as we experience the waxy feel or the sweet odor of flowers. It is not an appearance, for it does not appear the same. And yet I know it to be the same, which Descartes then says tells him something about himself, about how his mind works, about how he relates to appearances. I always, he says, learn something about myself in such analytical excursions. I understand myself better and better.

This thought, that there is a kind of mental activity that accounts for continuity, was formulated with a stunning grandeur at the end of the eighteenth century in the philosophy of Kant. Kant, too, was a representationalist. He, too, supposed we are acquainted only with appearances, which he termed phenomena rather than ideas. And he also recognized that there was no phenomenon of continuity to account for the continuity of phenomena. So he contended that there is a kind of mental work that takes place, a kind of synthesis, by means of which phenomena are integrated, fused as it were into wholes, and referred outward to objects—to the X that Berkeley found so unintelligible. Kant realized that we needed the X to refer continuity to, even if continuity itself was the product of the synthetic integrations of the mind. Kant's whole system involved a mapping of the integrative actions of the mind, though the mechanisms through which integration is effected are never themselves present to consciousness. They must be inferred in some way, and inasmuch as they transcend the content of experience, since they are not given in experience, Kant made use of what he termed transcendental arguments. An argument is transcendental when it reasons to the existence something deemed necessary to the possibility of experience being understood in a certain way, when experience itself does not disclose what is needed. The nature of transcendental argument has remained a complex problem for interpreters of Kant, but the point in bringing it in here is that it illustrates the recognition, on the part of a representationalist, that if we cannot assume what we need, we must work for it in some way. But in order to achieve what we need, we clearly have to bring in factors that lie outside experience, and that correspond to nothing given in experience. And perhaps we ought to consider what this violation of the canons of experience means to Berkeley, who used those canons to such effect in dissolving the real object = X in the establishment of his idealism.

I shall bring this out by describing a further economization in the representationalist scheme that we owe to David Hume, who had the gift and courage to take things to their furthest consequence, however absurd. Berkeley's system, he would have argued, quite transcended his own strictures. What better grounds have I for accepting the existence of a self—or spirit—than I have for accepting the external object = X? All that those strictures strictly allow me are appearances—or ideas, or experiences—or phenomena—and beyond that really nothing. Since Berkeley was at pains to argue that there is no idea—no experience, no phenomonon of the self—that spirits are not ideas for themselves—he already had to grant something as abstruse as the object = X that he had rejected. So in consistency he ought either to drop the idea of spirits or allow the external object to stand. And Hume argued that since *he* could find nothing in his experience of which the idea of a self or spirit could be a copy, he had no grounds for admitting the existence of such a thing.

> For my part, when I enter most intimately into what I call
> myself, I always stumble on some particular perception or other,
> of heat or cold, light or shade, love or hatred, pain or pleasure.
> I never catch *myself* at any time without a perception, and never
> can observe anything but the perception.

Hume was seeking, somewhat tongue in cheek, for a sort of metaphysical thread on which his perceptions were united—a thread that was at once a perception and a ligature between perceptions—and failing to find this, he concluded, with a certain stunning bravura, that he, and anyone who cared to undertake the same investigation, was nothing but "a bundle of different perceptions which succeed one another with an inconceivable rapidity, and are in perpetual flux and movement."

Hume's minimalist thesis has a certain grandeur, and it is not surprising that other thinkers, though with different motives, might have come to the same conclusions. The Buddhist philosophers, for example, arrived at a view in which the world itself was reduced to a sequence of mutually succeeding appearances, which meant that the world itself has but the substance of a dream; and they also concluded that the self itself was but a sequence of mutual succeeding appearances, so that the appearances are all there is, and the belief in an underlying reality on either side dissolves as a matter of mere superstition. The Buddhists found this to be an exceedingly liberating doctrine, though I am uncertain that a similar feeling would have been found in Hume, who was left somewhat uneasy by the dizzying picture he felt himself compelled to accept.

For Hume, there is no object *of* which the appearances are appearances, and no subject *to* which they are appearances, and though the discussion of his one-dimensional theory of the world does not belong to the present topic—the philosophy of knowledge—there is a question of whether he leaves himself room for the structures he requires. It is important that we appreciate that neither Descartes nor Berkeley would have been dismayed by the thought that the self is not given to itself as an appearance. Descartes, for example, argued that no image could be formed of the self, that the self was not spatial, hence could not be represented in spatial terms. And Berkeley was resolute in insisting that the self—or spirit—is not an idea, so that he was obliged to allow an exception to his thesis that to be is to be perceived—for if the self were perceived it would be an idea, a consequence Berkeley could not accept. Nor would Kant have been disquieted by the thought that the self is not a phenomenon or to be found among the phenomena that present themselves to it: The synthesizing activity of the mind is inferred but not itself given. And perhaps all Hume meant to stress was that a strict empiricism, used as a blade, so to speak, to cut away the redundant or dubious excrescences of thought, might just as well be used to cut away the concept of the self as to cut away the external object = X. But then there arises a serious question as to whether empiricism itself can allow us all we need in order to account for experience, or to account for the coherence of experience. After all, the world does not present itself to us as a disordered staccato of appearances: It really does present a kind of coherent whole. And where does this coherence itself arise from?

Berkeley's response to this is instructive, if only for its picturesqueness. An Anglican bishop, after all, Berkeley found in the problem of continuous existence an opportunity so radiant that he, like Saint Anselm before him, may very well have regarded it as an answer to a prayer. His thought was that the world is instantly stabilized when we consider that God continues to perceive objects when no one or nothing else does, so that even the falling tree in the empty forest has an auditor—an Auditor—when it crashes, and that no experience is ever lost. And in a way everything is suddenly restored to what commonsense realism requires: The latter's God's-eye view of the world reduces at last to, in the most literal sense, a God's eye view of the world. There is a world of stabilized and continuous objects, appearances still, to be sure, but appearances always at least to the divine mind. And now Berkeley has the religious believer's satisfaction in saying that without a belief in God there will be chaos, that faith is the only shield against anarchy. If

God does not exist, the appearances lose their unity and scatter, like a broken string of beads—like (though he did not live to see the Humean reduction) a bundle of perceptions. But then the question remains as to how, in Hume's view, we are to solve the problem of continued existence between perceptions. After all, there is the fact that the kitchen is there when I decide I want a cold beer, after my session of reading metaphysics in the living room: I turn the light on and there it all is, down to the photophobic roaches fleeing the unwelcome illumination.

But is this not enough—that when I turn on the light I experience the kitchen? What more, really, am I saying when I say that the kitchen continues to exist than that if I do certain things I will have certain experiences? Why, really, do I need God to underwrite all this? There is a position that philosophers of knowledge have at times found extremely attractive, which is in its way as austere as Hume, but without the vertiginous vision, without the abyss of emptiness his vision discloses. It is the contemporary version of idealism, and it is known by one of the synonyms for *idea* that we have encountered: phenomena. It is called phenomenalism, and I would like to close this section by characterizing it briefly.

The phenomenalist really is committed to the most radical kind of empiricism: For him reference to objects is always finally reference to sense-experience, namely the sense-experiences through which objects are given. Sometimes this was advanced as a kind of translational program, according to which all terms referring to physical objects would be replaced, without remainder, by means of a conjunction of terms that themselves refer only to sense-data. And a sense-datum language was then deemed sufficient to accommodate all our justifiable beliefs about the world. To be sure, this means that even Berkeleyan spirits, or what we refer to as minds, must be translated out in such a way that we refer, in referring to mental states, only to what meets the senses. But such reductions are not unfamiliar in recent or contemporary philosophical thought, behaviorism being a good example of such a program. John Stuart Mill once spoke of physical objects as but the "permanent possibility of experience" and this, by and large, is what the phenomenalist exploits: All we can mean, in talking about physical objects—or nonphysical objects, if there are any—is what experiences we would have in dealing with them: so describing such objects must finally come down to a vocabulary which refers to these experiences, or possible experiences. The piece of wax, for example, is defined with reference to taste, smell, feel, color, and the like. "Putting the wax by the fire" calls for a complex translation, but again we all know, more or less, what belongs in the description. And then we can describe what happens after this, describing the wax in terms of moltenness and the like. The entire transaction can be expressed in terms of actual and possible sense-experiences. And what else, then, do we need? Phenomenalism has a great appeal to philosophers. We no longer need postulate divine omniscience or spirits to account for continuity; we no longer need shudder at the edge of the Humean-Buddhist abyss. Berkeley was right about external objects. They dissolve, neatly and without remainder, into the experiences we have or would have: They just are those experiences or, more technically, they just consist in the sense-data the language of phenomenalism countenances as uniquely meaningful.

To be sure, no one has ever carried out such a translation. It is perhaps practically impossible to do so. There is virtually an infinitude of possible sense-data in connection with the simplest of objects—an apple, say. Every experience is thence incomplete: To experience an object completely would be to experience every possible sense-datum, and this is not available to a finite knower. Little matter. As with all such programs in philosophy, the question is whether translation *in principle* is fully possible. And the phenomenalist has little hesitation in saying that it is. Try, he may say, to think of something that does not refer to an actual or possible experience. Simply imagining such a thing calls upon the resources of phenomenalist intuition: It must refer to some experience or other. But critics of phenomenalism have not been certain of this. Quite apart from the cumbersomeness of a sense-datum language—an aspect of the language that may mean little to the phenomenalist who has, after all, no intention of *speaking* "phenomenalese"—the critics have been unconvinced that the translation can be carried out without referring, in the process, to certain physical constants, if only to time and space. Thus it may be conceded that to say that the kitchen exists while I am in the living room is to say that if, at the time I am in the living room, I were to go to the kitchen and turn on the light, I would have certain experiences. The question is whether I do not need some objective, not to say physical, notion of time in making this translation. And if, as may be pressed, I need physical terms to eliminate physical terms—well, that may serve in principle to deconstruct phenomenalism as a viable position.

But now the question is whether any of the rivals to phenomenalism are any better off in this regard—whether any of them can come to terms with those nonempirical matters of space, time, and continuity that empiricism in all its forms and despite its structures seems to require?

# 28

## *Matter, the World, and Philosophies of Knowledge*

CONSIDER, AGAINST THE ARGUMENTS of the last section, what Berkeley would have said he had achieved in reducing objects to appearances, and in then further reducing them to objects of perception that had no existence other than what they were perceived to have. *He* would have said that he had gotten rid of the concept of matter. For it would have been matter that was left behind once he had peeled away the various sets of sensory properties, the colors, the tastes and sounds and odors, through which objects present themselves to the senses. And Berkeley asked what meaning we could then assign to the concept of matter inasmuch as it answered to no possible sense-experience? It must be a thoroughly senseless notion (no pun intended) if no experience would tell us anything about it, and indeed, in ridding us of it and hence, in his view, removing what might have been perceived as the final obstacle against regarding the universe as spiritual through and through, Berkeley might have said he had only rid us of a kind of superstition—matter was an absolutely empty notion.

Now Berkeley was not fighting a straw man here. Matter really would have been construed in just the terms that he, using his special theory of meaning, regarded as empty, for it would have been a point of philosophical consensus that matter was invisible, a kind of locus of primary qualities, a kind of colorless and tasteless and odorless substratum distinguished from the sensory qualities the seventeenth- and eighteenth-century philosopher or scientist would cheerfully have allowed were "in the mind," with no ulterior existence. The physical world—the "real world"—was either a set of colorless, odorless, and so on corpuscles, as Newton supposed, or a kind of colorless and odorless extended substance, as Descartes believed. Material things were, according to Descartes, merely *extended* things, objects of pure geometry, changes in which underlay but were in no sense characterized or penetrated by colors and sounds and the like. In the final metaphysical picture he offered, Descartes said there were two substances, really, thinking ones like himself, and extended ones like the piece of wax, which clearly cannot be identified with the contrary sets of properties he noted at either end of the episode of melting. If we are to speak of change rather than replacement of one set of properties by another, there must be a thing that changes—but it cannot have, as proper to itself, the properties it gains or loses. And it would have been this, a kind of abstract extendedness, which Berkeley found at last to be an empty view. To require an underlying substance like matter would be—though of course it was Hume rather than he who drew this consequence—as great a piece of superstition as requiring an underlying self when there are only the changes one notes on introspection—one perception giving way to another with immense rapidity. Matter was an uncharacterizable "I know not what" that was, as it were, like conceptual ashes, something left behind when everything the senses tell us of a thing had been stripped away. Or perhaps to call it ashes is still to give it too much weight. Rather, the concept of matter was an artifact of a perhaps very primitive form of thought that insisted on there being something, though it could not say what.

Wittgenstein once used—with great effect against a certain theory of meaning—the example of a piece of rope with twisted fibers. It was the friction of fiber against fiber that gave the rope its strength and kept it from disintegrating into its constituents. Someone might have found this mysterious and felt that the rope could not possibly hold together unless there were a single thread running the whole of its length. This would have been the primitive mode of thought, that there has to be a single underlying something or everything will fall apart. Of course there *could* be a fiber as long as the rope itself. But there would be no need for such a unifying fiber for the rope to hold together. Look and see, Wittgenstein wrote, if there really is such a thing. And this might have been a welcome image for Berkeley—or for Hume. There need be nothing that holds appearances together, and certainly nothing that is the same from instant to instant, in order for there to be change. Why must there be a string, as it were, termed matter, on which appearances are strung like beads? What do we need it for?

Matter, in Berkeley's time, would have been something like the luminiferous ether in nineteenth-century physics, and it is worth pondering the difference between the way in which Berkeley eliminated matter and the way that physics itself got rid of ether. Matter, I have said, was postulated in order to account for change, in order to "support" the primary qualities, in order for there to be something that underlay the shifting qualities of the senses. The argument for ether was that light, conceived of in terms of waves, must have a medium in which to undulate. This medium must fill all of space in which light could be propagated—certainly it must fill the space between the Earth and the distant stars if their light was to reach us across the vast intervening distances. But was there any direct evidence for ether? It was colorless, odorless, tasteless, exactly like matter in the older view. And the Earth rotated in the ether, as in a surrounding fluid. If the luminiferous ether were a kind of perfectly elastic solid, then a beam of light, transmitted from a given point on the Earth, should require a different amount of time to return if sent along the path the Earth followed through the ether than if sent off perpendicular to the Earth's trajectory. In 1887, Michelson and Morley performed a crucial experiment and failed to find any difference of a kind that should have appeared had there in fact been a fixed ether. It did not matter if light went out in the direction of the Earth's motion, or in the opposite direction, or at right angles to it: The velocity of light is constant. And thus the postulation of a fixed ether became increasingly dubious—almost a matter of superstitition.

The Michelson-Morley experiment involved a complex piece of apparatus, the interferometer, and was repeated in various circumstances, from positions above the Earth as well as on the surface of the Earth, with no detectable differences. Berkeley used no apparatus at all, only a version of what came in time to be the Verifiability Criterion. I think he might have said on a priori grounds that there could be no test for matter, in the sense that if there were a detectable difference, then *that* would be part of the appearance, whereas matter is something for which there *can be* no appearance. But having defined intelligibility in terms of appearance, he in effect eliminated matter through analysis rather than experiment. Who knows but that the concept of matter, had it resulted from the same impulses as the postulation of ether—that there *must* be something—might have been tested for by some peers of Michelson and Morley? But it is striking that science and philosophy should be so close at this point that it is almost indifferent whether one uses analysis or experiment. Or almost a matter of indifference whether something is a philosophical concept or a scientific one.

There is an often recounted episode in the life of Doctor Johnson who, when informed that Berkeley denied the existence of matter, kicked a rock, saying therewith that Berkeley was refuted. But what do we prove to Berkeley's detriment when we kick rocks? He was not denying that rocks were material in any sense on which Doctor Johnson would have insisted. To be sure, Johnson might have found it difficult to describe himself as kicking something "in his mind"— but then the foot, the kick, indeed the whole bulk of Doctor Johnson as an embodied spirit, were "in the mind," and nothing internal to the experience would divide the lexicographer from the philosopher. What Berkeley was denying was a sense of matter that lay quite outside the domain in which kicks, stubbed toes, resistance and weight and hardness—data of experience all—had any meaning. It was a sense of the term that could be blown away without its absence being marked at all, for it was external to experience, totally and absolutely.

Yet it cannot perhaps be too heavily stressed that what has just been said about matter, so easily eliminated that its absence does not leave a hole in experience—it is not, after all, as though Berkeley had denied the existence of *rocks,* whose absence would leave an astonishing hole in the middle of experience—can be said of Bishop Berkeley's own entire picture of the world. There could not be a shred of differentiating evidence for its truth—its truth would never and could never be registered within experience. Experience would be just as it is whether it were true or false. No experiment could be set up to determine whether Berkeley was right or wrong. He may indeed have believed everything to be in the mind. Still, Berkeley felt distension when he overate and tipsiness when he took too much claret and engorgement when he felt, as he must have done, the proddings of the flesh in fathering the children on whom he so doted. He felt elation and he felt grief. He did not suppose that everything being mental shortened the distance by a single inch between Ireland and Newport, Rhode Island, where he lived for a time, or made the ocean any the less wet. He lived a full and useful life, building houses, publishing books, raising funds for a visionary university in Bermuda, praising the salubrious properties of tar-water, which he publicized with his usual panache. His philosophy made no difference in how he lived his life; it did not at any point because it could not at any point penetrate the fabric of his existence. It cast not a single differentiating shadow on the lives of men.

But what is true of the idealist is true as well of the representationalist. When Descartes concluded his meditations, he doubtless exited from the closed quarters of his philosophical seance into the same world he left, and though he may have continued to carry certain doubts, still, he needed a horse to carry him from point to point and a cloak to shield him from the chill. He perceived the world exactly as he had perceived it before he decided to be a representationalist, though representationalism was not itself a theory that could be tested against experience. It at best drew analogies from whatever science can tell us about perception, for what science tells us must take place in a way that does make differences within experience—that is the way it is with science—whereas what Descartes, an externalist after all, tells us must take place, however this is to be understood, is external to experience and no experience, no experiment can tell us it is true. Notwithstanding that, Descartes rode across the snow, fed his body, fathered a child, wrote his volumes, traveled to Sweden at the behest of a queen, felt the bite of a northern winter that ended his life there—and his philosophy made not a single difference in any of that. The world of the idealist and the world of the representationalist is the same, so far as conduct and content are concerned. The differences all are at right angles to that.

And so it is with the world of the skeptic. Hume, who loved his comforts, wrote his *History of England* sitting by a fire in a drafty library in Edinburgh, grew fat as he grew famous, played whist with his friends, and chased the giggling servant girls. "Abstruse philosophy," he wrote, "being founded on a turn of mind which cannot enter into business and action, vanishes when the philosopher leaves the shade and comes into open day, nor can its principles easily retain any influence over our conduct and behavior."

Doctor Johnson was, so far as he was an "abstruse" philosopher, a kind of naive realist, but as we saw, the hard rock he kicked was an idea for Berkeley without being by the slightest degree less hard. It was a representation caused by an external object, according to Descartes. Yet the experience of one was like the experience of the other. Their differentiating philosophies cast no shadows over their lives. Wittgenstein said, with exquisite depth, "Philosophy leaves everything as it was." Philosophy, as with poetry, according to a famous line of Auden's, "makes nothing happen." But since no experience can differentiate between the three theories of experience we have canvassed, it is clear that the differences between them must lie outside experience altogether. It can easily be seen that theories of experience, so conceived, must be meaningless when addressed from a positivistic perspective. Everything in experience is consistent with all three theories of experience, as it must be with a fourth or fifth, if they really are *philosophies* of experience. A theory of experience, if a philosophical theory, must lie at right angles to the whole of experience, leaving it intact and unmodified. So one has to go outside experience to find out which theory of experience is true. So far as experience is concerned, we are locked in its cave and cannot assign any sense *in* experience to going *outside*—for any experience that would mark the outside must of necessity be inside experience and hence not outside at all. The differences *seem* intelligible and momentous. It seems as though it makes as vast a difference as can be made whether the world is spiritual or material or somehow both. But there is certainly no way, corresponding at least to the ways in which we find out which of a pair of scientific theories is true, of ascertaining which of these theories is true. In a way we might echo another thought of Wittgenstein in saying that the greatest differences are really no differences at all. The way the world is, so far as experience can tell, underdetermines how it must be from a perspective taken from outside it. The world as we live it and know it is consistent with all possible philosophies of knowledge.

Herein, then, lies the difference between Berkeley's claim that matter does not exist and his claim that everything is mental. The former really is an internal claim about the world. That is why it is so much like the outcome of the Michelson-Morley experiment seeking to detect the presence of the luminiferous ether. The procedures are different, but the differences are not great. Someone might have said: If light is undular, there has to be a medium in which it undulates. There are no waves if nothing waves, as there are no grins if there are no mouths. That would be as near to an analytical proposition as one might find, and it is striking that it turned out to be false even so, scientists having to learn to live without something they felt they needed under their feet. Someone might have said, similarly, there are no colors unless there are colored things. But since things can change colors, they internally have no color. There must be some properties they have, however, or they would not be things. And Berkeley showed that this, too, was a piece of superstition, perhaps a grammatical artifact of no great moment since nothing fell when it was false. The world was poorer, no doubt, for lacking luminiferous ether, as it was poorer for lacking that marvelous but improbable propertyless sheet on which the properties of the experienced world were spread. Still, it was an internal improverishment. It is in a way too bad that there are no ghosts, no unicorns, no plaid snakes, no mermaids. But there it is.

The claim that everything is mental, on the other hand, robs the world of nothing at all, and this would have been one of the things that greatly recommended it to Berkeley. It is an external claim, in compensation, which can make no internal difference. And that, of course, is in violation of the very principle to which Berkeley appealed in erasing matter from the inventory of the world. That of course does not mean that we do not have to draw distinctions within the world between the mental and the nonmental. That is perhaps as important a distinction as we ever have to draw, and in a way it must have been precisely that distinction Doctor Johnson meant to reinforce in kicking the rock. *There* is something, Sir, that is not an idea. You cannot break your foot on an idea! Nor could Berkeley seriously have questioned that distinction. Whatever distinguishes my ideas of rocks from rocks themselves is internal to my experience of the world. He had to have used the word *idea* in a different sense altogether in saying that my ideas of rocks and rocks themselves, for all their unquestioned differences, remain ideas even so and are exactly alike. Their being alike must leave all the differences Doctor Johnson and the plain man he exemplifies would insist upon.

# 29

# Coherence and Reality

IN THE WIDE SWINGS WE HAVE BEEN MAKING, it may be observed and perhaps objected that we have quite lost sight of the theory of knowledge. But in truth what we have done is to move to a stage outside all theories of knowledge, simply because the chief positions in the theory of knowledge presuppose solutions to their problems as a condition for raising them. This is preeminently true of the Problem of the External World, as raised so vividly by Descartes. It turns out that it exactly presupposes the theory of representationalism, which sets up a gap between representation and reality it then challenges us to traverse. But if we *can* set it up we have, as it were, already traversed it, for the terms of the problem are the solution to the problem. That is to say, if the problem is genuine, it is solved—for there is reality and here is representation and we have straddled the gap between them in setting the problem up. Small wonder Bishop Berkeley said that men had raised a dust and then complained they could not see! The question of whether the problem is genuine is the question finally of whether representationalism is true. And that is precisely what representationalism cannot demonstrate. It cannot because it has no way of showing that it and not realism, or it and not idealism, is the true philosophy. There is nothing in experience to tell, hence no epistemologically acceptable way of telling. And since epistemology cannot solve the problems of its own validity, some other discipline, one whose structures are scarcely understood, must be appealed to. And if this discipline should solve the problem of which of the three theories of experience to which I have been appealing is true, epistemology will have nothing to do either, for in solving the problem of experience it will have solved whatever there is to solve in epistemology. It is not as if there are not answers to its questions. It is only that it cannot give them.

This means, I think, that until we find a position outside all known positions, from which they may be addressed, we must put the theory of knowledge on hold. But before turning away from it altogether, it must be said that while the different theories of knowledge cannot resort to investigative practices at all like those of science, still, each of them has to be able to answer certain questions that arise within experience, such as the nature of illusions. Even, for example, if one is an idealist or a realist, some way of characterizing illusions must be found. And it may prove instructive to canvass the differences from this point of view. For it is possible that a procedure will emerge that is neutral to the differences between these competing cognitive visions. And if each must subscribe to all the same distinctions, perhaps the urgency of deciding amongst them is drained away.

Let us begin with considering illusions. The concept of illusion arises in part because certain of our perceptions appear inconsistent with one another when they are in the first instance taken to be perceptions of the same thing. And perhaps the concept of illusion was invented precisely as a way of keeping a coherent view of reality. It is coherent for reality to contain straight things and bent things—like a box of nails—but not to contain things at once bent and straight, as in the case of the stick in water that looks bent to the eye but feels straight to the touch. Since it cannot be both, one of them is assigned the status of an illusion. My claim is that this was an absolutely remarkable invention, just because the world would be that much more difficult to navigate if every property things were perceived to have were believed to be part of those things. Coherence is taken to be the defining property of reality (though it would be an interesting and entertaining diversion to think of the concept of monsters, which are things at once human and horse, or woman and fish, and the like). It may be a problem to determine which of the properties is illusory or, for that matter, which events have been dreamed. It is true that the stick really could be bent, and its felt straightness the illusion. But then we would need a physical law to the effect that immersion in water causes sticks to flex, when this at the same time seems insufficient force to overcome the stick's rigidity. It is, in other words, not merely a *decision* that touch triumphs over sight, but that the continued rigidity of sticks fits in better with the background physics that defines the world. And its seen bending has a natural explanation in the theory of optics: If we put together enough science, it should seem a mere matter of course that an immersed stick should remain straight but look bent.

Even so, "is bent" and "is straight" are contrary properties, and sticks cannot *be* both. The question with which philosophers have almost obsessively dealt is the status of the property that does not really belong to the stick because it is inconsistent with the property that really does belong to the stick. This is as much a problem for the idealist as for the realist, though perhaps it is one of the advantages of representationalism that it can handle this question in a somewhat straightforward way.

To begin with, the representationalist will say that there is nothing difficult in representing the stick as both straight and bent. The representations, to be sure, are inconsistent with one another, but it is built into the nature of representations that they can be inconsistent in this way—the paper on which I write, "The stick is bent and straight," does not ignite! Still, the inconsistency is there, and the natural representationalist response is that one of his representations is true and the other one false. When I see a straight stick as bent, I see something—a representation—but what I see fails to correspond to reality. For the representationalist, the false representation is "in the mind" just as the true representation is. The only thing is that one of them fails to correspond to an external reality and so is false. And one of the great beauties of representationalism as a theory is that it allows itself enough by way of philosophical equipment to be able to handle the problem through the collateral notions of truth and correspondence. But reference to an ulterior reality is then almost a necessity for the representationalist, for otherwise he has no way of bringing consistency into the set of his representations: At least one of his representations must be false if he is to have a coherent set of beliefs. So some distinction between a representational system and an external reality is required. The false representation, as said, is housed in his mind, like the true one. But only the latter is, as it were, projected outward and taken to characterize the real world.

But just about the same amount of structure is needed by the idealist, even if it is his view that everything is in the mind. Everything may indeed be in the mind, but not every representation—or idea—can be true, and the question that faces the idealist is how this is to be accounted for. The standard view, roughly since the time of Berkeley, is that we take as true the largest set of self-coherent ideas, and those ideas then are false that cannot coherently fit in the set. There are, in effect, "wild" ideas, their wildness defined by lack of fit with the coherent set that defines reality for the idealist. The wild idea is no less real by Berkeley's criterion of "perception"—if to be is to be a mental object, or an idea, then there is nothing to choose between the set of ideas, each of which is a mental object. So Berkeley needs a second criterion to account for the advent of illusion, and this is taken care of by the provision that ideas fall into two sets—or into a set and a nonset, the coherence of the former being what defines the real world. The rest are *simply* "in the mind."

And much the same distinctions are of necessity imposed upon the realist. We may in fact perceive objects as they are, but if every perception is taken as true, the stick will have to be both bent and straight. Some respite might be gained by saying that it *looks* bent and *feels* straight, as indeed it does, but the realist insists we perceive the world as it is, and he is not anxious to dissolve objects into mere feels and looks—for then it is difficult to see how he can distinguish himself seriously from his rivals. So he too has to partition his perceptions; say some are of the stick as it really is and some are simply in us. And those that are in us will pretty much coincide with the "wild ideas" of the idealist and the false ideas of the representationalist. But this is going to be true of whoever sets out to solve the problem of illusions. There are, for example, or at least there once were, philosophers who sought to respond to the problem by the interposition of sense-data. Sense-data were really neutral as to whether something was in the mind or not. And it was sense-data that we sense, the thought then being that we "construct" physical objects out of the sense-data that are the immediate objects of the various senses. The sense-datum theorist (or phenomenalist, as he is sometimes called) then has the problem of deciding which sense-data belong in the constructed real object and which do not. In constructing the immersed stick, does the "straight" sense-datum felt, or the "bent" sense-datum seen, belong to the constructed stick? And of course there are going to have to be sense-data that do and sense-data that appear as if they do but do not "really" belong to the object.

Not only, then, do the differences between the theories of perception not show up in the world—not only do they leave the world as it is, characterizing it differently only from "outside"—each has to solve the same problems and each requires the same pieces of apparatus—some way of distinguishing between what belongs to the world and what does not. Each appeals to some intuitive notion of coherence, to some intuition about fitting or not fitting with some maximally ordered set that is taken to be the real. Nobody, so far as I know, has made great headway in analyzing the concept of coherence. The use of the concept is invariant to all positions, but it is a concept that means something only against the presuposition that reality itself cannot be incoherent, that if there is incoherence, it is somehow due to *us*. Small wonder Descartes complained of his wayward or vagabond mind! On the other hand, if minds are not real, they or some equivalent to them would have to be invented to house the representations, or ideas, or sensations that do not cohere with reality. And some kind of dualism seems forced upon us. Even, for example, if we followed the radical path laid out by the ancient Sophist, Protagoras—who said more or less that everyone is always right, that to each individual there is a world of which that person's beliefs are true, and who sought then to rectify conflicts between individuals by relativizing their differences to different worlds—we would have the same problem that we have been discussing throughout this section. The problems would still arise *within* worlds, even if we were to accept the existence of a plurality of them. Protagoras would have to achieve a certain consistency, and as illusions, even within a world, would surely be inescapable, Protagoras, too, would have to find a way of dealing with them. And it is difficult to imagine him doing so in a way very different from the one I have sketched.

Invariantly, then, as to epistemological philosophies, some appeal to coherence seems to serve as the criterion of reality, and someplace must be found to lodge what does not cohere and so does not form part of the real. Our commonsense picture of things has developed a rich set of categories—of dreams, fantasies, illusions, hallucinations, mirages—to enable us to build up a coherent picture. Inevitably, since reality is supposed to be coherent, coherence has been accepted by otherwise widely diverging philosophers as *the* criterion of the real. But how reality itself is to be characterized *from without,* that is to say, whether it is spiritual, as Berkeley believed, or something else, since that is not something that can be settled from within—and since such differences as we may consider leave the world, as defined by the coherent set of representations, unaffected—we have the choice of regarding the questions as the deepest questions there are or as no questions whatsoever.

# 30

## *Reality and Rationality*

BY ASSIMILATING THINGS TO OUR PERCEPTIONS of things, leaving no space between the thing and our perceptions of it for the skeptic to haunt, Berkeley may have congratulated himself that he had conquered the skeptic by giving him, as it were, no place to stand. Descartes had supposed that there can be no reasonable doubt that I have a certain idea—no interesting doubt at least as to whether it *seems* to me that there is a fire before me while I sit in my dressing gown scribbling meditations on certainty and doubt. Still, he argued, there can be no certainty that I really am sitting and writing, thus garbed, before the fire: There can be no certain inference, only a blind and rash impulse—what Hume later called a "blind and powerful instinct of nature"—compelling us to believe "the very images presented by the senses to be the external objects." Perhaps we cannot help but believe our senses, but still, Descartes would insist that he had shown, our experience could be just as it is and there is nothing there, in reality, corresponding to our experience. And so experience being consistent alike with the presence or absence of what our "blind and powerful instinct" compels us to believe, the world, for all we know rationally, is separated by an untraversable logical gap from our experience. If I guardedly say "It seems to me that I am sitting by the fire," and so on, I can make no interesting mistake. But if I say I *am* sitting by the fire, then, if I base this on the only evidence available to me, namely my experience, I can be wrong. And since the truth or falsity of this claim about the world is equally compatible with my experience being just as it is, experience cannot justify an inference to reality. I am shut off forever from what I blindly and rashly believe to be the case. Skepticism has no interest in blind, rash impulses. Skepticism forces us to admit that the blind, rash impulse can never be replaced with rational argument. Skepticism, finally, shows how paltry human reason really is, how greatly we are creatures after all of irrational drives and propensities, even where we had thought ourselves most rational.

So in a way, defeating the skeptic might have been regarded as restoring human beings to their rational dignity. And this was the compelling power of Berkeley's *esse est percipi* thesis. To be sure, it did not exactly restore rational dignity in furnishing us with the kind of argument the skeptic taunts us for our incapacity to provide. What it does, rather, is to show that no such rational argument is needed. We are as little separated from the world as we are from ourselves. If we are certain that we are perceiving a fire, ourselves suitably garbed before it, and so on, as Descartes insisted we are, then there is nothing further needed by way of argument to prove that the fire is there, for it is the essence of fire to be perceived as warm, orange, luminous, and flammiform. To be sure, we may be separated from our own experiences, and beliefs about them may be open to doubt. But no one, least of all Descartes, ever had raised such doubts. Beliefs about our own experience were regarded as canonically certain, largely, as we saw, because it had been regarded as the nature of the mind that he whose mind it is has instant, certain, and privileged access to its contents. With our own mental contents, there is no room for error as there logically had to be room for error in regard to anything external to our mind, whatever its nature.

Defeating the skeptic may not have been Berkeley's primary philosophical motive. It may rather have been to demonstrate the spiritual character of reality and the existence of God. But it was a strong incentive, he may well have argued, that we at least do not have to forfeit our rationality and trust our blind impulses. We do not because our impulses are right, and can be shown right. God vested us with impulses it would be blasphemous to doubt. The spontaneous belief that seeing is believing is one of the gifts of God. The skeptic is then a kind of devil—Descartes was right to think of him as a malign spirit.

But the discussion of our last section shows that work remains to be done by the idealist, work perhaps as little capable of achievement as the founding of the external world is on the representationalist position. Experiencing the fire and the embodied self before it does not as such guarantee that it is not an illusion, for it is quite consistent with its being an illusion that the experience should be just as it is but false. So the direct and immediate certitude regarding the contents of my own mind, which are supposed to follow from the very nature of mind, come to very little so far as the skeptic is concerned. No experience, however certain, even if certain to the point, if there is a point, at which doubt becomes unintelligible, will assure me that what I am experiencing is not an illusion—for its status as nonillusory is a function of a vast body of other experiences, none of them being had at the moment at which I have it, with which the immediate experience coheres. The most I can do is to predict that certain experiences will be had or might have been had. But until I seek to carry out experiments, there is no way of knowing. The gap that Berkeley's shrewd and magnificent argument has closed between experience and object reappears as a gap between experience and experience. If the first gap made us, in Berkeley's poetic phrase, sit down in a forlorn skepticism, we are not one bit less forlorn now. The problem of the external world has merely been replaced with the problem of experiences beyond the experiences I am having now! So the blind, rash impulse may after all, the providential goodness of God notwithstanding, be wrong.

How, then, are we to proceed? The answer is, whichever view we take of perception, whether idealist or representationalist or realist, our procedures must be the same. To say there *is* a fire there is to make predictions that go beyond and must go beyond what is immediately given in experience. The predictions are carried by the meaning of the word *fire*. To be a fire is to be hot. To be a fire is to be able to cook meats if large enough, to burn hands stuck in it, to melt lead that is left beside it, to smoke, to burn houses down if out of control—and to warm the chilled human frame if it sits at an appropriate distance under appropriate circumstances. Are all these things built into the meaning of the word *fire?* I suppose that depends on how wide our experience is and how extensive our body of beliefs. However extensive it is, we can imagine circumstances where predictions fail and we may suddenly have to make our minds up whether we were dealing with fire after all. Thus if we put a stick of lead next to the fire and it does not melt, then we have to ask whether it is a fire or if it is lead. We are back with the famous reservations on analyticity raised by Quine and others. There is no anticipating when we may have to modify the terms under which we use a word; no telling what, in advance, we would do, even to the point of saying we had undergone illusion, when things fail to work out as we forecast them to do.

There is no point in spelling out this familiar picture. It is enshrined in scientific practice, but it is no less enshrined in the most ordinary ways of being in the world. We really do sometimes act too hastily, as in the wonderful Indian examples, recoiling from a harmless piece of rope believing it to be a snake, grasping the worthless piece of nacre believing it to be silver. We trust too easily or too insufficiently. The world is a difficult, treacherous, and uncertain place—no less so, after all, if its essence is spirituality as Berkeley believed than if it is filled with solid real things as our impulses, blind and rash, insist that it is. Everyone must edge his or her way into the darkness, and there is not a single philosophy of knowledge that can spare us the pains of experience.

If everyone must proceed in the same manner, namely by predicting the outcome if certain experiences are taken as we believe them to be, then this practice does not discriminate among philosophies of knowledge. It is consistent with them all. It is the universal condition of cognitive beings to act in a darkness, or at least in conditions of less than full illumination, and to be obliged to overhaul the systems of beliefs in the light of recalcitrant experience. No philosophy of knowledge explains in any way better than another how we are to proceed or why we must proceed as we do. Each of them recognizes and has to recognize a gap between illusion and reality, however they propose to bridge it. And in the end all their bridges are alike.

Let us consider one more time the experience of the fire. Let us indeed suppose that I am certain of the content of this experience. I see the flames dance, and though I lack the words to describe fully everything that is taking place in the hearth, I harbor no doubts that it is a fire. Suddenly it begins to behave in ways I am unused to. The flames form the body of a being that looks like a man made out of flames. His eyes especially glare like embers. He reaches out a fiery arm to drag me into the coals. And then I wake up, there was no flame-man, no eyes, no fire—I have been asleep and dreaming. Retrospectively, the vivid experience was unreal. Happily, it fails to cohere with what I am experiencing now—too many blankets on a night turned unusually warm. I lie in the safe darkness of my bedroom as my heartbeat returns to normal. Whatever my philosophical beliefs, they do not penetrate the experience or induce me to change by a single degree the description I just have given of it.

To be sure, the idealist may say that what I am predicting and seeking to render coherent are *experiences*. And to a certain degree he is right. But the urgency has been drained out of assimilating objects to our experiences of them once it is recognized that in any case we must go beyond any given experience if we are to know, in whatever way we do or can know, that what we are experiencing is real. Perhaps "is real" means little more now than the inexhaustibility of predictions licensed by the claim that we are really sensing a fire—but if so it is a sense of the term that is invariant to the differences between the philosophies of knowledge.

The world, of course, may finally be spiritual, as Bishop Berkeley fervently wished it were and wished us to believe it was. Or, more in conformity with modern usage, it may all be mental. But if it is mental in the total way Berkeley required and insisted, it must be so in a way that cuts across the distinction we commonly draw between the mental and the material—between feelings, or beliefs, or thoughts, on the one side, and such things as fires or rocks on the other. That is a distinction, as it were, internal to the world, rather than external to it in the way in which Berkeley uses the concept of spirituality. But that internal distinction between mental and material gives rise to no epistemological problems of the sort that external characterization does. Mental and material are equally "real," if we persist in using the term as we just have. But as the distinction no longer seems to involve the philosophy of knowledge, we may bring this section of our study to an end and address this last division of our topic.

# PART IV

# The World

# 31

## *Substance*

*I*T IS DIFFICULT TO RECAPTURE or almost even to imagine what it was like in the missionary days of analytical philosophy, when it seemed that the task at hand was largely therapeutic, to rid the world of philosophy as of a sort of neurosis. That philosophy is nonsense, that it is a disease of language or of thought, that it demands radical extirpation rather than solutions or answers to its dark, portentous questions, may have been a hasty and enthusiastic reaction to the almost total absence of progress in reducing philosophy to tractability. And while the therapeutic endeavor met with resistance and bit by bit ebbed away—leaving behind a curious profession called analytical philosophy that seems to draw its nourishment only from itself—the truth remains that the history of philosophy and the personal history of any one of us bear some marked similarities. Any human being, but most particularly the neurotic, is the victim of patterns established in its earliest and most impressionable age. Hypotheses about the world are formed at an age when the child is ill prepared to form them, and by time the child is grown to a rational age, the patterns are long established. Early traumas and conjectures define the personality to the point where cure is hardly available this side of transformation: One has almost to be reborn a new human being in order to be clear.

Philosophy, too, suffers from very early decisions as to what the structure of the world must be if certain facts are to be understood. Even when one would no longer frame theories as once was done, the problems with which philosophers deal rest on archaic divisions they repudiate. How much of the so-called mind-body problem would remain were we to erase, really erase, certain concepts that gave it form but which have long fallen into disuse, is difficult to say. One of the concepts, for example, is that of *substance*. Philosophers have asked the question of how many kinds of substance there really are. The favored answer would be one, but Descartes suggested there were at least two and at most three, and Leibniz contended that there were infinitely many. One, two, three, infinity—those are philosophically attractive numbers. It is difficult to imagine a philosopher arguing that there are seventeen or twenty-three basic substances—but in order to appreciate that, it is necessary to see what sort of work the concept of substance was intended to do and what problems it gave rise to against this agenda.

Berkeley, for example, while he claimed to have repudiated the existence of matter—a claim, as we saw, that elicited a certain amazed indignation on the part of the great lexicographer, Samuel Johnson—really, at most, would have argued away the existence of material *substance*. And though by the time of Johnson's dictionary "substance" may have lost some of its technical meaning to become a useful word, as in expressions like "unknown substance" or "toxic substance," it is altogether feasible that what Berkeley got rid of— material substance—not only left everything else as it was, but even left materialism as a possible and viable philosophy. For materialism was not necessarily arguing over questions of substance. But since the very concept is remote and abstract, its origins buried in the philosophical unconscious—and since it bears testimony to Santayana's principle that those who do not know history are condemned to repeat it—a word on its use in the traditions of metaphysics will be prophylactic.

Substance would have been correlative with the term *attribute*. The attributes of something would be its properties—its color, say, or its texture or smell—and these may change over time, as we saw in Descartes's wonderful example of a piece of wax that melts, losing in the process its odor of honey and its characteristic waxy feel, to become something that is a gray, warm puddle, with just the smell it does have. The belief was that there has to be something that underlies these changes, that does not itself change when they give way to one other. And this would be the thing's substance— literally what is there, under the changes and hence itself unchanging. It would be, as it were, the piece of wax in *itself*. It is not difficult to see, in this respect, how the concept of a self—the "self in itself"—should have played the role of a substance. For much the same reason that it appeared necessary that something should underlie and support changes of attributes, it seemed no less required that something should underlie and support changes of *mental* state. And as we saw, Hume found mental substance no less dubious an entity than Berkeley found material substance to be. For Hume the mind was simply the fleeting particulars of mental life, and though there may be a problem of what makes these particulars all belong to the same mind, Hume might have said that we were hardly better off in postulating a mental thing to unite them, since that could make no conceivable difference in the way mental life goes on, all the less so since there is no experience as such of this underlying something. Mental substance "supports" ideas, feelings, beliefs, experiences, and so has logically to be distinguished from any of the contents it may indeed be said to support. So, correlatively, with material substance: It cannot be identified with any of the attributes it supports and cannot be characterized by anything it underlies. So it becomes a puzzle as to how to characterize it at all.

There is an initial question of whether in fact there are substances in this sense—attributeless underlying canvases, as it were, on which all that presents itself in an object is embroidered. There may very well be—but we hardly can have any evidence for them, since evidence would be in the nature of an attribute that presents itself, and it would beg the question to say that it was evidence for *substance.* But then it may be argued that it is not the kind of thing we know about on the basis of evidence, but rather a requirement of thought—that just to talk about change and sameness presupposes something to which sameness and changes are to be referred. To then say that substances exist is to say that this way of thinking is true. But that again begs the question against thinkers like Hume and

Berkeley and many others, who insist that we can very easily think of sets of attributes unowned by substances. And even if the postulation of substances were to be entailed by some conceptual scheme such as our own, it is still by no means established that that particular conceptual scheme is itself necessary—there are other thinkable conceptual schemes. Nietzsche thought that one of the great mischiefs of our subject-predicate grammar is that it commits us to substances—substance is what the subject refers to, as attributes are what the predicates refer to. But then he proposed that there is nothing sacrosanct about this particular grammar. Indeed, he proposed other grammars entirely which generate different metaphysics and perhaps no metaphysics at all. Russell once observed that if we reflected on the sentence, "It is snowing," we would realize that there is nothing that *does* the snowing. It is just, simply, that there is snow falling. And perhaps this could be put quite generally. For every sentence of the form "X is F," we could instead say simply, "F-ing is taking place." It would be odd that a mere change of language could cut off a whole conception of reality. But the eliminability of the concept is of less consequence to us at this moment than certain internal difficulties in the concept of substance that remain to haunt philosophy, even when, as today, relatively few philosophers subscribe to the concept of substance or its necessity. To these I now turn.

Aristotle characterizes substance thus: "While remaining numerically one and the same, it is capable of admitting contrary qualities." That is to say, substances remain the same while their attributes change: They go from solid to liquid, or undergo alterations in color, and these contrary qualities do not penetrate the substance that "underlies" them. But if change is defined in terms of one quality being replaced by one of its contraries, then that which underlies change does not *itself* change. For suppose it did change. Then, by the argument that holds that something like the concept of substance is required if there is to be change, there would then be something, more substantial than it, that remained the same while the substance underwent change. So, ultimately, there would have to be some single underlying substance wherever there are changes—and *it* must remain the same, unaltered and inalterable, forever. Such would have been the classical argument. But it then directly follows from that that substances cannot causally interact. For suppose they did. Then the substance that was acted upon would have to show an effect. It would have to change, for causes bring changes about. But since substances cannot change, they cannot be effects of causes. And so causal interaction between substances is impossible. Hence, finally, each substance is independent of each other. And this gets to be, in a writer like Descartes, exactly the definition of substance. A substance needs no other substance in order to exist.

At this point it becomes plain that only God could be a substance, a consequence seized upon by Spinoza, who saw God exactly as the single unchanging being that underlies all the changes that there are. But Descartes had notoriously insisted that the world is composed of at least two substances other than God—thinking substance, or mind, and extended substance, or matter. If, indeed, mind and matter are substances, they must have certain properties that are essential to them, and that they cannot gain or lose. Descartes argued that he could not think of himself as not thinking, and hence thinking was the defining trait of the kind of being he was. He could not think of matter as unextended—however small a piece of matter, there is always some modicum of residual extension. (As we saw, "bodies are extended," was one of Kant's paradigms of an analytic judgment). But more important than these considerations, if mind and matter are separate substances, they cannot interact causally. It is true that their independence, which follows from the nature of substance, was of great use to Descartes in his view that the self is immortal, in at least the sense that, if a substance, it is not in any way connected with changes in the body (a parallel obvious argument is available for a proof of the immortality of the *body,* since it does not depend for its existence on the mind, and so can survive it).

The mind-body problem, which is our heritage from the seventeenth century, is an artifact of the concept of substance.

# 32

## The Mind-Body Problem

INTERACTIONS BETWEEN MIND AND BODY—causal episodes in which a mental event and a physical event are linked in whatever way cause and effect are linked—must be among the most familiar occurrences there are. My finger is placed on a hot surface and I feel a burning pain. A beautiful woman passes my view and I feel desire physically. I see a penny on the ground and I bend to pick it up. I want to speak to a friend and I dial his number on the telephone. I have a feeling of fear and begin to shake. A feeling of elation causes me to jump and skip. These are as familiar and as obvious as putting an egg over heat and watching it cook, as hitting a piece of wood with a hammer and leaving a mark, as a rock striking a windowpane that shatters. It is only that the concept of substance seems to rule it out in the first set of cases, inasmuch as substances cannot interact causally. If there were no concept of substance, there would be no problem, while with the concept of substance there can be no solution and the mind-body problem appears metaphysically intractable.

It is true that Descartes argued that bodies have to be spatially extended and thought the mind itself incapable of spatial extension. The latter view is odd enough to mention here. He *could* deny the existence of bodies, since it was possible he only dreamed he had a body or that there were bodies at all; whereas he could not deny his own reality, so he could *not be* a body. For if he were a body, that is, spatially extended, he could deny his own existence, which in fact is impossible. Hence he is logically nonspatial. This, then, seemed to leave one of those insane "How possibly?" questions that lend a cartoon of credibility to insane philosophical positions. "How possibly could something less extended than a bare point cause the movement of a hand the size of a small ham?" "How (possibly) could waves reflected from the surface of a body cause a response in something smaller than the smallest physical thing?" The mock incredulity these How possibly? questions imply make it sound as if we were dealing with weird physical episodes, like a spot of dandruff causing the floor to collapse, or a mouse swallowing a beachball, or a broadax splitting a hair. And some of Descartes's own curious theories seem to take the premises of this disproportion seriously. He invented, for example, the concept of animal spirits, which were designed to mediate between spatial and nonspatial things by being sufficiently broad at the base to receive thrusts from matter while sufficiently fine at the apex to affect the airy nothingness of mind—like metaphysical cones, as it were. But obviously if it is going to be thin enough at one end to interact with mind, it would have to be mind, and if thick enough at the other to interact with matter, it would have to be matter—and the animal spirit is accordingly so mysteriously composite as to raise the question of why we should not ourselves be sufficiently composite, if animal spirits are, to be both mental and material at once? Invocation of animal spirits is accordingly a gesture of despair.

But so are all the efforts that take the concept of substance seriously enough to try to cut what Schopenhauer called the world-knot by metaphysical expedients. Consider, for example, the theory of epiphenomenalism. According to epiphenomenalism, the mind is impotent to cause anything to happen. The only causation runs from physical event to physical event, or from physical event to mental event, but never from mental event to mental event, or from mental event to physical event. But this "one-way interactionism" is as mysterious as the issue it tries to deal with. If causality is allowed to take place between substance A and substance B—but not between B and A—we have forfeited the principles of substance to begin with, and gone on to dismiss as illusory a great many of the causal episodes that seem on the face of it to be among the most familiar. Aside from hostility to the concept of the mental, it is hard to see what epiphenomenalism can have achieved.

Parallelism is the view that there are parallel series of events transpiring in the two independent substances, which cannot, because they are different substances, interact. Thus one's finger touching a hot stove is an event in the physical series, and one's feeling pain an event in the mental series, but one is not the cause or effect of the other. It is just a coincidence that the one event takes place when the other event takes place. Usually, in seventeenth-century thought, the parallels are kept going and harmonized by the mediation of God: It was a standing miracle and evidence of constant divine intervention that one should eat and feel satisfied, refuse to eat and grow thin, desire food and enter a restaurant. This version of parallelism was known as occasionalism, and its defenders used a curious image: The two series were like two clocks, one of which strikes ten when the other shows ten, though there is no causal connection from clock to clock, but rather they were designed to function in phase. The spectacular system of Leibniz is a vast elaboration on this point: The world is an infinite number of causally segregated substances, which he termed monads, but such is the perfection of God that the events in the infinite set of series conform like voices in an infinite choir, to a vast orchestrated harmony nothing less intelligent or powerful than God could have composed.

There is a certain baroque and stupefying grandeur in Leibniz's metaphysical scheme, as there is indeed in all the great philosophical responses of the seventeenth century to the problem of connecting minds to bodies against the fierce difficulties raised by the seemingly indispensable concept of substance. Spinoza's argument that there can be at most one substance, of which mind and body—or thought and extension—are modes, and such that (as he writes in a famous passage) the order and connection of ideas is the same as the order and connection of things, which in its own way is a form of preestablished harmony; Descartes's theory that mind and body, as distinct substances, can have nothing in common and so must be externally united by God who assures us that the order and connection of ideas and of things must be the same; and Leibniz's articulation of the universe into an infinitude of substances that are harmonized by celestial orchestration—all these are, as it were, marvelous pearls produced by the irritant of the concept of substance acting on intelligences convinced of certain innate differences between minds and bodies. And each of them becomes radically unnecessary when substance itself is given up—when it no longer seems compelling, no longer seems an a priori requirement, that some underlying we-know-not-what holds the world together, keeps things from flying into fragments and minds from disintegrating into unconnected ideas. It is almost breathtaking to observe how little happened when the concept of substance was given up, first by Kant's suggestion that it may not be an objective necessity but an internal requirement of thought, and then by the hammering criticisms of writers like Nietzsche, who saw in such concepts mere fictions. At first, pulling substance out of the universe must have seemed like one of those extraordinary tricks, in which a great juggler yanks the tablecloth out from under stacked goblets and glistening glassware without disturbing anything. And then it begins to seem as though it were like the emperor's new tablecloth—nothing happened because nothing was there and nothing was done. The glassware of the universe was not resting on something infinitely more transparent than itself.

The heroic irrelevance of the great useless positions on the mind-body problem is made vivid when one recognizes that it leaves unanswered all the deep questions of psychology and physiology that have to be answered if we are ever to understand how bodies and minds work. But at least, with removal of the concept of substance, a great metaphysical obstacle has been withdrawn from the possibility that mental states can be states of bodies, at least bodies like *ours,* and while there may remain some severe difficulties in conceiving of our minds being states of our bodies, room has been made for transferring the problem from metaphysics to science. On the other hand, there are certain intuitions regarding the differences between mental states, or minds, and the physical world that were shared by the great thinkers of the seventeenth century, and that remain compelling today. A good place to begin, then, is with what is distinctive about minds. The further question is whether whatever is distinctive in this way precludes the possibility of mental states being bodily states.

# 33

## *Persons*

$T$OWARD THE END OF THE *Meditations,* Descartes, surprisingly in view of his ruthless segregation of mental substance from material substance, contends that I am not in my body the way a pilot is in a ship—where this was exactly the way we would have supposed Descartes supposed we *were* in our body. In a famous polemical work of the mid-twentieth century, Gilbert Ryle's *The Concept of Mind,* Descartes's theory is ridiculed as a "ghost-in-the-machine" theory—though Descartes, even in the most dualistic pages of his book, is anxious to insist that the mind is not some spectral substance that haunts his body, as it were, until (I add), released by death, it sets out to haunt houses. The mind is not an especially vaporous inhabitant of a body built on mechanical principles. The mind is not extended at all, he wanted to say, though it turns out that he must have meant that extension is not an essential attribute of the mind, for in a sense his final conception appears to have been that the mind is one with the body, that mind and body form a certain unity, that the mind is embodied and the body inspirited—that when mind and body are together, they really are together, totally and almost indistinguishably. And this is not a theory the caricature of a ghost-in-a-machine can be got to resemble.

Here is the sort of reasoning he gives. A pilot only knows that his ship is stove when he begins to notice water pouring in. But when my body is stove, I know this, not by noticing that something is sticking into my arm, say, and that blood is coming out—I feel it immediately, so that, loosely speaking, body cannot be affected and I not know it. There are things I know to be the case only because I happen to, though they could be the case without my knowing it just as easily. There is a bird on my roof, but it could be there whether I knew it or not—it just happened that I came to know it by observation. Now of course a good bit takes place in one's body without one's knowing, or which one comes to know only by observation, and sometimes quite complex observation. One can have high blood pressure without knowing one has it, and it requires a special instrument to find out one has. But then, when I am thirsty or hungry or hurt, I know these things directly and without the mediation of instruments. In a sense, the pilot is in the ship but is cognitively external to what takes place in the ship. But there is a kind of knowledge—which sometimes has been designated "nonobservational knowledge"—that we have of our bodies, or parts of our bodies, but never of such things as ships.

Nonobservational knowledge was specifically the order of cognition held by Descartes to define the mind. The mind, according to Cartesian philosophy, was so structured that for anything to be true of it was ipso facto for the one whose mind it was to know that it was true. This in fact has often been held to be the defining trait of consciousness: To be conscious of anything at all is ipso facto to be conscious of the fact that one is conscious of it. This was part of what made the concept of the unconscious so philosophically troubling when Freud introduced it, or what made Freud himself feel that he had made an immense discovery in having found the unconscious. For here was something that one was conscious of in some sense—we are genuinely troubled by unconscious conflicts— but we are not conscious of this fact about consciousness. It takes place without our being aware that it is taking place. But perhaps normal consciousness has the internal reflexiveness that Descartes had insisted upon, so that to be aware is to be aware that we are aware.

In any case, part of what Descartes meant was that this epistemological feature of the mind was an epistemological feature of the body when we are one with it: that we know at least certain bodily states by feeling them, even if these modes of knowledge are confused and somehow clogged by the material circumstances of the body. Certain mental states are just bodily states of which the owner is conscious in the same direct way he is conscious of his mental states, according to the theory.

Descartes might have identified another feature of bodily existence to help nail down his claim. A pilot turns the ship by turning the wheel, and he turns the wheel by moving his arms. But he does not do anything of the same order to move his arms—he *just* moves them, immediately and directly, performing what I have spoken of elsewhere as basic actions. An action is basic when it is done, but not done through doing anything other than it. I lift a finger or shut an eye, directly. But I have to move my hair by moving my hands against it, and unless I have a special gift, I cannot move my ears unless I do so with my fingers. There is a traditional theory that in order to move my arm I must, somehow, execute a volition—an act of will. But it has rightly been argued, by Ryle among others, that this raises the problem all over again, namely, how do I form a volition? Do I form it directly? Or do I need another volition—and how do I form *it?* So there either is an infinite regression, or some volitions can be formed directly. But if I can form a volition directly, why cannot I in the same sense lift a finger directly? The concept of the basic action was introduced to identify that class of bodily movements that an agent has within his repertoire, actions he can perform immediately, that is to say, without the mediation of some other act or series of acts.

So the final picture Descartes leaves us with is this: If we augment his cognitive criterion with a performative one, and take into consideration the concept of the Freudian unconscious, the mind is such that of at least certain of its states, to be in those states is to be aware that one is. There can be mental states of which we are altogether unknowing, as in the case of certain repressed memories or feelings, but at least in the case of human beings, it would not be a mind if every state were like that, if we were, so to speak, always external to our own mental states. Indeed, it might be impossible. But there are also certain bodily states I am as directly aware of as I allegedly am of my mental states when I am directly aware of them—even if there are many, many states of our bodies that we know nothing about at all. The ancients knew nothing of blood pressure, and it took an immense amount of physiological knowledge before the concept of blood pressure could even be formed. The ancients knew nothing about enzymes, nothing about insulin, nothing about metabolism. About the body as a physical system there is immensely more to know. But about the body as *embodiment,* as one with the mind—well, the ancients doubtless knew as much as we. Ancient literature is concerned with feelings we still share and still understand, and though the ancients were aware that there are bodily obstacles to understanding one another's minds—Medea said there were feelings only a woman could know, and even the gods quarreled over whether men or women have the most intense sexual pleasures—there are certain common human traits everyone human knows. To be human is to have had those experiences.

Recently, the British philosopher Peter Strawson introduced the concept of a person. He was building up a philosophical picture of the world, and he supposed there were two main kinds of things that make up the world, persons and things. His thesis took the form of a linguistic analysis: There are two basic kinds of predicates, what he termed M predicates and P predicates. An example of the former would be, perhaps, "weighs 150 pounds." An example of the latter would be "dreams of glory." Mere things are describable by means of M predicates alone. Nothing is describable by means of P predicates alone, though if there were really disembodied minds, they might very well be so described. But a person is described through M predicates and P predicates. A person is the kind of being that at once weighs 150 pounds *and* dreams of glory. These two descriptions apply to one and the same philosophically fundamental kind of being. And in a way, the concept of person answers very closely to the final Cartesian picture. But in a way, it leaves all the problems unresolved. Mostly, we have no problem with applying M predicates. There is, on the other hand, some controversy over how we apply P predicates. But beyond that there is a question of whether there is not a closer relationship between P predicates and M predicates than that they should be true of the same person. Is there, for example, some M predicate that is a condition for a P predicate to be true? What relationship is there between mental and bodily properties other than being properties of the same individual? Suppose that my brain must be in a certain state if I am to dream of glory: What is the relationship between the latter and the former? That, one feels, is the question Descartes leaves us with in saying we are one with our body. He is not saying, merely, that we are persons, some of whose properties are mental and some material. He is saying, more strongly, that some of our properties appear to be mental and material *at once.*

Let me take these matters up separately.

No one knows, really, how much he weighs—or what his temperature is—without the mediation of instruments of mensuration: scales and thermometers. One can ordinarily tell whether one has put on or lost weight by how one's clothes fit, but weight is defined relative to scales of measurement, and no one's introspective powers count for very much when it comes to applying such M predicates as do, like weight, require such mediations. By contrast, a person would ordinarily suppose he can tell, with the immediacy the Cartesian picture of the mind made central, in what mental state he is—whether he feels happy or not, whether he believes in God, whether he remembers who lives next door. But in fact the mind is rather more treacherous than that: Memory is deceptive, we hide our feelings from ourselves and are capable of severe self-deception, and even our beliefs may seem so strongly in conflict with our behavior that we may decide, on the basis of self-observation, that we do not after all believe what we thought we did. A man may believe his wife faithful. But there is behavior deeply incompatible with such a belief, and if someone points out to him—or he hits upon the truth himself—that such behavior is his, he may very well question the actual state of his beliefs in regard to his wife.

Behavior, one might say, rather more than introspection, is the criterion in such cases. If this is so in common life, it is that much more so in the scientific investigation of the mind, where a certain revolution in psychological method was achieved when it was decided that the introspective reports of subjects were simply too vagrant and uncertain to provide sound data for psychological generalization, and experiments came increasingly to be designed in such a way that how one responds to stimuli, how one performs certain tasks, what one's reaction time is, can be measured with chronometric exactitude. Seventeenth-century philosophers, writing of experience, spoke of certain inner sensations as well as outer ones, the former being just those feelings that Descartes appears to have made paradigms of epistemic certitude, states of affairs in connection with which doubt was unintelligible. And in certain cases it is indeed difficult to imagine doubts arising, as in episodes of severe pain. The patient would ordinarily be authoritative when the doctor's proddings and palpations are to elicit answers to questions about whether something hurts and what sort of pain it is—throbbing, stabbing, burning? But there are hysterics—individuals who, as in Freud's well-known experience, claim to suffer afflictions that are anatomically impossible—paralyses that have no neurological basis, pains where there can physiologically be none. But there is no reason why inner sense need be any more authoritative than outer sense, and though the patient may, if philosophically stubborn, insist that he really does feel what he says he feels, our access to our mental states is not so privileged in the bulk of cases that we can allow the objective observations of science to be defeated by it.

So far, then, there is a considerable degree of consensus between what science requires and what mere human wisdom will allow. "What sort of creature am I?" was a question Socrates could raise in total sincerity, and "discovering one's true self" remains an entertainable project for those who feel that perhaps their true nature escapes them and that it can be found only through some discipline. And writers from Nietzsche to Skinner have contended that the terms we apply to ourselves—anger, envy, resentment, sorrow—are themselves grounded in patterns of meaning we learn from the group in which we acquire our language. For Nietzsche, the self is nothing but the society internalized and self-applied, and what we are is what the "herd" forms us to be. The act of instrospection, through which we are to ascertain, allegedly irrefutably, what our inner states are, is already defined in terms of social practices and public uses. Even terms like *toothache,* according to Skinner, will not apply correctly unless certain objective criteria are satisfied. To be sure, the dentist can be in error when he scoffs at our complaints. But the point in its most general form is hardly worth contesting— what we know about ourselves is governed by objective criteria with which it must at least be consistent.

Alongside these more-or-less standard and scarcely controversial observations, a more extreme range of positions has in one form or another been defended by philosophers. It is not difficult, for example, to pass from the scientific thesis that on the whole behavior gives us a better index of psychological truth than do introspective reports, to the more radical thesis that either there are no inner states to report, everything psychological being behavior, or the somewhat less radical "logical behaviorism" that psychological predicates are defined or definable through behavioral ones. For one thing, neither Nietzsche's nor Skinner's thesis about the acquisition of psychological language would survive either of these radical views: Both of them concede that there are aches and pains and feelings, the correct description of which comprises public criteria. Both of them agree that there are inner states, however unimportant they may be—and presumably they are considerably less important than Descartes would have supposed for purposes of philosophical definition. Still, they are there, and how we feel is certainly of the greatest human importance in the chief junctures of life. And while it may be conceded that the application of psychological terms to one another is in some measure based on behavior and in some further measure connected with rules of meaning shared all across a group, some difference remains between M predicates and P predicates. Behaviorism goes some distance toward blurring the difference. If "weighs 150 pounds" is applied on the basis of readings on a scale, and if psychological predicates are applied on the basis of readings on a different sort of scale altogether, then the only difference may indeed be a difference in the scales themselves. But in that case it is far from plain that there is any deep difference between M predicates and P predicates, or even that we need the category of "persons" in our philosophical scheme, as Strawson insists that we do.

It comes to this. If terms like *anger* or *love* were absolutely and totally defined in terms of behavior, there really would be no difference between them and the terms with which we describe people—terms like *blond* or *fat* or *tall*. But in fact we do not apply the terms to ourselves on just the same basis with reference to which we apply them to others. It is one thing to say that there can be doubts about how correct we are in such ascriptions, and that our self-ascriptions must square with the ascriptions others would make of such predicates to us. It is quite another to say that there is nothing more than that to love or anger. There really are differences in the way we ascribe such terms to ourselves and to others, whereas with terms that refer to temperature or weight, there are no such differences to speak of. And perhaps what distinguishes P predicates from M predicates is just that: For the former there are two distinct ways of applying them, and one of these ways only the person to whom they in fact apply can use. Only she or he knows whether there is the feeling or the state of mind required by correct application of the term in at least a number of important cases. P predicates involve a double criterion, and one of the criteria is under the control of the individual to whom the terms apply.

But that would still leave the question of the relationship between mental states and bodily states. We may grant that there are mental states in the sense that only on the basis of something like inner sensation or internal experience can someone say with any certainty whether a given description holds. Almost any theory of what a person is is compatible with that. The person could be a compound of mind and body, and the mind could have nothing to do with the body, even if behavior were explained with reference to it. Yet such an explanation would be puzzling and difficult. We are, after all, things in the world with a certain chemistry and evolutionary history. The problems of mind and body are not merely problems of the meanings of M predicates and P predicates. Perhaps there is something to which we must refer in explanation of both the feelings and the behavior when, for example, we ascribe the complex predicate "is angry" to ourselves or to another. And what could this something then be?

# 34

# *Behaviorism and Functionalism*

BEHAVIORISM, IN ITS CLASSICAL and uncompromising form, was a rare example of a science that undertook to create itself in the philosophical image of what a science should be. It was an effort to put into effect the positivist thesis, first, that the meaning of a term is defined with reference to some set of observations, and secondly that a term must be meaningless unless one can specify the observations that would go to verify a sentence in which it occurs in a primary way. Now, of course, the concession to "internal sensation" is consistent with this positivist demand, inasmuch as the presence or absence of pain (for example) is something that can be observed directly. But the problem is that such observations appeared restricted to at most the one individual in whom the pain occurred, and given that science requires publicly defined language—if only in order that experiments can be repeated and theories confirmed by more than one investigator, at different times and perhaps different places and under various circumstances—"internal sensation" was regarded as scientifically worthless, all the more so in the light of the extreme untrustworthiness of introspective reports. The "language of science" had to be public, and there were even proofs, most notably in the writings of Wittgenstein, that a "private language" is impossible. Terms whose designations could be observed by at most one person would of necessity be in a "private vocabulary"—but that meant that only terms whose designations could in principle be observed by more than one person could have a place in a public language—the only kind of language there could be.

The precise argumentation of the "private language" thesis remains a matter of scholarly controversy, and it provides a comfortable thicket for the commentators on the later Wittgenstein, but its impulses are clear enough. They return us, inevitably and instructively, to the epistemological preoccupations of the preceding section. When it seemed essential to science that it be reconstructed on foundations of unimpeachable certainty, it seemed that only the immediate data of the senses provided such foundations, and the effort accordingly was made to erect the totality of science—of "meaningful discourse" in positivist ideology—on just such foundations. And this meant that all scientific language had to be reconstructively defined in the idiom of sense-data. There was a massive effort by theorists of knowledge to show how it was possible to define, if only in principle, the entire vocabulary of science in these terms. This was known as empiricism, and it is striking how behaviorism turned away from empiricism, so construed, and found its bases instead in only what was publicly observable. Behaviorism thus took it for granted that there was no problem of the external world—there was only a problem of the internal world. And the foundations that had been sought by empiricists down the centuries were dismissed and replaced only with what every qualified observer could observe in the same ways. And in the case of psychology, this meant behavior. So, inevitably, the effort was made to define the relevant vocabulary in terms quite opposite to those that recommended themselves to empiricists: the external responses of subjects to scientifically controllable stimuli. And psychology as a discipline massively addressed itself to the discovery of regularities in stimulus-response (S-R) patterns. As we saw, the behaviorists were tempted to something more radical than this wholly unexceptionable research program: Sometimes they thought that all there was to mind was behavior, and sometimes they went so far as to insist not simply that introspection is scientifically unreliable but that it does not or cannot occur, there being nothing to introspect and only behavior to extrospect.

But S-R correlations were really only correlations and offered no explanatory insight into the subject's responses. At times the behaviorists would endorse this limitation, saying that it was not the office of psychology—perhaps not even the office of science—to do more than establish correlations; and heroic efforts by sympathetic philosophers of science attempted to show that scientific laws really are only shorthand for correlations. But certain results in psychology seemed to cry out for something deeper and in a way interior. A famous set of experiments set subjects the task of determining whether two abstract shapes were different representations of the same figure or not: Was the subject, in effect, shown diagrams of two distinct things or rather of one and the same thing in two distinct orientations? It turned out that the time it took the subject to answer the question was a direct linear function of the size of the angle between the figures—the wider the angle, the longer it took to decide. It became almost irresistible to conjecture that an "internal" rotation must have taken place. And psychologists themselves, the grip of behaviorism by then having loosened, began to speculate that there may very well be internal images, or at least internal computations, for otherwise one could not account for the remarkable results of the experiments. Of course this did not especially rehabilitate introspection. Subjects may or may not have been conscious of *performing* a rotation. What it did rehabilitate was the possibility of an internal representation, whether subjects were aware of it or not. It was as though there were a vicarious rotation, as there would be were people actually to rotate pieces of paper. Only this rotation takes place "in the mind"—conceived of now as a representational system.

But in fact there had been a gradual erosion of behaviorism well before the striking experiments on mental imagery. Perhaps the initial onslaught came from linguistics, especially from the thought on language acquisition of Noam Chomsky. It was Chomsky's view that in order to account for a child's acquisition of a first language, a great deal of internal representation—a "language of thought"—was presupposed, in which the child could formulate a "theory" or "grammar" for the language at hand. Chomsky felt that only human beings have this power, since only humans, in fact, despite great efforts by primate psychologists to prove the opposite, exhibit linguistic competence. B. F. Skinner, the great advocate of behaviorism in its more extreme versions, had sought to explain our power to use language in specific behaviorist terms—as a matter of conditioned responses. Chomsky, a severe polemicist, wrote a famous, scathing review of Skinner's theory of linguistic behavior, intending to demonstrate its woeful inadequacies and the need to postulate what behaviorists could not countenance—an internal representational system. Once more, this does not especially vindicate introspectionism. A child has very weak powers of introspection at the time it generates the theories of its first language, and in any case if we knew introspectively how we form linguistic theories, we would not have required a Chomsky as discoverer. The degree to which the prestige of Chomsky's theory reoriented psychological investigation since the 1950s can hardly be overestimated. That prestige was such that the way was open to viewing the mind as an internal system of representation, operations which explain the behavior of subjects of various species, from humans to dogs to rats to pigeons to fish to insects.

But perhaps the great stimulus to the new theories of mental structure were provided by the computer. The computer offers a remarkable example of a piece of technology that not only revolutionizes life but revolutionizes the ways in which we think about ourselves. In fact labeled "thinking machines," computers seemed to offer a wonderful model for the way the brain works to process information, and the metaphor that we ourselves are computers and the mental conduct is essentially computational began to dominate the way philosophers and "cognitive" psychologists began to represent human beings. The computer is like us, according to the metaphor, in that its input is analogous to our perceptions, its output analogous to our behavior, and that just as we have to postulate enough internal structure to explain how input is transformed into output, so, with human beings, we have to postulate enough structure to explain how perceptual inputs are processed to result in behavioral outputs. Any philosophy of mind and body must accordingly be capable of being a philosophy of computers. Today this is the dominating image in the discussion.

Perhaps the first really novel theory of mind and body in centuries arose against the realization that the computer, while made of materials measurably different from the materials of which we are made—with silicone chips the operative ingredient in them, where the neuron is the operative ingredient in us—may nonetheless be metaphysically our twin. And with this realization came the thought that the same mental operations may have different material embodiments, so that little as we may physically resemble one another, we and the computer are *functionally* the same.

Functionalism is a theory that is very attractive to philosophers, for it enables them to discuss certain aspects of the mind in abstraction from any knowledge of the brain. For since much the same mental operations could be realized through material systems as different from the brain, in terms at least of the substances it is made of, as the computer is, philosophers have supposed that in some sense the substance—no pun intended—is immaterial. The thing is only that the material that embodies mental processes must be organized in a certain way: But so long as input is processed into output, the same output for the same input, it does not matter in the least, the functionalists contended, what the transformative mechanism is made of. It perhaps could not be made of rocks or steel girders. But no one knows in advance what it could be made of: Visitors from another planet may prove to have vegetable brains and be nearer of kin to cabbages than to mammals or computer mechanisms or us—but so long as information may be taken in, processed, and their behavior reflect this fact, they could and would be our functional counterparts. The important thing is that whatever the mechanism, it must be able to support such functions as memory, language, perception, and, in a sense, thinking. So far only the brain and the modern-day digital computer do these things. But the computer today is quite different from the earliest computers, the transistor having replaced the vacuum tube, the microchip the elaborate circuitry, with immense enhancements in terms of speed and energy. Still, a sufficiently cumbersome vacuum tube system might be able finally to do what its sleek electronic descendent can do, if there were energy enough to drive it and to keep it cool. The *matter* has changed immensely, but the functions remain the same: The wheezy old computers still support the same order of functions as the new.

Functionalism has, oddly, raised severe problems for certain materialist theories of the mind. Thus it is difficult to insist that the mind is nothing but the brain, hence nothing but that material system, if the mind itself can be functionally defined and then given something that supports all its functions but is otherwise different from the brain. How can the mind be identified with the brain when it can also be identified with the computer when the computer and the brain cannot be identified? Identity is transitive: if $a = b$ and $b = c$, then $a = c$. Of course, functionalism itself may be false. It may seem available only to a superficial knowledge of brains and computers. It may be that there really is only a distant analogy between mental functioning in human beings and input transformation in computers. Already today, for example, computer scientists are contending that computers circa 1987 really are inadequate to model mental functions like speech. There is already the sense that something far more complex takes place in brains than in even quite advanced machines.

Today, for example, there are exceedingly elegant theories that suppose something called "parallel distributed processing" takes place in the brain, and that computers built along those lines would really resemble the brain a great deal more than present-day computers. Still, if these scientists succeed, as they almost certainly will, in integrating, or connecting into a single system, numbers of computers working in parallel, and so get something greatly more like the brain than a single computer is, functionalism may still be a possible theory. The mental processing in question would still be embodied in (a) the brain and (b) the connectionist computer. On the other hand, nobody knows whether even the connectionist system of parallel distributed processing will be enough like the brain to give us a body for mental processing as *we* humans do it. It is possible to argue, though of course only as a possibility, that only the human brain is complex enough to house the human mind.

And functionalism then would be false at the level at which it would be philosophically interesting for it to be true, namely, that "computers 'R' us."

It is certainly premature to argue that computers *already* "R" us. Against the strong claims of artificial intelligence theorists that machines really do have and do not merely imitate mental functioning, a famous argument has been mounted by John Searle, which can only be sketched here. Searle works with a model touched on early in this book, invented by Alan Turing, according to which if no distinction can be observed between the output of a machine and the output of a human being, given the same input, then there *is* no relevant difference between them. If the human being may be said to think, then so must the machine. Searle takes the case of understanding language: If the output of a machine, putting out certain sentences when certain other sentences are put to it, cannot be told apart from the output of a human being, with just the same sentences, then there are no grounds for distinguishing invidiously between the human and the machine in point of linguistic competence. And this Searle denies.

He imagines a case where he is in a room into which strings of marks are inserted on pieces of paper, he having been taught certain rules whereby when these marks come in, other marks go out. The marks in fact are Chinese calligrams. The input and output are Chinese sentences. Let it be assumed that Searle's output from what has come to be known as "the Chinese Room" is indistinguishable from that of a native speaker of Chinese. Does indiscriminability of output then mean that there are no distinctions to be drawn between Searle and a native speaker of Chinese? As between input and output, there is no difference, and by Turing's argument, Searle must therefore know Chinese if the native Chinese speaker knows Chinese. But Searle insists that he really *does not* understand Chinese. He really does not, which then means in part that linguistic competence cannot itself be understood in terms of rules for processing sentential inputs into sentential outputs. One must in addition understand what the sentences mean. Searle says he lacks that understanding. And if his behavior mimics the behavior of a machine, then so does the machine lack understanding—even if at the level of behavior, nothing discriminates between the machine, Searle, and the native Chinese speaker.

In one way this returns us to the issues of behaviorism itself. Externally it may seem as though someone knew Chinese, measured against the rapidity with which he responds, sentence to sentence, to sentential stimulation. But *internally* it is not that way at all: In some sense, if not by inner sensation or introspection then somehow, we know when we understand and when we do not. Searle is as clear that he does not understand these sentences—would not so much as know they were sentences had he not been informed—as the classical epistemologist knows when he is in pain.

In another way this returns us to the preoccupations of understanding and meaning of an earlier section. What is it to understand a sentence? Perhaps it is to be master of a rule that tells us that a given sentence is true under given conditions. Of course this is not enough. In a general way one must have a language in order to understand a sentence. Persons who have a language may be mistaken that they understand certain sentences. They may act in a certain way that elicits the response of the narrator in "The Lovesong of J. Alfred Prufrock"—"That is not what I meant. That is not what I meant at all." But at least the misunderstander knew it was a sentence, even if he missed the cues that inevitably go with it in different points of culture and that form the context against which understanding a sentence involves more than even linguistic competence—something like *cultural* competence, one might say. In any case, this is what Searle lacks. The marks he "processes" are meaningless squiggles. The only rules he knows connect meaningless squiggle with meaningless squiggle. And the question finally is whether the computer understands more than this: whether the computer in effect does more than respond with electric pulses to electric pulses. Maybe all the *brain* does is respond with electric pulses to electric pulses. The brain may sit in the skull as an extremely compact computer, designed to respond with pulses to pulses at an amazing rate of speed. But then what can the relationship between mind and brain be?

Even before addressing that, we have to say that functionalism, as a theory, really is less a philosophical theory than a scientific one. One has to wait and see what the future output of computer science and cognitive science is. But even if machinery is produced that, according to the Turing test, matches human competence output for output, the question would remain as to whether it embodied a mind. Perhaps the best we can do is to see what it is that would be embodied if it *were* a mind. What, in brief, is mind?

# 35

# *Neurophilosophy*

*B*EHAVIORISM IS, AMONG OTHER THINGS, a theory of learning, of how the behavior of a subject is modified by conditioning. It presupposes, accordingly, a degree of plasticity on the part of the subject, and seeks to represent how a history of conditioning produces a very different subject at the end of that history. Perhaps behaviorists have learned something themselves in the course of the controversies between them and functionalists—perhaps they will agree that in an important respect, the computer offers us a good model of what takes place when input is processed into output through some inner computational process that it would be of the greatest scientific value to be able to replicate. Still, there is a question of how a behaviorist who has learned this would represent the fact that he has learned it in the austere idiom of S-R correlations. And for that matter, it is difficult to see how the functionalist could represent his own activities in the theory he so forcefully defends. And here one must remark on an important difference between psychology and the other sciences, which remains however much the psychologist seeks to mold his practices against his beliefs about how science is. It is not important for physics, or chemistry, or even biology, to take special account of physicists, chemists, and biologists (though as we saw in Part I, it *is* important for cosmology to include cosmologists in its picture). The law of falling bodies will have as great an application to a Nobel laureate who falls from a roof as a brick, the relationship between acids and bases applies as much to the inner chemistry of chemists as to anyone or anything, the DNA of biologists is of a piece with the DNA of living creatures generally. So their respective sciences apply to themselves by default, but they need make no special effort to bring themselves under their own laws and theories. But if the laws of psychology are inadequate to represent what psychologists themselves do, there is a grave defect in those representations. For psychologists themselves are, after all, subjects that learn and represent.

Often science represents the world as though there were no scientists in it, or as if their being there made no special difference and made no demands on the sciences themselves. And for a good many of the sciences this attitude of severe externalism makes no special difference. The scientist, one might say, casts no shadow over the world. There are, of course, theories in physics in which the circumstances of observation so affect the phenomenon observed that they have to be reckoned into the final description of the world. But psychology often adopts an attitude toward its subjects so distant and "objective" that it forgets that the psychologists themselves are part of the reality they address. Skinner, to his credit, insisted that one criterion of the adequacy of a psychological theory was that it explained the very putting forward of that theory, and hence the practice of the theorist. But he had an oddly limited view of what it was to be a theorist.

As scientists, this is what psychologists do. They form beliefs about subjects, they make observations, they test their beliefs against those observations, and they put forward corrected theories. In fact their theories may be false and their observations skewed, and there may not be a single solid truth in the entire literature of psychology. Even so, a psychological theory that had no place for forming beliefs, making observations, testing beliefs and making inferences would be woefully inapplicable to psychologists, and hence woefully inapplicable to the subjects of psychology so far as they resembled psychologists to begin with. But where in behaviorism or in functionalism as representations of psychological subjects is there room for just the kinds of representations in which behaviorism and functionalism consist? I am insisting that psychologists are human beings, and that it is with their humanity that they should begin or at least end. But it has been characteristic of advanced psychology to exclude this fact from itself. It is, in a sense, we who should be models for computers if we are anxious that computers be like us. But that means that a psychological theory must finally represent its subjects, especially its human subjects but in many instances its animal subjects as well, as if they themselves behaved like psychologists: forming beliefs, making observations, testing views, learning as they go.

But this is just the way we tend to represent one another in the ordinary episodes of life. We seek to rationalize one another's behavior by ascribing beliefs in the light of which that behavior is understandable. We explain one another's behavior in terms of the rich complex of desires and beliefs and values and previous experiences that went into the formation of those beliefs, values, and desires. We say that what another person does is altogether comprehensible, given his or her learning history, the traumas undergone, the adjustments and adaptations of life. It is thus that we explain the functionalists today, who have gone through a century of psychological speculations, from James through Watson to Skinner and Neisser, not to mention Freud and Gestalt, to come to the views they now hold and that they teach to their students and test in their laboratories and write about in journals. In brief, there is very little difference in structure between the behavior of scientists and ordinary men and women, as there is very little difference in the way we represent the behavior of scientists and the way we represent the behavior of the most ordinary persons. To be a person at all is at the very least to be a system of representations. And the real task of psychology is to explain how representations come about and how they enter into the explanation of behavior.

This view of the matter has sometimes been called folk psychology. Obviously, we want to make clear that there is a difference between folk psychology, so understood, and what one might think of as the commonplace generalities with which we, as ordinary persons, satisfy ourselves in dealing with ourselves and one another, and that pass as a kind of commonplace wisdom. We say that young people are going through phases. We say things like Women want to be dominated. Or we say things like Boys will be boys. Or like Haste makes waste. Folk psychology in this sense is a set of adages, prejudices, and self-comforting attitudes that may be false and silly and that may come to be replaced by a better understanding than what we inherited from our mothers and fathers. A good many of our beliefs about men and women are false or modifiable. But *that* is not folk psychology in the sense that philosophers have tended to use it. In their sense it is folk psychology simply to use beliefs, desires, values, perceptions as if they were explanatory notions. Like the adages of folk psychology in the other sense, folk psychology in this sense will be replaced—not by better psychology but by something altogether different: a kind of neurophysiology. For in the end all that there is are modifications of nervous tissue.

This is the view of theorists who designate themselves neurophilosophers. The neurophilosophers' view is a new kind of materialism in the sense that it insists that we are nothing but a material system, and that introspection, should it occur, really is of changes in neural patterns. It is not that there are no beliefs, desires, hopes, perceptions, fears, moods, and affections. It is rather that these are nothing but neural states of those to whom they are to be ascribed. And in the end folk psychology is destined to give way to a neural science in which only matters neural can be described. So in a sense, but only in a sense, neurophilosophy is a program of linguistic reform. The language of commonsense explanations of human conduct is in effect stagnant and moribund, and belongs to an earlier era of human intelligence that we have grown, or are about to grow, out of. And in the new era we will explain whatever there is to explain about human beings strictly and solely in terms of neurochemistry. And in the new language we will have only such terms to designate ourselves and one another as have a place in the latest neuroscience.

But visionary as this program is, there remains a fact that it must not overlook. Neuroscientists are scientists, and, as scientists, they strive to represent the world. Any neuroscience that is to be as rich as neurophilosophy requires will have to represent neuroscience in neuroscientific terms. That is to say, it will have to represent the beliefs of neuroscientists, their efforts to test these beliefs against observations: They will experiment, confirm, disconfirm, observe— and because they are human, they will have to care about how things work out, will be pleased when they succeed and dashed when they fail—and all of this, of course, must be represented in the idiom of neurons, firings, the transmission of neural impulses and the like. But beyond all this the fact is that neuroscience, just because it is a science, will be a system of representations. It may represent only neurons, firings, neural transmissions, and the like—but it itself is of a different order altogether. The future of science, if it is to be of *science,* is the future of representations. And while we cannot easily say what the content of those scientific representations will be, we at least can know, now, that they will be representations. And these representations must be housed *somewhere.* Neuroscientists, like behaviorists and functionalists, belong in the world they also study, and their representations too must belong in the world.

Of course, those representations may themselves be neural states of neuroscientists. But this returns us to the classical question of mind and body, and the complexities of the concept of identity.

# 36

# *Intentionality and Representational Materialism*

IF THE ARGUMENT OF THE LAST SECTION IS SOUND, neurophilosophy is in hostage to what it had believed it redeemed, namely neurophysiology considered as a science. For a science is a system of representations in which practitioners of the science participate and which they modify in the course of conducting the experiments and making the observations in which the practice of science consists. Acting, perceiving, inferring all involve representations: one believes that P, one infers that Q if P, one sets out to test if Q is true, one observes that it is false, in which case one modifies one's belief that P, or one finds out that it is true, in which case one regards one's belief that P as confirmed. All these processes have a common propositional content, we might say: One believes that P, infers Q from P, tests in order to see if P is true, and so on. And the questions that then face the philosopher are what to do with this content and where these representations are to be housed. Neurophilosophy set out to eliminate such representations, thinking them testimony to a stagnant theory of mind—folk psychology—but, as we saw, they all reappear in the characterization of the neurosciences themselves. So they cannot coherently be eliminated from our representations of ourselves: We must represent ourselves as beings who represent, as what Descartes might have termed *ens representans*.

Now of course the representations could be segregated from the body and regarded as the properties of a separate thing called a mind. That in a way is what Descartes appears to have believed in the early *Meditations*. But that raises all the difficulties of interactionism and leaves out all the questions of how bodily perturbations cross the boundaries between mind and body to cause representations in the mind, or how mental perturbations should cross in the reverse direction to move the body this way and that. And little by way of progress could be imagined, even though serious scientists, like the neurophysiologist Sir John Carew Eccles and the philosopher Sir Karl Popper, have brought considerable ingenuity to the demonstration that it would be possible for a disembodied mind to act on a body. For Eccles, of course, it is a scientific conjecture and as such there is little to do but see whether anything like this conjecture should prove experimentally sound.

But there is another and rather more plausible scientific position, one that may preserve the insights of neurophilosophy and really erase the sorts of boundaries and interactions an Eccles-type dualism would have to deal with. This, too, is a kind of scientific theory, and it is preemptive, since no one knows how to show it to be true. At best one can argue for its possibility. This theory I shall call representational materialism. It holds that when someone believes that P, for example, then he is in a sentential state that stands to P in much the same the way that an utterance of P stands to an inscription of P. It is the same proposition whether written or spoken or believed, whether it is made up of sound waves, layers of ink, or nervous tissue. As far as the mind-body problem goes, the view I am advancing is that the body is itself sententially structured. Perhaps, even probably, what is sententially structured is nervous tissue, which is perhaps all that neurophilosophy requires to vindicate its chief insight. All that changes is that the research program of the neurosciences is now modified as follows: The task of the neurosciences is to show how nervous tissue represents.

Representational materialism insists, in effect, that there are two kinds of matter in the universe, matter that is representational and matter that is not. It endorses a metaphysics that holds the world to be such that parts of it rise to represent itself, including, of course, the further fact that those parts not only represent the world but represent that they do so. Representational beings—ourselves and animals—are like openings in the darkness, like lights going on, illuminating the world and themselves at once. But having paused for that rhapsodic digression, let us sketch some of the main features of this sort of materialism.

In the first place, if it is true, it gives a natural explanation of certain widely discussed logical features of mental states—features that have been said to be the criteria of the mental—namely, the intentionality of mental states.

Let us restrict ourselves to beliefs, though the observations about to be made hold for states other than beliefs as well. Regarding beliefs, then, a number of things have been said. First, if a man, Tom, believes that P, a sentence in which S is its subject, then it will not follow that Tom believes P′ when P′ is the result of replacing S with some other term that means the same as it, or that refers to the same thing as it. Tom believes Clark Kent is a weakling. Now Clark Kent in fact is Superman, and Tom does not believe Superman is a weakling—indeed he believes that Superman is superhumanly strong. Now, ordinarily we can substitute names that stand for the same individual without altering the truth value of the sentences in which those substitutions are made. If Clark Kent is Superman, then if Clark Kent is a weakling, so is Superman. Or, if Superman is superhumanly strong, so is Clark Kent. But that rule does not hold for belief-sentences, as they are called. Clark Kent and Superman are one, but a man who believes that Superman is superhumanly strong can still believe Clark Kent a weakling. Such things happen all the time. It is the nature of belief that this should be possible. Oedipus believes Jocasta will make him an ideal wife, but he does not believe his own mother will make him an ideal wife, though Jocasta is, tragically, his own mother. The truth is often hidden from us and is such that if we knew it, we would have to change our beliefs, intentions, hopes, expectations, desires, and fears.

Now, if the propositions one believes were in fact sentential states of oneself, there would be a wholly natural explanation of these features of intentionality. Let us begin by considering written sentences, as the easiest examples for us to work with here. Consider first:

Clark Kent is a weakling,

and then:

Superman is a weakling.

The first thing to notice is that these two sentences are the same with the exception that the shapes *Clark Kent* occur in one and the shapes *Superman* occur in the other—and these are very different shapes. If the first sentence contained one sentential shape and the other a different one, then clearly there would be no guarantee that a person who had a sentential shape of the first sort would ipso facto have a sentential shape of the second sort. He *might*. But he might not. The greater likelihood would be that he would have a sentential state represented by the first sentence, and a sentential state represented by

Superman is not a weakling,

if, among his sentential states, there are any that have Superman as subject. But then, if there are such states, the likelihood is that the person in question has never really connected Clark Kent with Superman. Had he done so, it is almost certain the two sample sentences would not figure in him as a representation of the world.

There is a second consideration regarding intentionality. Pretty much any normal member of our culture has some beliefs about Superman—that he is a good person, that he is sweet on Lois Lane, that he wears a cape, has an *S* blazoned on his jersey, and flies like a bird. And, of course, that he and Clark Kent are one and the same.

We have these beliefs even though there is no such being as Superman or, for that matter, Clark Kent. So it does not follow from the fact that we have these beliefs that there exists such a person. And there is a great difference between sentences like

Jane believes that Superman is kind,

and

Jane noticed that Superman was kind.

The first sentence can be true even if Superman does not exist, whereas the second sentence is false if Superman does not exist. You can only notice what is there, but you can believe in anything at all. And again there is an analogy to written sentences. I can write *Superman* without Superman having to exist. And for the same sorts of reasons, you can have *Superman* written or inscribed in your representational system whether such a person exists or not. If we think of what we believe as a kind of writing in the soul—or, to be serious, as a kind of neurological script—then we can understand certain logical truths regarding intentionality. The first is that it applies only to representations, hence to things that can be true or false, containing components that refer or fail to refer, that designate or fail to designate, that correspond or fail to correspond. And the second thing is that it applies to material objects—to layers of ink, or incisions in wax, or to patterns of light or to sets of sound waves or—we conjecture—to neural states of *ens representans*. It may be true that intentionality is the mark of the mental—but only because the mental is in the first instance representational and in the second instance material.

The materialist premise of intentionality has, I think, very largely escaped philosophers because they have studied intentionality in abstraction from the question of what sort of reality sentences have. Here we have much the same oversight that has infected neurophilosophy and made it so vulnerable to self-refutation: Neurophilosophy regards science, if it regards it at all, as though it were not real, did not take place in the world, were logically weightless.

But if science is itself a natural process, something performed by flesh-and-blood persons, then if those scientists represent, representations must be states of flesh-and-blood beings, and representationalist materialism gives us at least the beginnings of a good theory of how minds can be states of bodies.

It is, to be sure, only a beginning. And perhaps we have to devote some thought to the problem of identity that is raised when we say that a belief is a sentential state of an *ens representans*. Is this, for example, the "is" of strict identity? Well, let us reflect. Consider any sentence you choose:

> Clark Kent is a weakling,

say. What is the relationship between that sentence and the particles left on the paper by the impact of typewriter keys? Is that strict identity, or what? Do we have two things or one? My sense is that if we cannot answer the question for written sentences, we are hardly likely to be able to answer it for neurosentences, where our ignorance is so profound.

The beginning of an answer is as old as metaphysics: We have here matter and form. And the same form may be materialized in various ways: in layers of ink, in clusters of sound waves, in neural tissues, and the like. These kinds of matter are clearly different from one another, with different physics and distinct chemistry. But the form is identical, one might say, however it is written and in whatever medium. Indeed, if one thought of the mind as the form of the body, one would have a theory as old as Aristotle's and as fresh as Wittgenstein's thesis that in the human body we have the best picture we could have of the human mind. If it is the same form, however, that is embodied in ink, sound, and neural tissue, it is clear that we are dealing with more than shape, for in an obvious respect, writing and speech have different shapes, and both are different from whatever shape neural tissue must have to be a token of the same sentence as we write or speak. Moreover, the same sentence may have different shapes even when written: as in,

Clark Kent is a weakling,

and its misspelling,

Klark Cent is a weakling,

and in,

CLARK KENT IS A WEAKLING,

as well as in,

Clark Kent is a weakling

and in,

*Clark Kent is a weakling*

—not to speak of the same sentence spoken by a man, a woman, a child, a man speaking in falsetto, and any number of different accents and dialects and with speech impediments of every order. If written and spoken sentences may vary, it is hardly to be expected that neural transcriptions should be invariant from person to person. Learning to read the nervous system, accordingly, will have to be as complex as learning to read the handwritings of very different persons, mastering different typefaces, learning to hear the same sentence spoken in the countless different voices.

In any case, the laws of neurophysiology, if these speculations are sound, will be like the laws of writing or of speech. The important insight of representationalist materialism is that we are built on the principles of texts, of words made flesh, and that a complex trade-off must be made between what a sentence means in the text of one's life and what it means as such. And the former is a function, one might say, of how the texts of our lives have been written.

# 37

# *Representational Beings*

IN THE PENAL COLONY, Kafka describes a curious and horrifying punitive practice in which the convicted criminal has inscribed in his flesh the nature of his crime, like a barbaric tattoo. It is an odd coincidence that the criminal is *sentenced* to be in a sentential state, written on by needles and in blood, which, if he survives, perhaps scars to be like the Scarlet Letter writ large. Such a marked person—like those savages one used to see illustrated in adventure books, whose entire bodies were covered with what were doubtless symbols—is only representational in an external way, for the representations with which he is covered do not penetrate his essence. But this would be true even if the inscription were not merely on the skin, hence outside, but somehow inside, his internal organs somehow bearing the stigma of his crime. Some primitive peoples believe in divination through the examination of the liver, and it might be argued that those livers that bear news of the future are in sentential states the diviner has learned to read. But even if this were true of our livers as well, this would not make us representational beings—*ens representans*—unless those representations, as just said, penetrated our essence. And the question then is how to turn that expression into something philosophically acceptable.

In the *Theaetetus,* Socrates offered a model of the mind as a piece of wax on which the world makes its various marks. If the marks are clean, the wax being pure, we have clear images, whereas if it is dirty, or impure, the images themselves are blurred. Locke, too, thought of the mind as a kind of tablet on which experience inscribes representations that correspond to it—Locke insisted the tablet was blank in order to give metaphoric emphasis to the thought that we know nothing until we are acted on by the world, arriving here with no innate or preconceived ideas. These models, primitive as they are, would give us a model of ourselves as representational beings and even as sentential beings if the "impressions" were in the form of propositions. Socrates thought they must be images, being taken in by the metaphor, one supposes, of a seal leaving an imprint in sealing wax and not asking how adequate from the perspective of mental representation a set of pictures would be. Locke specifically thought of writing, but representations in his case were "ideas" and hence, one feels, images or pictorial representations. And in his case too the question arises as to how adequate for mental life as we know it—for "human understanding" as he sought to characterize it—ideas would be. The thoughts that sentences must be the basic representation and that we are linguistic entities come late to philosophical awareness, and it is part of what sets our own century apart from the rich but inadequate history of speculation on the content of the mind.

Still, it would not mean much that representations were sentential if all that was involved was the registration on a kind of screen of sentential shapes. One could imagine, with no great difficulty, the dashboard of an automobile that transmitted sentential signals— "Seat belts are unfastened"; "The door is unlocked"; "Check the gas tank"; "Don't drive while drunk" (the car being equipped with sensors that signal an alarm when the driver's breath is boozy). The displays could all be sentential without our wanting to say that the car was a sentential being, or even a representational being, though that might be hasty.

Let us just consider an ordinary gasoline gauge, assumed to be in working order. When the tank is empty, it reads "empty," whether through a red light, or a needle pointing to *E,* or the word *Empty* flashing or the word *empty* as a kind of noise, like an alarm, repeating itself until the tank is filled. The system is so designed that the gauge "says" empty only when the tank really is empty, so it corresponds to what makes the signal true, the gauge being accurate, in fact, and in working order only when the representation is caused to go on when, and only when, it *is* true. Then this comes pretty close to a standard model of knowledge: We have knowledge when, and only when, our representations are made true by what causes us to have them. Do we want to say that the gauge "knows" that the tank is empty, or that we have a model cognitive system in the tank and the gauge where the one registers changes in the other? Does the thermometer know the internal temperature of the patient? Does the sphygmomanometer know the intensity of the pulse beat? One might say no, on the grounds that these instruments are not conscious of their readings, but perhaps just having those readings might be a kind of consciousness of the state of whatever it is that they register—the amount of fluid, the body temperature, the intensity of a pulse. Well, then, the instruments are not conscious of being conscious—they are not self-conscious: But we ourselves may not in this sense be conscious of all our representations, taking in, as perceptual instruments, vastly more of what takes place in the world than ever comes to conscious attention. How are we to draw the line, if indeed we are to draw it at all, between ourselves and these mechanisms? Why are they not *ens representans* if we are? And the answer is that more has to take place than the passive representations of external stimuli, even if like the gasoline gauge, we are "wired up" to register changes in the external world, or the world to which we are attached by our sensory apparatus. The representation must modify the *ens representans* in some way other than that which consists simply in having the representation. A pattern of light modifies a piece of sensitized film, which bears its imprint forever. But nothing else happens. *We* are not merely a *camera obscura,* with the play of light on our inner surfaces explained by the play of shapes and shadows coming through the aperture of the senses. We are not like a wind organ, piping tones as the breezes play on the keyboard of the senses. But we *are* partly like that, or the problem would not be quite so vexing.

The answer, I believe, is that we are a number of interrelated such systems, and the systems are exactly those postulated by folk psychology.

In the first place, we really do represent states of the world, ourselves included, in the sense that our beliefs themselves are caused by what makes them true. We believe we are hungry when we feel stomach pangs, we believe we are soaked when our skin feels wet, we believe the sun is shining when we see that unmistakable brightness through the window. Of course illusion is possible in all these cases. There is the power of autosuggestion. There are honest mistakes, as when the director next door has all his lights on at two in the morning, simulating sun, making a movie in his backyard. As a perceptual system, these mistakes are to be expected: The belief system is activated by look-alikes, much as a turnstile may be activated by a slug or the telephone ring when the lines are struck by lightning. At certain distances the eye does not discriminate silver from oyster shell or ropes from snakes. And, indeed, it is due in part to this that intentionality is possible: There is a representation that is not caused by what it is of, mainly because the representation is connected with some system of representations, which cause the subject to believe it is silver when it is mother-of-pearl (or, if a pessimist, mother-of-pearl when it is silver).

Moreover, there are certain innate or acquired propensities to do something when we have a certain belief: to eat when we are hungry or believe we are; to dry off when we are wet or believe we are; to get up when we see the sun, even if that belief is wrong and we wonder why, if it is high morning, we still feel so sleepy. If the automobile were so connected to signals in the world that when the tank was empty, the motor would stall at the first service station—or even better, if the car would turn into the first service station, other sensors "informing" it that it was safe to do so—it would begin to resemble us in consequence of its complexity, with representations translated into actions. And we might even begin to think of ourselves on the model of such *auto* mobiles rather than pieces of wax or photoreceptive tablets or whatever. We might say that just as the car will not turn right until the "coast is clear," so we act in such a way as to ensure that we will act again, governed by considerations of self-preservation.

There really is no special need to extend these images. Beliefs are representations ordinarily only in systems of memories and beliefs that process incoming stimuli in such a way as to cause the belief that is consistent with those memories (themselves representations) and those other beliefs that are in part representations of representation, which is to say: interpretations. Whole continents of representation are activated by the simplest signal—a buzz, a scratch, a shape or color, or an odor. To perceive is ipso facto to interpret what we perceive, and the wax tablet of Socrates is finally too inert to accommodate this constantly shifting network of representations. A better metaphor would be a spider's web, where perturbation anywhere sets the spider scuttling toward its source. The point is, however, not to look for a metaphor, or to say that the best metaphor is that the mind is a text that is constantly being rewritten and revised as experience after experience, perturbation after perturbation, is induced by the world upon us.

Let us now become somewhat schematic. In the characterization just sketched of representational entities like ourselves, four main kinds of episodes may be distinguished, depending on whether representational states are causes or effects or both or neither. Here is an array of the four sorts of episodes:

| | CAUSE | EFFECT |
|---|---|---|
| 1. | R | R |
| 2. | R̸ | R |
| 3. | R | R̸ |
| 4. | R̸ | R̸ |

An R means that that the cause or effect is a representational state. An R with a stroke through it (R̸) means that the state is not relevantly representational. An episode of type 4 may be illustrated by the usual kinds of causal episodes discussed by philosophers—a billiard ball moving when concussed by another, a glass pane breaking when struck by a rock, a match bursting into flame when scratched. A good example of a type 3 episode is when someone performs some action, moving an arm, say, because he wants to signal someone, where his arm movements somehow satisfy his representation. A good example of case 2 is any ordinary cognitive transaction, someone believing that it is raining out because it really is raining out. Type 2 episodes figure prominently in the wax-tablet sort of metaphor that for centuries dominated our models of the mind and of human understanding generally. And a good example of type 1 episodes is someone believing something because he believes something else. Perhaps he believes that sounds he hears are caused by rainfall and so believes that it is raining. Or he believes that Socrates is mortal because he believes that all men are, and Socrates is after all a man.

The problem we have been dealing with in this section is due to the preeminence in the philosophical tradition of episodes of kind 2, where we are depicted as passive recipients of representations from without. As if we really were wax tablets or *camerae obscurae* or photographic plates. That gives rise to the centrality of epistemology in the philosophical picture of human beings, where the agonizing question is how we know whether any of our representations answer to external causes, and where we are obliged to answer the questions from within—that is, on the basis of sets of representations. Of course, that exercise would be impossible if there were not episodes of type 1, episodes of ratiocination, where we infer certain things on the basis of certain others, leading to the model of human beings as rational or, latterly, as computational, and where our nearest of kin is the computational device par excellence, the high-speed digital computer. Put together, type 1 and 2 episodes give us computational processes and input devices, in that order.

But with episodes of type 3, we enter the world: It is the modality of action, where we modify the world to conform to our representations of it if we can. One may construe this as output, to complete the persuasive metaphor of ourselves as computers, granting that the output in our case involving the movement of limbs and the execution of tasks of varying degrees of complexity makes us rather more like the robot than the mere computer, whose characteristic output is a display or a printout. What we have to add to this picture is, first, that any characteristic episode involves all three of these episodes, and that there are many, many such compound episodes at every instant of life. And secondly our "output"—our actions—modify our representations in a process of learning as we go. Having inferred that it is raining, we rise to shut the window and seeing the bright moon remember that we had neglected to turn the sprinkling system off before retiring. And we leave the window open and go out to turn the necessary valves. And life goes on and on.

And as it does go on, everything necessary thereunto goes on as well: The blood circulates, metabolism occurs, the brain is swept by showers of electrical discharges, muscles flex, neurons fire, the bladder distends; countless episodes of type 4 transpire at every instant. Some of these can effect the life of representation: If the blood-sugar level falls, representations are blocked. If coma supervenes, life goes on without any episodes of types 1, 2, and 3 to speak of. Of immediate interest to us is the fact that neurophilosophy wants to advance the thought that there are only episodes of type 4. And in a sense they are right. Representations are after all materially embodied. So whenever there are episodes of types 1, 2, and 3, there are episodes of type 4. It is just that the reverse is not true: Not every bodily state is a representatonal state. So nothing happens in an *ens representans* without there being a type 4 episode.

But does that mean that the entire history of a human being can be mapped onto type 4 episodes, and written simply in terms that require no reference to representation? In the *Monadology,* Leibniz asked us to imagine a machine so constructed that it could "think, feel, and have perception." Then, he says, let us have the machine enlarged "and yet preserving the same proportions, so that we might enter it as into a mill. And this granted, we should only find on visiting it, pieces which push against one another, but never anything by which to explain a perception." Well, we are in fact such machines, and because nothing happens that is not characterizable without reference to representations, we can be entered and our entire operations given in terms of "pieces pushing against one another." And of course that will be true. But it would be like entering a text that we do not know how to read. We can identify the various characters. We can describe the frequency with which character goes with character. We can be, like Searle, in a Chinese room. And we may not even know they are characters or that what we have is a text. What we then have to do is to learn to read, however this is done. My ambition, as projected in these pages, is that we should enter the mill that is another person and learn to read the text of his mind. In one sense, we would know immeasurably more about ourselves if we could do that. In another, I think, we would know very little about one another beyond what we do know.

In his stupendous biography of Flaubert, Sartre used the Leibnizian image of entering a mill. Perhaps he came to know as much about Flaubert as anyone, Flaubert himself included. But the knowledge came from letters, the recollections of others, from books, and conversations and speculations on human psychology. Perhaps it would enhance the biographer's art were he able to enter the mill of other persons in the more precise Leibnizian way, ferreting out secrets, suppressed memories, and unconscious feelings. Still, what would be disinterred in this manner would be but the kind of things we know from conversations, letters, writings, and the recollections of others. The inside and the outside are one.

# 38

## Causal Analysis

THERE EXISTS NO SATISFACTORY ANALYSIS of the concept of causality in the philosophical literature, and it is possible to argue that it really is among the primitive concepts. Hume implicitly denied it primitivity by trying to analyze it into other notions, such as conjunction, and it might be prudent to sketch his thought at this point. What Hume insisted on was that there is no experience of causation as such, but that what we call causality is, rather, certain relationships between experiences. For example, when we believe A causes B, we are talking about the experiences of A and of B, and we are saying that these exemplify types of experience—the A-like and the B-like—which have been experienced together sufficiently often that the mind anticipates the B-like when the A-like is experienced—fire is so experienced that one anticipates smoke. It is this movement of the mind, this stretching forward, so to speak, toward B, that explains, in Hume's theory of experience, the vague notion of a connection in nature. Because we have, he argued, experienced the A-like and the B-like with great frequency, or with enough frequency, a certain habit or propensity has been instilled, which the mind then projects outward and reads as if it were a propensity in the world. But all there is, so far as the content of experience is concerned, is the repeated conjunction of the A-like and the B-like. But repetition (one is hesitant to say "causes") causes the conjunction to be read as a connection.

In Hume's view, then, the concept of causation dissolves into our evidence for it: "A causes B" summarizes a body of conjoined experiences, and the conjunctions would then support an inference from B to A on any given occasion. It becomes exceedingly difficult to see what there is in Hume's analysis of causation that differs from the concept of induction. And this is especially so when we subtract the psychological component of habit and propensity and mental disposition that Hume enjoyed supposing was consistently projected outward and read back as a kind of necessary ligature. All there is to the concept when this is abstracted is the fact of constant conjunction. To be sure, there would usually be a presumption of temporal order—causes do not succeed their effects—but the important point is that the component of connection is replaced with that of conjunction. Or: "Connection" is just shorthand for constant conjunction. It then becomes a problem how many conjunctions constitute grounds for a connection—and then a problem of what we *mean* by a connection other than repeated conjunctions. As a centerpiece of his critical philosophy, Kant argued that causality is not derived from experience—hence there is, just as Hume insisted, no experience of causality. What there is, rather, is a *form* of experience— things are experienced as connected—and the concept of causality is part of the a priori fabric of the mind. Hume's notion of habit is thus replaced with Kant's notion of a form—but then Kant did not break the concept of connection down any further, so that for all philosophical purposes, it remains a primitive notion.

Perhaps what we can derive from Kant is the thought that we do not experience the world as a kind of stream of particulars, a mosaic of As and Bs. Just to be an experience is to be connected: Conjunctions, then, are those experiences that, even when experienced as connected, are not connected as such. Hume's approach sought to explain how we build up a single causal belief—that the A-like and the B-like are related as cause to effect. And he would necessarily have difficulty in accounting for single causal episodes, episodes in which A causes B but the A-like and the B-like have on no other occasion been experienced as conjoined. Kant does not find it necessary to build up our causal beliefs. We *begin* with them, as it were, but we may find that they have to be dismantled when the evidence goes against them. In a way, the difference between Hume and Kant is like the difference between Aristotle and Galileo (or Newton) on the topic of motion. For Aristotle the deep problem of physics was explaining motion. For Galileo and Newton, bodies are in motion already: It is only changes in velocity that require explanation. For Kant the world is experienced as a causal fabric. For Hume, it is not experienced that way at all—causal beliefs have to be worked for.

Kant's analysis works rather well with the fact of innate disposition in humans and animals, certain things neonates do and avoid that they did not learn to do or to avoid. Over time we learn a great deal, but the structures within which learning takes place may be innate, perhaps must be innate. But then a combined Hume-Kant position would be that there are inborn propensities in humans and animals and learning, then, becomes a matter of habituation. But Hume might then add that still, all there is to the notion of connection is that the mind should anticipate certain things, other things being given—and all causation is is a name for this psychological truth.

But now consider episodes of type 4, as discussed in the last section—billiard balls moving on concussion, glass breaking when struck with sufficient force by objects sufficiently hard, matches igniting when scratched on surfaces sufficiently dry, and the like. Whatever we may come into the world with so far as expectations are concerned, it will hardly have to do with objects invented too recently to have affected our genetic equipment. Hume, who of course had no clear knowledge of evolution, puts the matter differently: His point is that until we experience shattering, glass as such conveys no notion of its brittleness. A savage looking at a match would see only a stick with a painted head, and it would come as a complete surprise, almost a wonderwork, were it to burst into flame upon scratching. Things, especially manufactured things, do not wear their causal powers on their faces. And only experience tells us what those causal powers are. No one would know, looking at an aspirin, that it would clear headache. No one smelling oil of clove would know it eases toothache. Or that foxglove is good for certain forms of heart disease. Or quinine for fever. And Kant, of course, would concur: We do not come with our causal beliefs as part of our a priori equipment, only the belief in causality. And this explains our believing that striking causes flame, hitting causes breakage, concussion causes movement. We spontaneously experience the world as a rational whole, where things happen because other things happen, where something like the Principle of Sufficient Reason governs experience. Like Hume, however, Kant saw causality as a feature of experience. He was reluctant, for metaphysical reasons, to speculate whether there were causes in the world in itself, apart from our experience of it. But then it is extremely difficult to see what content such a speculation could have, especially since all that he says about causation is worked out with reference to the structure of experience. Perhaps, then, we could not think of the world as other than causally ordered, just because *that* is the structure of thought. But whether it is causally ordered apart from the way we think about it is almost a meaningless question.

On the other hand, with Kant as with Hume, something is left out of the picture. The mind itself must, objectively, incorporate causal features in that we really do, without having learned to, expect certain things, other things being given. If there is an internal propensity in the mind, which explains our acquisition of causal beliefs, why are there not similarly internal propensities in the world, explaining why it supports our causal beliefs? Just to build up their theory of causality, Kant and Hume, though speaking of experience, have to go outside experience—for we never, as it were, catch causality in the act. Perhaps all we mean by causality here is that something happens rather than something else. It does so because the mind is simply made the way it is made. And so it is with the rest of the world: It works the way it does work because *it* is so made. No one need have made it this way. There need not be some prior plan or design as thinkers in the eighteenth century felt it was necessary to postulate. What made Darwin's theory of natural selection so intellectually thrilling was that it showed how the world could have got the way it is without having been made to be that way by anterior design. Still, Darwin needed to appeal to such basic transformations as nutrition and generation. And organisms are so made that certain things will nourish them, and so made again that they reproduce.

But having said this much in the direction of a kind of causal realism, it remains true that what has been said applies most obviously to type-4 causal episodes. It is also true that we represent because we are made a certain way, and that representations can be causes or effects—or both—because of the way representational beings are made. But there are factors other than causation that come into play in episodes of types 1, 2, and 3, and it is a beginning in our understanding of how we, as representational beings, are related to the world and to one another to draw attention to these further factors.

Let us once more think of Hume. Hume's concern was with what corresponds, in experience, to our knowledge of causality, and his answer was that it is to be found in repeated associations of representations, or ideas. We experience the first billiard ball hit the second, and we then experience the second move. This associated pair of experiences, repeated often enough, gives rise to an expectation. But any single causal episode is simply a pair of representations, which happen to come into experience sequentially, and which happen to be reinforced by similar sequences in numbers sufficiently large to cause the habit of expectation. It is important to stress that Hume's account bypasses the problem of diverse substances. For Hume it is a matter of philosophical indifference that the paired events experienced should belong to different substances. So for Hume a mental event might be believed to cause a physical event if they are, first, experienced sequentially and then enough repetitions of the sequence occur that a habit of expectation be built up. The issue of "how possibly?" drops from sight. Hume might ask what we really know about billiard balls except the fact that when one moves against the other, the other moves. What do we really know about matches except that when they are struck, they burst into flame?

What more is there, really, to know? So what difference would it make if the paired events occurred in distinct substances? The causal beliefs in the best of cases involve purely external relationships between events. The world just happens to be one way rather than another, and our causal beliefs just follow the drifts of happenstance.

One cannot admire Hume too extravagantly for this brilliant account. By grounding the entire causal concept in causal experience, he isolated a whole complex of metaphysical anxieties, and then allowed them to wither away. By the time philosophers began to examine his views critically, the metaphysical anxieties were long gone; no one worried any longer about different substances. Determining whether one thing caused another became more or less the problem of induction, and the analysis of causation thus turned into the analysis of scientific method, the method, specifically, of holding certain variables constant and allowing others to change, in order to see which were the independent variables, these then being treated as causes. A variable gets to be the cause when changes in another variable are or can be tracked to changes in it, everything else being held constant. And of course with this shift to scientific method, the psychological premises of Hume's account themselves fade away. We no longer speak of habit. Expectation is no longer a form of psychological anticipation. There is simply "rational anticipation," that is, what one might be justified in expecting, given the evidence there is. Causality dissolves into covariation. And philosophers like Russell went so far as to suggest that causality is an outmoded concept and certainly a prescientific if not an unscientific one. Science has only to do with covariations, and the so called "necessity" that Hume had sought to explain through habit perhaps instead is to be explained through the mathematical fact that relations of covariation are represented in equations. The necessity becomes a kind of mathematical necessity. To say that A causes B on this account is in effect to say that the relationships of variation between A and B can be represented with a differential equation.

Now it is possible that we can learn to live with such an analysis of causality in dealing with the natural world, the world in which changes in sets of objects are correlated with changes in other sets of objects. Our relationship to nature is such that perhaps this is all the connection that we can grasp, an external connection. The deep ties and ligatures escape us, and even if we had access to them, it is difficult to see that we could proceed any differently than we in fact do—notice correlated changes, build up bodies of rational expectations, seek mathematical representation, make calculations. In the period before Hume, philosophers wanted something more. They really did want a kind of necessity, which Hume sought to explain away with reference to habit. They wanted causes to entail effects the way premises entailed conclusions in deductive arguments, or the way in which theorems are entailed by axioms in deductive systems. They wanted the world to be rational, as if a logical system. And Hume wanted to say that you cannot deduce effects from causes. Only experience will tell what happens when what else happens. There are no internal logical relationships. The world is not a rational system but a mosaic of repeated patterns. We notice. We do not deduce.

But can this be the same with us? Do we not, just being us, have an internal understanding? Hume was exceedingly ironic on the thought that in our own case we caught causality on the wing. Why, he wanted to know, do our arms go up when we raise them, though other parts of our bodies just do not obey the mandates of the will? His answer was that we do not know. All we know is that things happen as they do happen. It is as mysterious, if it helps even to say that, as anything in nature. Hume seems to me to be absolutely correct in this argument. Philosophers in the next century, Schopenhauer, especially, insisted that while all we know of the world is our representations of it, of ourselves we have another kind of knowledge, altogether nonrepresentational. For him, we are the only examples we have of things in themselves—we *are* a *Ding an sich*—and in our own case we have immediate access to will. Will is the necessary dynamic force missing from the concept of causation construed, as Hume did, in terms of externally connected representations. But the problem remains why our arms move when we will them to move, unless we are paralyzed, and why some but not all persons can wiggle their ears when they will them to wiggle, and why nobody can break down carbohydrates as a matter of will.

Nevertheless, there remains, as I have said, something left over when we subtract the factor of causality from the first three sorts of causal episode, which Hume missed. He missed it because he insufficiently appreciated the structures of representation and the facts of intentionality.

# 39

# *Mental Causation*

CAUSE AND EFFECT MAY NOT, just as Hume argued, be logically connected but only externally conjoined. But let us consider the case where someone believes P because he believes Q. He believes someone is happy because he believes that Jones is happy, and so he believes it false that everyone is unhappy. He is a logical person and so puts his beliefs together in this way, and it would altogether misrepresent the structure of his thought to say that these various beliefs just happen to be associated in his mind. Or that he has come as a matter of habit to expect it false that everyone is unhappy because he believes it true that someone is happy, or that he simply has associated "someone is happy" with "Jones is happy." He has certain beliefs because he has certain other beliefs, but the beliefs really are internally related through their contents. "Someone is happy" *follows* from "Jones is happy" by what is called natural deduction, and by the same sort of consideration, "Nobody is happy" is false if "Someone is happy" is true. One's beliefs form a logical system, or can, and hence in addition to whatever may relate them in terms of causation, there is the further fact that they are logically related. If the person here is a logical person, these logical relationships help to define him as such. Logic, in his case, has a psychological reality. He has been programmed, perhaps is initially so wired up, that he believes *something* is F when he believes that A is F. He does not just associate them. He has deduced the one from the other. They really are connected in the way the universe at large may not be, or cannot be known to be connected. More is here than simple conjunction of mental states.

Pretty much all that the classical empiricists—or for that matter modern psychologists—allowed by way of mental structure was the association of ideas. Since association really is an external matter— the ideas associated need have nothing to do with one another, as the classical experiments on salivating dogs by Pavlov demonstrated—one's representations of the world build up brick by brick, as it were. Even in the psychology of language, the most by way of structure empiricism would allow was the association of a sign with its meaning—*dog* with dog—where almost by definition the sign had nothing really to do with its designation, inasmuch as *chien* and *Hund* are associated by other conventions to the selfsame animal, and language is tied to the world loosely and as a matter of convention.

But when we have thoughts, we have the transformation of mental states into one another. A conclusion is not *associated* with a pair or set of premises—it is reached by transformation rules on those premises. Of course there is mental association. And of course there is creativity—conclusions being reached by leaps. Even so, transformation of state into state characterizes most of human and, I would say, animal reasoning. Aristotle thought that logic specifies psychology, and there is a sense in which he remains right, even if it is also true that the validity of logical formulas is not underwritten by psychology. What logic does, whatever the grounds of its validity, is to describe the way the mind functions when it functions validly. And to function validly is to move from state to state in such a way as to preserve truth. This transpires, of course, below the threshold of consciousness, and in beings who may never have *learned* logic. In a somewhat similar way speakers conform to the principles of a grammar they may never have explicitly learned. It has, as we saw, become a powerful metaphor for mental process that it is computational—but whether or not this is true, computation itself involves transformation of state into state. When someone believes there are four persons in the yard on the basis of seeing two pairs of persons there, he has not associated four with a pair of pairs: He has computed it.

We are entering here upon vast, unexplored, and little understood territory. But enough may have been said to suggest that in causal episodes involving representations, the mind moves on two tracks at once—a logical track and a causal track. In a sense, speaking physiologically, all there is is one state and then another, however, states themselves are to be characterized. But these states are structured, if my argument is sound, and the process from state to state is to be explained through structural transformations. If the transformation is a logical transformation, as in any instance of reasoning, the states at either end must be sentential—for logical transformations are transformations of sentences into sentences. It is this that enables truth to be preserved, for only sentences, after all, bear truth values.

It is this second track that is missing from Hume's account of the mind. We are, it must be conceded, owners of richer mental lives than those involved in obvious ratiocination or even mental association. In dreams there are some very complex transformations from unconscious states to conscious ones. In these cases, and in many, many others, rules of transformation—which must be identified along with whatever makes the succession of states causally possible—connect state with state. Just think of what is involved in understanding a simple narrative, which any normal human child is capable of. Think of what is involved in understanding even a simple poem. There are structures and structures of thought other than rational thinking. The mind has a textual density as rich as the texts we learn to master in literature. The principles of these texts are scarcely understood by philosophers or psychologists. But they take us very far indeed from the crude model of association.

But as much may be said of the other two cases of causal episodes involving representational states as causes or effects. Consider the case of belief. Let us say that a certain sound causes us to believe that it is raining outside. Why that sound and not some other? All that Hume allows is the external relationship between cause and effect. Why don't we believe it is raining when we taste peanut butter? Or touch silk? The answer, in part, is that beliefs are true or false, and that when we have a belief that amounts to knowledge, not only is the belief caused by something, but what causes it is also what makes it true. There is a semantical as well as a causal relationship between representational states and the world, including, as part of the world, ourselves when the beliefs are about us. And this semantical relationship is what is missing again from Hume's account. We have the concept of knowledge because we need there to be not simply representations but true ones, and not only true ones but those that are true because of the way the world causes us to have those representations in the first instance.

Beyond that, there is the case of action, where a representation causes something to take place. I want to move my arm and my arm moves. If all we had were external relationships between cause and effect, it would be perfectly imaginable that wanting my arm to move would cause my eye to close. And if this happens frequently enough, a habit of expectation arises, and so on. But this is not the way it really works. We count a causal episode an action only when the effect not merely is caused by the representation, but makes the representation true. In action, we modify the world to conform to our representations. In knowledge the world modifies our representations to conform to it.

Folk psychology explains our conduct with reference to inference, knowledge, and action. All of these involve us as held together within ourselves by logical relations, and held together with the world by means of semantical relations. The materialist is right, in that unless representations were embodied, perhaps even neurally embodied, making the neurophilosopher right, representations would and could make nothing happen. Causality holds between material states. But the idealist is right as well: If no representations were embodied, we would be mere physical systems. It is the metaphysical relationship between matter and representation, and then the causal relationships through which representations are effective, that a representationalist materialism of the sort I have been advancing here must work out. But once there are representations, a factor or set of factors enters to complicate the materialist position. Truth becomes, as it were, a causal force (so, of course, does falsity). The way we represent the world becomes a factor in the way the world is.

Evolutionary theorists have told us with great power and imagination how minute advantages of color and metabolism, of size and dexterity, explain why one species survives and another perishes. It is curious that the power to represent has played so little role in evolutionary explanation, but it must have given certain animals some degree of adaptational advantage. Through their representations, moreover, they began to change the conditions of survival better to suit themselves. If the representations were consistently false, it would hardly be expected they could have survived. Nietzsche once said that evolutionary success is no criterion of truth, but that itself is open to question. Why should not the power to form true representations have been a factor in the emergence of animals in whom representation is as great a mechanism of survival as metabolism or protective coloration?

Still, the minimally representational beings that infer, know, and act may be very far down the evolutionary scale. It is clear enough that the line that separates us from the nearer animals is not that we represent and they do not. To understand human nature is minimally to understand us as representational beings—*ens representans,* as said. But more than that must be understood to explain the differences between animals and ourselves.

# 40

## The Realm of Spirit

IT HAS SOMETIMES BEEN MAINTAINED that human beings are so distinct from the rest of nature that we are not subject to the ordinary approaches of the natural sciences, but require, instead, a cognitive address of a quite distinctive order. Sometimes it is said, for example, that the natural sciences *explain* phenomena, meaning, by and large, that they are brought under causal laws. With human beings, on the other hand, there are no causal laws and hence no explanations. Instead there is a kind of *understanding* available: We understand one another in our uniqueness. There is, according to such a view, a deep distinction between explanation and understanding—between (since the theorists in question have mainly written in German) *Erklären* and *Verstehen*. And there is a corresponding difference between what are referred to as the natural sciences and the *human* sciences, or, once again using the German labels, between the *Naturwissenschaften* and the *Geisteswissenschaften*. *Verstehen* is a procedure by which we internalize somehow the representations of those whose conduct we wish to comprehend. Sometimes this is thought of as an act of interpretation.

The distinction in question has often been buttressed with some exceedingly vague arguments. Sometimes, for example, its defenders speak of the uniqueness of human occurrences, as over and against the regularities of nature. But nature is filled with irregularities and uniqueness. Even with supercomputers, it has been found impossible to determine the orbit of Pluto. After all, there is only one universe, without our needing other than the methods of the natural sciences to speak of its beginning and its end. And beyond that there are enormous regularities in human behavior. Nothing in a way could be more predictable than the way human beings behave toward one another. The possibility of any social existence is predicated on just this. Human lives vary very little from person to person, and while there are certainly exceptions, there is a certain folk wisdom that speaks of phases through which children go, of how men and women in love can be expected to do certain almost standard things, and how we do one thing when we are young and another when we are mature. The seven ages of man—with, to be sure, some modest deviations—are lived through by those who live long enough.

Sometimes, too, it has been argued that being covered by causal laws is out of the question because it is inconsistent with human freedom. But, again, whatever freedom is or means, if we in fact are free, this is perfectly consistent with there being causal explanations of human behavior. If we say, for example, that men and women do as they do because they want what they want and believe what they believe, there is little reason to insist that the "because" is anything different from the "because" of causal explanation: We are caused to behave as we do by our beliefs and wants and, of course, the things we care about. Various clever arguments have been advanced that beliefs cannot be causes of the actions they account for, but for present purposes they can be ignored. The main reason for ignoring them is that the concept of cause itself remains so underanalyzed that it is not very clear what we are saying when we deny causation to beliefs and wants. For certainly it is true that everything else being supposed constant, individuals with the same beliefs and wants and cares will act in much the same way. It may be argued that everything is really very seldom constant, but that holds for nature as well. The carefully controlled environment of the scientific laboratory does not reproduce the chancy fabric of nature—but human beings in laboratory conditions show some remarkable regularities in their responses.

This being said, it seems to me that there also really is something to be said for the distinction. There is, to begin with, the epistemic fact that in order to explain human conduct, we have to take into consideration the way humans represent the world, themselves included, so that what we are is very often inseparable from what we believe we are. A woman who believes women really are inferior to men is going to be a very different woman, in consequence of this belief, from a woman who believes herself the equal of men or their superior. If we are representational beings, then what we are is in large measure how we represent. Representations form systems. They hang together in ways that entail that two persons with a belief in common but everything else different do not even have that common belief. Beliefs occur in systems, then, as sentences occur in texts. And it is not at all difficult to imagine graphically indiscernable sentences which mean very different things because they occur in essentially different texts. To understand a person's conduct is accordingly to identify the representations that explain the conduct, and then to interpret this against the dense background of beliefs that compose his picture of the world. Explanation in the case of human behavior may be—in fact I believe it is—just causal explanation. But the identification of the causes requires some separate operation, call it understanding if you will, which consists more or less in identifying the point of view of the agent in question. A point of view is something that causes, other than representational causes, cannot be said to have. So perhaps the distinction we want is between the natural and the representational sciences, the latter being those sciences that deal with representations as causes and effects and that seek the causal laws of representation. One difference, certainly, between the representational sciences and the rest is that they deal with truth, falsity, signification, and entailment *as part* of what they deal with. All sciences aim at true representations. But a science which deals with scientific representation as its subject aspires to true representations or representational truth, where truth and such relationships enter into the structure of what this sort of representational science undertakes to represent.

This may still not quite capture the intuition on which the concept of the human sciences rests. For after all, animal psychology is increasingly dealing with animal representational systems—with the mental maps and schemata that must be ascribed to animals if we are to make sense of their conduct. And animal psychology is certainly a natural science, even if representation figures prominently in its clarification. What more, I think, that is needed has to do with representations having a history in the case of human beings, where nothing quite like this can be said of animals. To be human is to belong to a stage of history and to be defined in terms of the prevailing representations of that period. And the human sciences must, among other things, arrive at historical explanations of historically indexed representations.

There are many, many causal laws to which human beings are subject that involve representation not at all. The laws of nutrition, for example, or elementary immunology, will be the same from culture to culture, though complex adapations may have worked themselves out under local conditions. The point is that adaptation and genetics alone suffice to account for the $R$-$R$ laws under which human beings, as causal systems, fall. But equally, there are many, many causal laws involving representations as causes and effects which involve culture and history not at all. More and more cognitive scientists are uncovering the, as it were, natural wiring with which human beings are equipped as a matter of biological heritage. What cannot be sought in the genetic material is the contribution history and culture make to our identities. The DNA of Renaissance humanity cannot have been significantly different from that of humanity of Europe in the nineteenth or in the present century. But the historical circumstances are immensely different.

Philosophers, particularly analytical philosophers and philosophers of science, have done very little to clarify these deep differences, and they have not pondered the complex interrelations between individual representational systems and the cultural or historical representational systems that define the circumstances in which we live. Metaphysically we may be free, but we are hardly free where it most matters to those who defend the autonomy of the human sciences: We cannot live in historical circumstances other than those we in fact live in, and we can scarcely imagine what it would be like to have been a peasant in the Middle Ages, or a poet in the Renaissance, or a member of the proletariat in the nineteenth century, or fervently to have supposed the revolution we were making was ushering in the golden age. We hardly, for that matter, can imagine what it must be like to believe in Santa Claus. We know what the belief is like, but we do not know what it is like to hold it. And when it comes to the *future,* we have hardly an idea. Fictions about the future are almost always merely projections of *present* attitudes into the interplanetary ages.

And here, too, there may be a difference of a kind between the human and the natural sciences. The natural sciences may assume that differences of time and space do not penetrate the laws of physics: that objects fall at the rate they do fall wherever and whenever they are released; that the better behaved planets now and forever sweep out equal areas in equal times; that objects attract one another inversely as the squares of their intervening distances. But who knows what the historical future will be? There are limits assigned by historical locations in human affairs that have no counterparts in the natural world.

With this we begin to enter the domain of what Hegel fittingly called spirit in contrast to nature: the area of politics, law, morality, religion, art, culture, and philosophy itself. Having brought the readers to this point I must leave them, for the bulk of philosophical reflection has itself not crossed this boundary, and until it does we are very much on our own. This side of the boundary is philosophically explored territory, the geography of which I have sought to describe. The realm of spirit is dark and difficult *terra incognita* so far as philosophical understanding is concerned, though it is as well, so far as human understanding is concerned, the most familiar territory of all. It is in the realm of spirit that we exist as human beings.

# Index